PSYCHOANALYTIC CONVERSATIONS

PSYCHOANALYTIC CONVERSATIONS

From the Psychotherapeutic Hospital to the Couch

M. Sagman Kayatekin

ROWMAN & LITTLEFIELD
Lanham • Boulder • New York • London

Published by Rowman & Littlefield
A wholly owned subsidiary of The Rowman & Littlefield Publishing Group, Inc.
4501 Forbes Boulevard, Suite 200, Lanham, Maryland 20706
www.rowman.com

Unit A, Whitacre Mews, 26-34 Stannary Street, London SE11 4AB

British Library Cataloguing in Publication Information Available

Library of Congress Cataloging-in-Publication Data

Name: Kayatekin, M. Sagman
Title: Psychoanalytic conversations : From the psychotherapeutic hosptial to the couch / M. Sagman Kayatekin.
Description: Lanham, MD : Rowman & Littfield, 2016. | Includes bibliographical references and index.
ISBN 9781442238343 (cloth : alkaline paper) | ISBN 9781442238350 (electronic)

∞ ™ The paper used in this publication meets the minimum requirements of American National Standard for Information Sciences Permanence of Paper for Printed Library Materials, ANSI/NISO Z39.48-1992.

Printed in the United States of America

CONTENTS

FOREWORD

This is an exciting book about psychotherapies.

The psychoanalyst author describes in straightforward English what happens when a gifted therapist meets with a troubled person and says to that person, "Please tell me about yourself in as honest and clear fashion as you can. And I will try my best to understand what you say, and what you struggle with. I will tell you what I see, hear, and understand about you slowly and in detail. To do this, we will meet regularly between one and four times a week, at about fifty minutes in each session, for as long as it takes. We must both be literally safe during this enterprise. We must both keep these appointments regularly. You have to pay my usual fee. Through this joint work and its words, frustrations, and pleasures, your words about your pain and about your joy, I believe you will find that this process will be useful to you."

This psychoanalyst uses all the wisdom that the fields of psychoanalysis and psychotherapy have accumulated over their 130 years of study of human behavior, development, conflict, and growth. This psychoanalyst does this in the particular way that he has integrated these important techniques and information into his own mind and body. Then he applies this to himself and to the patient—in a common language.

Just as every parent knows that no child grows up without pain and conflict, without hard work and love, without hatred and excitement, learning and curiosity, so will these therapeutic hours be filled with such events.

This psychoanalyst describes to the patient what he understands about that patient's struggle, and he notes to himself his part in this patient's struggle with himself in this conversation. He communicates parts of what he comes to understand about even his own struggle with this conversation, as he thinks this will be illustrative and the patient would find this information useful.

No parent of a child can facilitate his child's growth without support; support of an economic nature, support of internal or external other loved people, support of regular structures, of a place to live, a teacher, a place to work, food and clothing, and safety—all are important for human growth.

The psychoanalyst in this book describes what happens between himself and his patient in clear and affective detail. He does this under importantly differing conditions. These include instances when these conversations and procedures are taking place in a solitary office, with its privacy and aloneness. He describes when these talks need to occur in a hospital setting, with all of its supportive personnel for both the analyst and the patient, where the hospital has a whole constructed atmosphere surrounding the task of attempting to welcome and support honest communicative efforts with and by nurses and other therapeutic groups of staff and patients, with medical consultants and their therapeutic pharmacologic medicines, and in modern, open hospitals with teachers of many different mental health specialties. All of these attempt to support the patient's and analyst's safety, as well as the self-understanding and mutual responsibility between patient and therapist and staff.

And since people grow up in families and with close relationships, he describes how he attempts to help these relationships and help the patient to use and understand them. The therapist attempts to communicate to the patient's family, with the patient's permission, his understanding of that family, of their origins, learned behaviors, human conflicts, imperfections, struggles, and feelings. The analyst learns to respect those families' terrors, and their strengths, and their occasions for joy as well.

All of this takes much of the mystery out of therapy and analysis. None of this suggests that such work, such growth, can be achieved without difficult, painful conversation. None of this can avoid the analyst therapist being at times as tangled up in his patients' or his own emotions. This complicated mix of understanding includes mutual hatred and love, grief and fright (though very differently modulated between analyst and patient) as in any developing human being in an important intimate relationship. But despite its travails and imperfections, the clear and mutually voiced benefits allow important strengths and long-term growth to develop, which is seen in each of this book's illustrative analytic therapeutic reports.

I recommend this book to any patient and family members of a patient, to any therapist, and to any analyst. It will make mental illness more understandable to a patient and to a family. It makes the hard, exciting work of a therapist and analyst clearly understandable, something from which patients, family members, and therapists can learn. And it shows what can be done with important help from the community of therapeutic support for the patient and therapist in a modern psychiatric hospital, as well as from the privacy and personal struggles in an office setting over time.

Daniel P. Schwartz, MD

ACKNOWLEDGMENTS

This book is a distillation of some of my learning.

I learned from my analysts, teachers, and supervisors, and from many clinicians whose works I read. And I learned from my colleagues, students, and patients. And in the pursuit of becoming a more refined psychoanalyst, I learned from myself. I am indebted to these teachers of mine.

Two of my outstanding teachers were not persons. The first one was the microcosm of the psychoanalytic relationship, be it in a therapeutic dyad or in family work. And the second one was the unique human ecology of the psychotherapeutic hospital. These extraordinary environments, with their structures, traditions, and rules, became important teachers of mine, as much as persons, articles, or books. I am much obliged to both.

Yet my deepest thanks go to my wife, Emel. She wholeheartedly supported my relentless search of psychoanalytic knowledge, and helped me articulate my ideas. This book is dedicated to Emel, with love and gratitude.

PREFACE

What Exactly Does "Psychiatric Illness" Mean?

AHMED: THE BEGINNINGS OF AN INTERMINABLE SEARCH

I met Ahmed in the late 1970s while I was working in a psychotherapeutic hospital. A twenty-year-old college student suffering from severe obsessive-compulsive pathology, Ahmed had intrusive sexual fantasies about every man, woman, and child he met, and was tormented by incestuous fantasies about his grandmother, mother, and sister. Besides these horrifying sexual fantasies, he had fears of stabbing his family members, thus he tried to stay away from them to avoid a chance accident. Moreover, he was tortured with innumerable compulsions; he washed his hands many times a day, turned lights on and off, and would count to forty repetitively as he paced the floor.

I was a young resident then, curious and eager to learn. As I was getting to know him, an aspect of his intimate life caught my attention. Ahmed had an unusual masturbation ritual: he would ejaculate into an old-style cloth handkerchief and after about a week, he would hand these handkerchiefs over to his mother. Well aware of what the handkerchiefs were used for, his mother would wash, iron, and fold them and return them to her son.

Unable to empathically understand these intriguing bits of information, I wondered if these perplexing series of actions were symbolic of some of the dynamics in the family. I began playing with a set of ideas. What role did the mother have in this pathology? Was there a causal relation between Ahmed's regressed relations with his mother and his obsessive decompensation? If there was no causal relation, was his mother worsening his illness by furthering the regression?

I was trying to develop a formulation about this unusual pathology, but as a young doctor with abundance of therapeutic zeal, I was also frustrated with our inability to help him get out of this torturous existence. Helplessly watching Ahmed go through endless compulsive rituals evoked a painful sense of sympathy, anger, and hopelessness in the staff.

To complicate matters further, Ahmed would get mad at anyone who would try to interfere with his compulsive rituals; he would swear at them and threaten to attack. One afternoon, he began throwing cobblestones that he had ripped from the pavement of the hospital yard as the nursing staff tried to approach him and invite him to dinner at the unit. The nursing staff had to physically restrain him.

Ahmed, no doubt, had the capacity to incite affect and action in others. He was tortured, and he was a torturer.

Ahmed's relation with his mother as it was symbolically condensed in the handkerchief exchange and his capacity to evoke strong countertransference feelings in me and the staff implanted some embryonic questions and ideas in my mind. Ahmed served as a symbol for many other patients of mine that evoked my curiosity about how to make sense of psychopathology beyond thinking about it as an "illness" located in the individual as it was espoused by contemporary theories of general psychiatry, or as a "conflict or deficit," again located in the patient as suggested by the dominant psychoanalytic theories of the times.

The idea of formulating beyond the important but constricting concept of the "person" or the "patient" naturally raised a series of other questions about how one can place the person in a historical human context that is alive, a person who is affected by the illness, conflict, or deficit; a person affecting others and the role of the others in the genesis and sustenance of the illness and recovery from it. These questions and their answers, which lead to many new ones, became a perennial interest of mine. This book is about such questions that I pursued and answers that I have found so far.

CAVEATS

The Psychotherapeutic Hospital in the Background

My training in psychiatry and individual psychoanalytic work gave me a solid foundation of understanding the human predicament as I faced it day in and day out, in the person of the patient. But probably if it were not for my hospitalist work, where I met the unusual human ecology of the psychotherapeutic hospital, I would still be at a loss over some questions, which I believe I have some satisfactory answers for.

In the hospital, as I met the patient and his family and witnessed the patient's transference repetitions, I came to learn to think about him as a person in a context; a person in relation to another, others as persons and as members of groups. This book is about a person who can be an "I" only if he can be in relation to a "You," and furthermore, develop a sense of "We and They."

I am well aware that my ideas are conjectures awaiting their refutations, as the renowned philosopher Karl Popper (1963) described it so poignantly. Yet as I experience it in my daily practice, my conjectures that are derived from my own experience seem to be reasonably reliable guides in my everyday psychoanalytic work.

Videre, Facere, Docere

"See one, do one, and teach one" is an old adage of medicine, the mother of all healing arts. In the healing art of psychoanalytic therapies, we have a fair share of "facere-do" and "docere-teach," but the "videre-see" aspect is a big absence.

The vast majority of our teachers and colleagues do not present their work. Beyond a few anecdotal vignettes, the workings of their clinical minds is a mystery. One's own personal analysis is a partial remedy to this deficit but it is not a proper substitute for the direct exposure to the work of our teachers and colleagues. We are kept in the dark on how they formulate their patients and strategize their techniques in approaching the clinical problems through detailed case presentations. In psychoanalytic literature, this awkward trend persists; it is a troubling fact that detailed stories of psychoanalytic therapies are sorely lacking in psychoanalytic literature (Volkan 2014).

In a paradoxical way, the most established and self-assured form of psychotherapies, psychoanalytic work, may be the only healing art form where one is expected to start practicing it without ever witnessing how it is done.

This conspicuous lack of "presenting" is a serious educational deprivation, and perhaps in a paradoxical way, it even prevents us from learning from our own experiences. It is a well-known phenomenon that we learn from our work when we present it to a supervisor or peers, or when we write about it, as this monograph reminded me as I tried to rewrite my case histories.

Thus, a main purpose of these stories is pedagogical. I am hoping to provide my readers with an account of my work in a manner that will allow my colleagues to critique it and in the process, sharpen their thinking.

Privacy and Docere

As I was working on this monograph, I faced the perennial educational challenge of how to present a lively account of the clinical encounter as it unfolded over time, and at the same time protect the privacy of my patients. To achieve both, I made a compromise. I amalgamated many patients with similar pathologies, developmental histories, and dynamics and disguised and distorted them. Thus, the "patients" in these stories are somewhat fictional and the only real person in these series is myself. Yet, despite the fictional character of the patients, I believe that the collection represents a realistic depiction of the therapeutic process as I experienced it at the time.

Clinical Observation and Theory

I find the idea of "atheoretical observation" naïve. We all see the world through the lens of implicit or explicit theories of ours (Canestri 2006). With this supposition, I tried to create a cycle where I assumed that I had an initial theory to be able to see what I had seen, and then I tried to go from my clinical observations toward critiquing and refining my theory, making it as explicit as possible, and then from this new level of theory, went back to the clinical observations.

With this caveat in mind, I attempted to highlight my approach mainly through the lens of experience-near clinical work. Clinical theory, as I learned it from others, and as I came to understand and shape into mine through experience, is present in between my descriptions of the clinical material, and it occupies the central stage in the final sections of the cases.

Utilitarian-Integrative Theory

Throughout my career, a centrally important task for me was to develop an understanding of theory that had practical implications regarding how one could therapeutically impact and change the course of pathology toward a healthier adaptation. In this ongoing search, a wide spectrum of psychoanalytic schools have been great teachers of mine. In all of these readings and interpretations of various schools, I tried to stay away from an eclectic or dogmatic approach. I tried to follow the dictum of "integrative pluralism" (Richards 2003) and be as cohesive and integrative as I could possibly be.

The Format

Throughout the book, I kept the "intrapsychic/interpersonal/groups" as the central theme. And, instead of the "novel"-like structure of the case reports of authors like Vamik Volkan (1984), I chose a "short story" format that fits my personal style better. Thus, every case can be read and critiqued individually.

The Audience

In the exposition of one's ideas, I am equally opposed to an obscurantist elitism and to an abridged populism. I tried to write in a manner that I hoped would be helpful for psychoanalysts and psychoanalytically trained therapists and perhaps would be of interest to the well-informed lay person.

In Sum

With these caveats in mind, I invite you to join me in reviewing my psychoanalytic work with some of my patients from the past few decades. I start with psychoanalytic therapy in the hospital, then move to family work. Then comes the complicated matrices of milieu and team. Following that, I switch to our offices and present some stories of individual psychoanalytic therapy, family work, and psychoanalysis in my office setting.

1

PSYCHOANALYTIC PSYCHOTHERAPY IN THE PSYCHOTHERAPEUTIC HOSPITAL

Al—The Armor, the Open Guts, and the Skin

Here, I will focus on individual psychoanalytic psychotherapy in the psychotherapeutic hospital through Al's story.

Psychoanalytic psychotherapy in a hospital setting is much more complicated than its counterpart that is conducted in our private offices. In the psychoanalytic office work, we have a window into our patient's world through the thin slices of fifty-minute sessions. Whereas in the hospital, the psychoanalyst, through the observations by nurses and other hospital staff, is directly informed about a much larger segment of the life of the patient, as the work is discussed regularly within the members of the clinical team. On the other hand, patients have much more information about their therapists as they live together under the overarching roof of the "therapeutic community," and they are aware of the other patients of their therapists, and develop intense, ambivalent therapeutic sibling relationships.

In the psychotherapeutic hospital, the patients develop multiple transferences in the ordinarily regressed environment of the hospital and displaced/multiple transferences float around the dyadic space of the individual psychoanalytic therapy. There is a subtle but powerful competition within the therapists, and the dyadic individual psychoanalytic work faces idealization and devaluation in comparison to the work of other members of the team who develop their unique relations with the patient.

Both the therapist and the patient have multiple roles that create different ways of relating to one another: as a therapeutic couple, as members of therapy groups, as citizens of a community, and as they work together in family therapy.

Membership in a variety of groups is a potential trigger for various degrees of regression (Kernberg 1973). This unavoidable phenomenon, regression (Blum 1994), is a source of information and learning, but at the same time creates a potential for relating destructively and punitively under the guise of treatment. In sum, working as a psychoanalytic therapist in the hospital requires substantial modifications in the analytic stance as the work of Daniel Schwartz (1986) demonstrates, and it may even be thought of as an impossible art (Bell 1997).

With these complicating factors in mind, let us turn our attention to Al.

Al was a single college graduate in his early thirties when he was admitted to the hospital. He was the only child of a wealthy couple. He had been in an extended psychoanalytic treatment that lost traction after some years of good work.

The maternal lineage of Al were immigrants who had settled in North America during late nineteenth century. Al's maternal great-grandfather was a wealthy businessman and a prominent social figure. His son, Al's maternal grandfather, inherited his father's business but partly because of the Great Depression, lost almost all of their fortune. Alongside this decline, there were rumors of the maternal grandfather running pyramid schemes and having extramarital affairs, and Al's mother grew up in relatively modest circumstances with a deep sense of shame about the financial and moral damage her father had done to their family. Furthermore, beyond losing the immense wealth of the family, their father, in the memories of Al's mother, was a person prone to rages and had issues with boundaries; he would walk around the house in his underwear and Al's mother would hear her parents having sex at night because they wouldn't close their doors. The maternal grandmother was another bleak figure. After brain surgery for a benign brain tumor, she developed dementia in her fifties, and Al's s mother took take care of her for some decades until her death. In the family constellation, Al's mother was seen as a good girl, someone who did not cause any troubles during her youth. She became a prominent lawyer in an international firm. Her younger brother was less shiny of a figure; he dropped out of college and had serious financial difficulties beginning with his young adulthood. Al's family took care of him during most of his adult life.

The history of Al's paternal lineage was rather sparse. The paternal grandfather was described as a "big goofy guy" who was seen as the gullible yet hardworking son of a family that owned a large farm operation. He married the daughter of a neighboring farming family and Al's father was their only child. Despite being socially awkward like his father, Al's father was academically talented. He attended a top university, and after graduation returned home to take over the large farm operation. With good luck, hard work, and good business sense, he developed the business to the level of a local major enterprise.

As the children of parents with dramatic histories, and who were somewhat misfits themselves, Al's father and mother felt like they found their soul mates when they met at a party and began dating. They married in a matter of months. Al's mother lost her first and only baby to a serious, life-threatening complication during pregnancy, and then the young couple adopted Al from a neighboring poor family.

As Al entered his toddler years, his mother perceived some peculiarities in her son. He was a precocious talker who was able to talk in sentences around his first year, but at the same time, in his mother's eyes, there was some awkwardness in his motor development. Compared to his peers, he looked rather clumsy and not that well-coordinated. With this perception, Al's mother focused her projective interest in her son and to remedy this perceived deficit, she implemented a self-styled rehabilitation program. Through playing some ball games with him, she hoped that Al would develop a better coordination and in his mother's opinion, Al responded to this intervention. In a few years, her anxieties about Al's neurological development disappeared. He was rehabilitated.

Attending kindergarten became a nightmare; Al would throw terrible fits as his parents tried to leave him at the elite kindergarten in their neighborhood. After hopeless struggles, the parents would yield to his wishes, bring him back home, and one would stay with him. To resolve this impasse, an immigrant family was brought to the house. The father and the mother of this implanted family took care of the household chores and their two infant sons became companions for Al. This was very helpful for the working couple and Al had the experience of having two peers in the house. It was a kindergartener's world in vitro. Ordinarily the kindergartener-preschooler would find this new world of peers outside of the house, whereas Al's parents brought a sample of that new world to the inside of their large estate. Again, he was rehabilitated.

The immigrant family left the house for the schooling of their children around the time Al started elementary school. It was a painful loss for Al, but he had partly healed the early failures of his parents through his adopted family and this helped him sail smoothly forward for a few more years. To the pleasant surprise of his parents, his elementary-school years were rather unremarkable. Al's mom and dad finally felt like they were doing a good job as parents. Al was somewhat shy and reserved but was overall seen as the top of his class—a very intelligent and promising child.

When the developmental turbulence of the teens hit, Al began struggling mightily. He couldn't meet the interpersonal demands of puberty—the budding sexuality that differentiated friendships between girls versus boys; a sense of belonging to some subgroups; admiring, envying, and competing with peers. Al became increasingly disjointed from the path his peers were taking. He treated his classmates in confusing ways—from being the good, asexual, unaggressive prepubertal boy who was seen as a very kind, somewhat solitary person to someone who came across as smug, sarcastic, and demeaning. The budding sexual and aggressive body and mind of a young boy and the vicissitudes of a new interpersonal world were flooding his intelligent mind, and he began struggling academically. This was a terrible blow to his sense of self-esteem; he was hit at the core of his pride—he was no longer the top of his class.

He was lost at home too. In his own words, he was the "best friend" of his mother, privy to information about the most private aspects of her life. On the other hand, he was in a hostile deadlock with his father. Al's mother, who was employed as an attorney by an international firm, took long trips nationally and internationally. This lifestyle allowed some space for her from her serious marital problems, but she was, at the same time, leaving Al and his father alone with each other, and the two were deepening their antagonisms. Al was becoming like the oppositional toddler he once was, impossible to manage, ready to pick fights, argumentative on almost every subject. His father, a prominent businessman, after working long hours would come home and would try to accommodate Al's endless demands. He was terribly unhappy in the marriage and was now talking with Al about his marital dissatisfactions. And there were rumors that both parents were involved in extramarital affairs. Al's family was crumbling, and he was in the midst of a terrible parental conflict.

A few years into his teens, Al's maternal uncle appeared in his life. After this uncle dropped out of college, he had some failed business ventures, and during Al's teenage years he joined Al's family and became an older brother figure. His brother-in-law's presence at home was a relief for Al's father, as his brother-in-law became another man that could help tackle Al's growing antagonism. For Al, this arrangement was similar to his younger years when some peers were brought into the home. Now in his teens, a chum-like male figure was provided for him. The world that Al needed to seek outside was brought in. Again, he was rehabilitated.

The uncle and Al had a special relationship. They deeply enjoyed each other's company, and after Al's uncle straightened his finances and left Al's home, their connection was not lost. They were like brothers, and Al would stay in his uncle's home for extended periods.

Within this awkward, "as-if" adolescent environment in a family that lacked a sense of tradition, pride, and cohesiveness, Al managed to graduate from high school and decided to take a few years off. He spent most of his time hanging out with his wayward uncle, playing video games with some introverted friends he contacted through the Internet, and was playing the drums—something he was exceptionally good at—and was invited to join the high-school band. He had practiced with the band for a few months but dropped it when being with others became a draining task. After a year, he got bored and decided to go to a local college. These years were even more troubling than his adolescence; he couldn't join any groups at school; his isolation became profound. He would spend a lot of time at his fractured parental home, and despite his incredible intelligence, he barely managed to graduate.

After graduation, Al tried to work for a sales company but failed in a matter of months and was fired. With the hope that maybe he was a nerd genius and may flourish in academia, he applied for graduate training, but was expelled from the program after a year. These populated human environments made Al profoundly anxious, and his mind would just shut down.

Now in his mid-twenties, Al was at a loss. He had failed almost all of his latency and adolescent tasks of establishing relations outside of the family, an identity as a person, and as a member of a group. Unable to hold a job or pursue an academic track, with no friends, not having dated anybody despite deep longings to befriend and be intimate, Al finally came to the agonizing acknowledgement that maybe there was something seriously wrong with him. He severed his ties with his parents, moved to a different province, started a volunteer job, and began psychoanalysis.

For a while, his psychoanalysis proved to be beneficial. He was feeling less depressed, had a few budding friendships, and there were some short liaisons that seemed meaningful to Al. He felt more comfortable in the workplace and was considering going back to academia for a graduate degree.

In the third year of his psychoanalysis, for reasons that were not clear to him or his analyst, Al decompensated. He quit his work and regressed to a level where he was unable to have an ordinary life other than attending the five-times-a-week psychoanalysis. He was stuck in his home, playing Internet poker in some tournaments and making some significant amounts of money because of his superior intelligence, reading a few favorite novels repetitively, eating fast food, and contemplating his death by suicide. His psychoanalyst tried to intervene with this terrifying negative therapeutic reaction by changing his medication regimen and with several short-term hospitalizations. All of these interventions were helpful for short periods, after which the treatment lost traction again. Eventually, Al was referred to a long-term psychotherapeutic hospital where he became my patient.

Al in the Hospital

In our first session, Al said he knew that this hospital was amongst the best, but the philosophy of our system which we prided ourselves in, the concept of the "voluntary, open hospital" (Schwartz 1983), was a façade! The idea of patients coming here on their own will and that we were an open system was an illusion. In his opinion, our hospital was not too different from the locked units where he had several involuntary hospitalizations.

Surprised by this opening statement, I reminisced about a Russian colleague who had recently visited our hospital. She knew quite a bit about open and closed psychiatric systems of Russian/Soviet psychiatry and had made similar comments that our open system may not be as open as we thought. Just like my Russian colleague, Al was telling me that we could be entrapped in a hospital without locks, in a system that had benevolent intentions and in certain ways, being confined with locks was easier to comprehend. Al's life history was a perfect example for this paradox; he had an "open" childhood that was devoid of any overt trauma or barriers; it was a family that didn't punish or traumatize him sexually, emotionally, or physically, so it was a mystery to him why he was, in his words, "so screwed up" and felt entrapped within himself and his family. We would visit this fascinating quandary many times in our work.

After this important philosophical opening, Al began painting a colorless picture of himself that I would repetitively hear for many months to come: he had no sense of an identity, felt agonizingly empty in the inside, and worse, he had no accomplishments in his thirty plus years. He wasn't even a pitch dark bad person like Theodore Kaczynski, who, at the very least, caused some impact through destruction. Al was verbose and would occupy the whole session with this monochromatic narrative if I did not interject a few questions.

At the very end of our first encounter, as he stood up and was leaving the office, Al asked whether any of my patients had committed suicide. It was a classical moment of adolescent tricking and brought a series of reveries to my mind. As teenagers, my two sons were in the habit of asking quick questions as we were passing each other in the hallways of our home or on our way out. These were what I considered trivial questions about buying something or going to movies with their friends. And, not having my thinking hat on, I would say "of course" and then would later regret approving that request: it was a big mistake because they had posed the same question to my wife a minute ago, and she had said no. During my work in hospitals, I had fallen into a similar trap many a times; had made many comments that I later regretted, and these again usually occurred in similar conditions where I had answered a question posed by a person as I was passing by him. Now Al had caught me with a familiar sense of surprise. I made a split-second decision and told him that we needed to talk about this further, but acknowledged that I had lost some patients to suicide. I didn't want to look too grandiose.

Second Session

The next day, I was sitting in my office waiting for our second session, feeling like we had had an ordinary first session where we had introduced ourselves to each other. I noticed that he was walking around my office, acting as if he was inspecting the building and appeared as though he was unable to come through the door. Intrigued by this unusual scene, I had a fleeting fantasy that he was flying in circles above my office like a predatory bird, and with some hesitation, trusting my intuition, I opened the door and said, "I am here." He came in.

With lengthy and articulate monologues, Al started talking about the attractive female patients in the hospital, and his lack of a core sense of self. He stated that even being someone like Bobby Fischer—a genius nerd who was accomplished in one area, would be preferable to where he was in his life. It caught my attention that for some inexplicable reason Al had moved from the ideal of malignant Kaczynski to the benign nerd of Fischer in a matter of a day. I thought maybe he noticed that he had not evoked a deep sense of fear in me, so he had mellowed the image down. I had only speculations about the dramatic change. He said that he had a decent education and money that could sustain him for the rest of his life, but nothing beyond that. He was living with a sense of painful emptiness.

With the intention to explore his previous therapeutic attachments, I asked about what his thoughts were on the work with the therapist he had before he came to the hospital. Al recalled feeling like a burden to his last therapist after some years of helpful work. It felt like he was an irreparably damaged person. After so many years of psychoanalytic work, now he was sent to our hospital. He was tired and was here because of his parents and would prefer to commit suicide. It was an unexpectedly early moment of intensity in the therapeutic encounter. I had no awareness of the dynamics in between the two of us and the historical roots of it. Nevertheless, I knew I had to say something about what felt like a frontal attack. I decided to let my mind speak for itself, and countered by saying maybe he was wondering about the grandiosity of me and the hospital, whether we could save him. Al said he sure was interested in that.

Al was inducing strong emotions in me from early on; a sense of curiosity about this interesting new patient, and a wish to tell him that he could be helped. He was also evoking a mild sense of disgust with the way in which he was picking the skins of his fingertips and to my puzzlement, throwing the pieces of skin into the emptied cup of coffee he had in his hand. Somewhat pleased with the way he disposed his skin, at the same time I thought that he was not even leaving his dirt in my office. I had some tentative ideas about the metaphoric meaning of this bodily/

verbal presentation. Was he telling me that he was so dirty and toxic that he should not deposit his skin to the floor of my office, or was he telling me that his skin was so invaluable that it couldn't be deposited here? It probably was both.

Toward the end of this second session, as I was listening to his interesting and articulate speech, I swallowed my spit, as I do countless times every day without being aware of it—an ordinary bodily event like breathing, coughing, or sneezing. He immediately stopped and asked whether I had something to say. I was meeting with the striking paradox of Al's outward indifferent appearance and internal, deep, vigilant attention to the other person. I recognized that I was excited with the prospect of a great patient. I thought that Al was an interesting and evocative patient who would make me work and think hard.

When I recognized it, the idea of a "great" patient worried me. I had an oft-repeated observation over the course of many years that a sense of therapeutic overexcitement in me was usually a bad prognostic sign. I never fully understood this phenomenon, but I wondered whether it was taken as a sign of neglect or abandonment by the patient. Or was it simply because the unique person was lost in the excitement as he became a great project to be worked on. Or perhaps it pointed to the evocation of some projective nidus in me.

We Come to a Halt

These intense, early, verbal, and nonverbal transference-countertransference excitements came to a halt in a matter of a few weeks, and Al fell into a noncohesive, kaleidoscopic presentation for the following months. He filled the therapy hours with monologues, quoting extensively from classics of the Western literature like Homer, Shakespeare, or the Bible as he was walking up and down in my office. I was amazed by his capacity to recite the texts verbatim and with his eloquence. But there was no hint of a conversation. He was on a stage, performing for me or maybe for himself. When he was not in a monologue, he would sleep for the full hour. And in between we had some ordinary psychotherapeutic dialogues, but the initial mutual intensity that excited me had evaporated.

As we were going through these cycles of drama and somnolence within the office, in the larger, containing, and constraining world of the hospital Al was avoiding contact with others and isolating himself either in his room or in his daily routine of long car rides. He was constantly ruminating on what he had not accomplished, and how he and his parents were an elemental root to this deeply unsatisfactory place where he was in life. As soon as he woke up, these repetitive, ruminative themes and thoughts flooded his mind, and he would listen to these broken records throughout the day.

As a therapist I was cognizant of my relatively quiet and patient personality. During my early youth, my parents were often distracted by the needs of some chronically ill family members, so I was accustomed to being overlooked. Thus, during this early phase of our work, I was tolerant of the inattentiveness, the relative absence of Al. Slowly though, as I listened to Al's monologues or watched him sleep, as I became more aware of his pattern, I began noticing the differences with my history and our current script. In my early youth, my parents ignored me due to their circumstances, yet in my countertransference response to Al, I was now recognizing how Al's "ignorance" of me had an actively aggressive element.

It was dawning on me that his dramatic reluctance to come into my office in the second session and his monologues were not just due to the anxieties of a fearful man, but that he was also pushing me out of my office by turning me to a spectator or an inanimate object in the room. I had images of Al as a recluse—a solitary being who could also attack viciously like a solitary predatory animal.

The dramatic acting before the second session was a synopsis of our work to come; he was circling above my office.

Let's Just Talk

Over the course of these initial months, being a part of this quite unusual therapeutic encounter, and somewhat intuitively, I developed a therapeutic hypothesis and a strategy; I was going to allow Al to tolerate my presence as another person in the same room with him, just like we allow a newly adopted animal to get accustomed to the routines of our home life. In this instance though, I had a fantasy that I was as equally wild to his uninhabited world.

So I elected to change my stance from the unnatural asymmetry of psychoanalytic "free association and evenly hovering attention" to the natural, ordinary togetherness of two persons, obliged to be together four times a week for fifty minutes, trying to strike a conversation without getting too afraid of one another. I narrowed down my therapeutic interest, listening, and speech and expanded the sectors of ordinary human interest, listening, and speech.

The shift from the analytic asymmetry is an uneasy stance for the therapist, and I knew very well that sometimes it could be quite risky. I had personally witnessed some close colleagues ending up in serious boundary violations with their patients when, with an intention of being more helpful to their patients, they shifted the ordinary asymmetrical analytic frame. But I was hoping that I could keep it under control.

Through my readings I also felt supported by some other analysts such as Jacob Arlow (2002) when he wrote about analysis being a conversation, or when Heinz Kohut in supervision advised Paul Ornstein to be comfortable with the spontaneity in the relationship (Ornstein 2008). Anna Freud's comfort in having human interaction with Arthur Couch in their analytic sessions (Couch 2002) was extraordinarily freeing for him (and as I read it, for me), and it was of note that Anna Freud, in what may sound like a paradox, was much freer in ordinary conversations in the sessions than she was outside of the sessions where she had a respectful, formal distance with her patients.

Gradually, as Al became more tolerant of the psychoanalytic asymmetry, the stilted listening (Arlow 1995), this nonanalytic, ordinary conversation space shrank to a much smaller proportion. Over the course of our work of many years, Al would, when switching to that mode, forewarn me and say, "I am going to ask a question to you just as a man" and then pose a question as if I was an older chum. Occasionally I would do something similar and say, "This is not a therapeutic comment but just an ordinary comment coming from an older man" and make my comment.

First Attempt to Move Out

While he was creating a defensive and protective wall within our developing therapeutic relation, Al was attempting to further his relation with other members of the community. It was as if he did not have the capacity to simultaneously be a part of the family (i.e., his dyadic relation with me) and his peers. Al was, from the beginning, very comfortable in various clinical groups where a clearly demarcated task and time frame existed. On the other hand, he was terror stricken in nonstructured settings.

Having a brief conversation with someone outside of the groups, in a friendly, ordinary way felt like an impossible task, so he tried to deepen and expand conversations with peers outside of the group therapy meetings. This was a wearing task. Having lived in severe isolation for so many years, he had no experience in doing this. And during his earlier years, his peer milieus were brought to him; he had not sought them out.

Feeling more anchored in his relation with me, Al ventured out to the community. He was noticing the subgroups in the community, and trying to understand what would take one to become a part of those. Faced with the ordinary adolescent dynamics that he and his family had fiercely avoided, Al was sailing without a compass and was rudderless. At one point he tried to identify with anorexic patients and began experimenting with anorexia by restricting food to the point where he fainted and needed a short-term medical hospitalization.

These attempts to tackle his bypassed developmental tasks, reach out to people, befriend them, develop a sense of group identity, would exhaust him. After these tiring forays into the jungle of human relations, Al would stay in his room and read his favorite books and watch some movies repetitively. These familiar, passive, repetitive activities would give him a sense of soothing. Or he would revert to his old habit of solitary and long car rides, where he could be with himself, stay in local hotels, and take brief absences from the intensity of the hospital.

First Attempt to Hatch

It was about six months into treatment and as he became more tolerant of contact with fellow patients and needed much less time for recuperative isolations, Al began flirting with a female patient. This behavior gradually caused a stir in the patient community and in the staff; it was not consistent with guidelines of life in the hospital. Yet Al acted as if he did not understand the potential implications of his behavior and continued to pursue this young woman and made light of his peers' warnings. In his attempt to get out of the box of his pervasive isolation, he was probably following the boundaryless relation of his mother around her sexuality—the only available pattern that he could draw out from.

He had touched a conflicted area of mine as his individual psychoanalytic therapist. During my teens, I was an inhibited adolescent who was seen as "mature." I was the image of a good boy who did not create any problems for his family. I would stay away from adolescent "bad behavior," which in its worst was smoking cigarettes in Turkey of 1960s. It was a deeply conflicted place for me. I longed to be a bit more mischievous but was, at the same time, proud of what I and probably others perceived as being a mature little boy.

With this template in the background, despite sharing some concern about his actions, I partially identified with Al and saw his attempts as comparable to the developmental struggles of a teenager and as potentially useful for Al, as long as he didn't get into an intimate, sexual relationship. I was probably developing what Heinrich Racker (1968) would call a concordant countertransference.

Then a rumor that they were indeed in a sexual relationship began spreading. In the larger setting of the hospital, this was a moment of crucial differences within the staff around the formulation of the actions of Al. Some of my colleagues were getting worried and were inviting me to consider whether this was a displaced transference, and I had to interpret it as such. On my end, not discarding that as a potential formulation, I was also considering the possibility that this was mostly unrelated to Al's relation with me; he was developing multiple transferences (Gabbard 2000) in the milieu, working on his adolescent tasks and his actions had loose connections with the therapeutic dyad.

However, what felt like developmentally risky but appropriate mischief to me, began feeling like an intolerable transgression to the larger community, and Al and his girlfriend became the main topic in the milieu. They were severely confronted by their peers about the inappropriateness of their sexual "pairing." Al and his girlfriend adamantly denied the allegations, but the girlfriend, out of a deep sense of shame and anger, immediately discharged from the hospital. Al crumbled and made a suicidal gesture; he tjem swallowed some over-the-counter medications and was treated in a local emergency ward overnight.

Back to Home

About nine months into his stay, Al felt devastated. Feeling like all of his attempts to be different from his usual self, to be more social, had failed, he assumed a position that was more isolated than the time he first arrived. He reverted to the old pattern of spending a lot of time outside of the hospital, driving his car for hundreds of miles to soothe himself as his father used to do when he was a teenager. He stopped talking with most of his peers and disappeared from the milieu. He was confused and did not understand whether he had transgressed boundaries in a way that needed such a strong response. In my opinion, Al clearly had transgressed some boundaries but the hospital was working in a retaliatory fashion secondary to group regression.

Back in his schizoid cave, Al had fantasies of hanging himself or blowing his brains out. But he managed to restrain himself mainly through the help of a solid friendship he had developed in the arts department where he would spend countless hours throwing pottery and talking with his art instructor. It was a repetitive, soothing activity where he would stop his ongoing self-critical thoughts and find some peace. His increasing attachment to me and intense family work also helped him, and the nursing staff did not forget him either. In contrast to the familial stance of not being bothered by his parents when he isolated or pushing them away if they tried to approach him, nursing continually "bothered" him by inviting him back to groups and to the milieu, tolerating his rage when they approached him. The nursing was serving a containing function, metabolizing his anger and detachment and returning it to him in digested and digestible ways (Bion 1962).

After several weeks, the heat had dissipated in the milieu but came back with full force to the dyadic analytic space. He rekindled in me some beloved Turkish proverbs: he was "stubborn as a mule," inviting passionate fights with his father and mother and me, whereas at the same time he appeared "docile and innocent as a lamb" in his relations with his peers, giving the impression that he was a nice kid. He never was able to have a cohesive image in the microcosms of his family and peers. These were two different and contradictory sets of group transference scripts—a negative one to his family and positive to other groups.

First Transference Dream

Al reported his first transference dream around this significant juncture, at the end of a psychotherapy session. He was at the shores of the lake in his hometown. He was a member of an odd group that looked like androids. There was a commander of this group and they all had robotic relations—nothing emotional or sexual. They got into an elevator that took these robotic characters under the lake, and they came out to the surface at the other shore where Al found himself in the hospital. Once in the hospital the scene changed. He had a young female peer on his lap, they were attempting to make love, but there was another man on top of her. Al was enraged over the fact that this man disrupted the sexual intercourse.

I was fascinated with this elaborate dream, and thought that it was a wonderful depiction of what had happened and what was coming our way in our work. In the following session, I told him that this was a very interesting dream, that I had heard a theme of him moving between being robotic and sexual; it vacillated between what he experienced with his father and his mother. And maybe it was a projection of what will happen in our work further down the road. It was a truly creative script, I said, and asked Al to associate to the dream.

He was deeply disappointed with my response and refused to comply with my invitation to associate to the elements of the dream. He thought it was a great dream for psychoanalytic exploration, whereas he had gotten a flimsy response from me. For him the dream was an "aha" moment, a moment of orgasm, and I had missed that opportunity. He left the session in rage.

In my mind I had the memories of his previous analyst asking him to reveal sexual fantasies for "aha" enlightenments. This approach had lead Al to a hope that things would be resolved at some intellectual orgasmic moments of discovery and understanding. I was offering none of those to Al. Feeling defeated and deflated, I carried on with this mundane, sometimes boring analysis, as life usually is within our offices.

Negative Transference

Gradually, in the dyadic space, Al became deeply resentful about his treatment in this expensive hospital. He was demeaning my mind and technique, mocking my accent, physique, and on occasions was threatening to destroy my office. It was a significant change: he was treating me with some affective valence, albeit a negative one, that was intensifying day by day. Despite a growing sense of frustration and anger with his barrage of insults, I was still able to keep my composure. My formulation of my stance was, I was being "neutral" toward and "containing" of an emerging negative transference. Meanwhile, my colleagues were getting concerned about the yelling and screaming that was coming out of my office.

Al was in the habit of taking long drives and sometimes staying at nearby hotels for several days to soothe himself after intense involvement in the therapeutic work. Around this extended crisis, during one of the self-soothing drives, he disappeared for some days after which we heard from a local hospital that he had overdosed and was treated in their intensive care unit to monitor for potential liver failure. After medically clearing, he was transferred to their locked psychiatric unit and was treated as an inpatient for a few weeks. We were all relieved that he had survived but this act had a massive impact on the hospital; unlike his first overdose, this was perceived as a serious attempt to take his life. About a year into the treatment, now it was my time to be evaluated within the milieu of my peers. For the following several weeks, Al and my work with him became a main topic in various settings of the hospital, from regular team meetings to general staff conferences, to the grapevine and hallway discussions.

It felt like I, Al, and our work were under scrutiny, and we were shamefully exposed. Gone were the days when I was acknowledged as a competent clinician who had a capacity to work with difficult patients as it was proven in my work with Al. There were remarks coming from my colleagues that maybe I was not working with the "aggression" properly. In parallel, there was an enormous pressure coming from the patient community and the family of Al about how the treatment was going and that maybe Al should change therapists, or we should get a consultation from an outside psychiatrist with "proper credentials." I felt attacked, scared, enraged, humiliated, and vengeful and defeated. It was an agonizing, perfect transference-countertransference storm.

In time, the "criticism" of the staff and community and myself toned down to a "critique." As it regularly does, the hospital was providing a milieu for the patient, and in a parallel fashion, it was providing a milieu that would potentially critique me or serve the function of the "third" as I was, naturally and necessarily, lost in the dyad during a regressed enactment (Muller 2011).

After his readmission to the hospital, with the help of my self-analysis and critique coming from my peers and the patient community, I became more aware of and comfortable with firmly interpreting brutal, enraging, aspects of Al. He in turn, felt that he was capable of evoking affects/

reactions in me and thus his agency/potency was affirmed. He told me that he had no sense that he had the capacity to affect me with a vulgar image: "To me you looked like a man who had my arm up to my elbow in his a**, and you were not saying a word."

After he came back, along with his unrelenting negative transference, in a paradoxical but expected way, Al began displaying more affection toward me. He was showing evidence that he had some remorse over his attacks and the damage he inflicted, and in some subtle ways appeared as if he was trying to repair the damage.

It was a little over a year when finally we connected on an alive plane of therapeutic togetherness. It was a surprising recognition for me that while I was noticing his cocoon, I was unaware of mine. We had knocked at each other's doors many a times, called each other out, asked to be invited in, repeatedly, and when we finally heard him through his suicide attempt, his action speech, we had met each other. We were both awake and ready to talk with one another.

I and You—The "Rubbish List"

I was back from a vacation, and as he was walking toward his chair, Al said he missed me. When spontaneously I told him that I missed him too, Al was surprised and so was I. He said that what we said was a reason for him to kill me and quickly switched to a recent event that had deeply touched him. The day before, he had written a lot in his journal and felt that his narrative was beautiful. He was writing about recognition; his theme was "the only way to become human is acknowledging others and being acknowledged by another person."

He had decided to open up these writings to some fellow patients, and he told me that he could not stop his tears when he read this essay to his peers, and as he was reading his beautifully narrated piece to me, he was in tears and so was I.

After this moving moment, Al told me that he was mad at me because he thought I was too passive in the family sessions we were having on a weekly basis. He felt like I was leaving him alone with his parents, letting him fight his fights.

This was clearly a different plane of relating compared to a couple of years ago. Others and I were becoming persons, in enjoyable, and thus painful, ways.

Al was learning to become more comfortable with the proximity of myself, his parents, and some peers in the community in a peculiar way. It was a process of inclusion and exclusion. The "rubbish list" as he coined it, summarized this beautifully. The "rubbish list" was a list of people, either patients or staff, whom he would pay no attention to. Al, who appeared as if he was ignoring anyone and everyone in his vicinity, was in fact vigilant to everybody; he was watching their minor gestures, paying attention to their narrative, inflection of voices, the subtexts, and so on, as was exemplified by our first session. With the "rubbish list," he was attempting to develop some boundaries around his limitless vigilance to everyone around him, and was trying to create social niches of "belonging."

As he was attempting to differentiate himself from his peers, in the sessions, he was playfully talking about bodily fantasies of peeing, spitting, hacking a good loogie, and passing gas. He was feeling powerful with his recently doubled bench press. He would show me his biceps and triceps. I was listening to his fantasies and empathically remembering these wonderful teenage dirty boyish pleasures and the grandiosity of adolescence. He was pointing to my therapeutic silent stance and to my hard-to-hide vicarious boyish enjoyment of his development, and we were trying to differentiate my reactions from his dad's perceived absence and intrusive interest of his mother. As we were noticing the abandoned, neglected, mistreated sides of him, we were also recognizing that his parents had put him up on a pedestal; he was the crown prince of the family. The narrative of Al and his family was becoming more complicated.

I was deeply surprised when I heard from the staff that he had taken a step outside of the hospital. Al had joined the local golf club, and he had also joined a small band as the drum player. He was a great drummer in high school and now he was rekindling that old skill of his adolescence. He was reluctant to share any of these developments with the staff and me because he thought these were signs of progress, and Al was worried that I, as his analyst, would get excited about this development. In the past, his dad would get excited when he heard such news and that would lead to Al's losing interest in what he had accomplished; he didn't know whether his accomplishments belonged to him or to his dad. So he was progressing in secret.

I told him I understood where he was coming from. I was thinking about "excitement" in the therapist, a phenomenon that I was well aware of with many other patients and recalled that it had appeared relatively early with Al, during the first few weeks of his treatment in the hospital.

Session

In between two patients, I was reviewing my notes about a presentation so I did not notice that Al was standing at the doorstep of my office. With a teasing, cynical tone he said, "You should be thinking about me." Coming out of the daze of my preoccupation, I found his comment irritating but at the same time loving and warm.

Al again complained about how I was being somewhat lukewarm in the way I was approaching the family sessions. He wanted me to join his attacks on his parents and be more open on how troubled his parents were: after a few productive sessions where they could listen to one another and elaborate on various themes, creating a story of the family, he had initiated a vitriolic attack on them, one that I had to intervene with and stop. Despite considerable reflection and analysis with my cotherapist in the family sessions, I still was at a loss on why he was recently attacking his parents so viciously; it felt unwarranted and out of the blue.

I pointed to his haughty and condescending comments about his family and said he is sadistic toward them, as he can be toward himself and others, including me. Al said his anger and sadism were secondary to his fragility. I told him that I thought it actually was primary; in my opinion, he was genuinely sadistic, grandiose, haughty, as well as fearful of human relations and loving others. Al produced a big grin and said primary sadism was an interesting idea; he had never thought about. He truly liked it!

Masturbation Fantasy

Some months ago, Al had revealed a central, repetitive masturbation fantasy: Al is having sex and at the point of orgasm, either he or his partner dies. Just like his first transference dream, this was another invaluable map into Al's internal and interpersonal world, and I thanked him for revealing his masturbation fantasy, and stated that this was a precious gift and stored it in my mind for future usage. I noted to myself that love for Al meant death of one as symbolized in his masturbation fantasy.

Building on how he viciously attacked the parents after a few loving sessions and the masturbation fantasy, I made the interpretation that if we were both to enjoy something between the two of us, one of us had to die. And I made a rapid, intuitive intrapsychic interpretation to myself; just as it was impossible to love another person and himself, it was also impossible for Al to love his body and mind at the same time, as his fantasy was insinuating. He was acting under the fantasy belief that you are a disembodied mind or you are a mindless body. One part of him had to be dead for the other part to be alive. He was struggling to put me and himself together and his mind and body together, and us as bodies and minds together.

After this session, where I felt like I had come up with exciting and impressive interpretations, some of which I had articulated to him and some I kept to myself, he attacked me for several sessions in a row, accusing me of having no formulation of his problems. His masturbation fantasy was a good guide for sure!

Moving Up

It was clear that our work was becoming less heated and that there was more reflective space available in the minds of both of us. There were dreams, fantasies, stories of Al's life, and he was developing a significant number of relationships in his life. We were moving toward ordinary psychoanalytic work without any deep anxieties about psychosis or death of self or others.

Al was making me reflect on the old, somewhat forgotten concepts of fixation and regression. I was thinking that even though there was a paucity of references to these in our recent literature, my work with Al was a testimony to the validity of these concepts. I was witnessing him moving upward from a lower borderline schizoid toward a higher borderline obsessive organization, moving from primitive defenses like splitting toward more neurotic defenses, a place where one could hold opposite images about self and others in his mind together without a need to expunge one side. These recognitions were reminding me of the influential theoretical classification of Otto Kernberg (2005) about neurotic-borderline-psychotic levels of organization and clinical conceptualization of Vamik Volkan (1987), where he wonderfully described the progressions and regressions as the therapy unfolded along the continuums Kernberg talked about. All of these developments, forward and backward, were evident in his dreams and associative material and in his developing deep ambivalence toward me.

Hi!

I noted that he greeted me after a vacation with a "hi" for the first time, and I recallled that he had anticipated my departure before I left. And I noticed the significance of him bringing a bottle of water to me during a session during a hot summer day when my air-conditioning had broken down. These were subtle but significant changes.

Al said that as his therapist, I should be like him, a bit more intelligent and articulate and then felt envious of this self-image projected into me. He was appreciative of my resilience, of the fact that I endured his relentless and brutal attacks for so many years. He was aware that very few people could tolerate him. And, after so many years of what in certain aspects felt like a warfare, now it almost felt like I belong to him. I pondered how correct he was; after great battles, soldiers who try to slaughter each other become brothers (Kayatekin 2008).

In parallel with these subtle but significant shifts in his relation to me and his parents, Al became more playful and mischievous in the hospital. He would pay out of pocket for community events like trips, buy DVDs, and pay for dinners. In all of these events, he was surpassing the patient budget, destroying all the rules of patient financing in ways that made his fellow patients and the staff mad. But in contrast to his sexual transgression during the first year that caused an immense stir and almost led to his expulsion, now he was seen as mischievous. He was learning how to become a part of a peer group.

In the past, Al had populated his internal world with robots in his dreams, with cartoon characters in his fantasies, parental ghosts who were haunting him through ruminations. Now, these spaces were being occupied with complicated, three-dimensional persons. This enlivening was emotionally taxing for Al. In this new world, he goes through "funks" where he feels he is sliding back. These happen, as he recognizes with my help, in an interpersonal context. A hurt, an excitement, a separation.

Something related to others. He learns to differentiate depression from sadness, hurt, and hopelessness.

His tantrums have become more sporadic, and we have the opportunity to explore their contexts and find ways of making sense out of them; if I do not understand his thinking, his formulations, he is enraged. Those are the moments when he again doubts his own mind and mine and his old fears are awakened. Either he can't explain it properly or maybe I don't have the capacity to comprehend, either of which is devastating for Al. He yells at me, stating that he is wasting his money over this useless treatment. These are painful but at the same time helpful guides for me to understand his raw spots.

In one of these yelling storms, somewhat tired of it, I rather spontaneously told Al that he was making important points but he had no right to yell at me, and also I did not appreciate his scowling when he was trying to get his points across. Al was deeply surprised, and he agreed that we could talk about his hurt and anger through different means. This action interpretation on my part was another turning point in the treatment. Our sessions became more of a conversation.

As we were entering the fourth year of our treatment, my countertransference was less taxing. There was a clear increase in my affection toward him, a decrease in the sense of dread, and dwindling of the wishes that he would not show up for sessions or be discharged from the hospital. These internal shifts were occurring in parallel with our ordinary analytic work, our mutual "hi's" as he enters the session, and my still unreciprocated "bye's" as he leaves them. The ending of the sessions were not yet acknowledged by Al.

In his dreams, themes of castration were becoming more prominent, pointing to his upward move from annihilation anxieties (Hurvich 2003) toward castration (Winnicott 1949). His balls were being ripped; his penis was chopped off. And then in our sessions he would talk about a six-foot-penis fantasy (his and my height). To his surprised ears, building on the dream images, I developed a bodily metaphor; I told him that it felt as though he was playing with me as if I was his penis/mind. He would bolster my ego, make me think that I am a great therapist, and then he would make me lose my mind/erection by attacking and castrating me. He agreed with these thoughts of mine, again with a big grin.

Thinking back about another dilemma that I was perceiving in him and playing with it in my mind for a while, I interpreted openly; if he were to get his penis, he had to lose his mind. They couldn't exist together. His desire to live, be it sexual or aggressive, did not have a chance to coexist with his enormous motive to think and be curious about the world. Al was impressed but was at the same time taken aback with this interpretation and said he needed some time to digest these ideas.

First Love

As he was tolerating his attachment, his transference love and hate for me as contradictory feelings that may exist side by side in his mind, Al was developing a capacity to have his parents and me in his mind at the same time. In parallel, he was moving into the world of love and bodily intimacy; several years into his treatment, at the age of thirty-five, Jane became Al's first girlfriend.

Jane was a deeply shy person, a high-school dropout, working in a local grocery shop. She was adored by the town's folks as one of them and had a niche in the local community. Al came to know her during his walks on the streets of the town, and they slowly developed a friendly awareness of one another. Once Al began working part time at the grocery store, their somewhat awkward friendship became intimate; they were two peas in a pod, seen on the streets of town, in movies and eateries. Al's upper-class family looked down on this relationship and Jane's divorced, indifferent parents were uninterested.

Al was surprised with their bodily intimacy. He was deeply uncomfortable with touching other people and being touched; he could barely tolerate touching himself. Now there was a young and attractive woman whom he had to touch and who was touching him in the most intimate ways and further, Jane seemed like she was enjoying him.

As Al was getting used to the ordinary pleasurable experiences of love, affection, togetherness, and sexual intimacy, as he was becoming more capable to cathect in a new object relation, "separating" from his parents, his family was becoming more differentiated and his parents more comfortable in their individual identities. His father was becoming assertive and capable in confronting Al in moments when he needed to be. Now in his early seventies, his father was coming across as someone who could tackle Al, and his mother was talking about her admiration of her husband. The Oedipal structure finally was firming up.

Reparation

Al was more active, lively for several sessions. And then he slept in the last session. I pointed to the sequence of the sessions and wandered whether he had any thoughts about it.

Al: Maybe I am tired of talking.

I: You go out to open and then revert to solitude?

Al: Maybe, but it may simply be related to how long it takes for the poison to take effect!

It was a stunning comment; and I asked him to expand about the metaphor of poison. Al said he felt very powerful recently. He was noticing that others could impact him and he could impact others in different ways. It was a textured impact of a different nature though. Did not have to be godly but could be of human dimensions. Not too destructive but still hurtful.

After a stretch of exhilaration over the recognition of his capabilities, he would, as expected, develop anxieties about castration and death and would fall back to "depression." When I highlighted these sequences, he would tell me that he was afraid of losing his balls and penis and convey some of his fantasies that either he or his dad should end up dying. He was simultaneously afraid of and enjoying these fantasies.

Moving Out for Good

Al was getting more comfortable with the idea that he may be attached to me, and I may be to him. As he was developing a capacity to be with peers in the community outside of structured treatment settings, Al's love for Jane was deepening, and they were thinking about getting engaged. Al was surprised, as was I, by how passionate and poetic he had become about this relationship; he told Jane that he "wanted to sit in the same room with her, breathe the same air, and be together with her all the time." I was touched by his tenderness and said that I found this narrative very poetic.

As he was leaving the session, he said, "Maybe I love you too."

I: "Hum uhm . . . that's probably true."

His last-minute loving comments, his keeping the perverse aspects of the narrative to the main body of the session, was probably an embarrassed acknowledgement of a father/son love. It was somewhat similar to our very first encounter, when he had inquired about my patients who had committed suicide at the very end of the session as he was on his way out. But then we were talking about his death, whereas now we were talking, in passing, about his love. It was quite a change.

After becoming sexually intimate with Jane, he began complaining about the joys of sexuality: "If sex is like this, I must admit that it is not too appealing. I haven't missed out on anything," he said, and again made allusions to how he was longing for an orgasmic session in therapy, an "aha" moment and his faked therapeutic orgasms over the course of many years of our work. He enviously referred to other patients in the hospital who would talk about the immensely painful, sad, joyous sessions that they had with their therapists, making me feel wondrously amused and nevertheless a bit worried about my technical capabilities. As I was helpless in responding to these wishes of his, Al was telling me he needed a blow job whereas our work was something in between a colonoscopy or a masturbatory session. And I interpretatively agreed with a "hum uhm." He was reminding me of how Ogden brilliantly pointed to sexuality as a metaphor and a Rosetta Stone of the person in their attempts to understand the world when he proposed that "human beings interpret all perceptions in terms of sexual meanings" in the process of creating experience (Ogden 1990, 19).

By now it was a solid four years of psychoanalytic work, and I was recognizing that, to my disgust and pleasure, he was finally capable of throwing the skin he would peel from his finger tips on the floors of my office in contrast to how he used to deposit all of these in his coffee cup for many years. It was love.

Dreams

As his transferential relation with me further deepened and love with his girlfriend became more intimate, his dream life became more polychromatic. Early on in our work, he had what he called "Al dreams"—dreams where he would be in an ecstatic state of mind, walking in Heaven. The content of these dreams had no connection to his daily life, and he would just feel happy. As our work progressed, his dream life shifted to scary dreams about aliens who were invading the earth, and Al was in a position of defending the world.

Dreams around this period were about the hospital, where he saw some friends from high school and college, and some fellow patients in the hospital and me. In his dream world, the hospital was somewhere in between his high school and college years. A pervasive theme was his fear of going back to parental home from the hospital.

Before an upcoming vacation, for the first time after so many years, Al told me that he will miss me and it hurts him badly. He feels like a butterfly coming out of his cocoon, trying to get out of a protective and nurturing shell that was helpful, necessary for his survival for many decades, but now it was to time to come out of it, leave it behind. It was a scary and exciting effort. He feels good and cool nowadays but also has a feeling of disgust as he recognizes his vulnerabilities. And this brings another downward spiral; he is ordinary. He is not God or devil. It is so relieving and so detestable. For the first time, after a session he says goodbye to me, and I reciprocate. He had finally enveloped the session with an initial "hi" and a final "bye." He was developing a skin.

Schizoid Armor, Open Guts, and Skin

Al's acknowledgement of his attachment to me, Jane, his parents, and some important others was going hand in hand with him "developing a skin": a boundary that is not impenetrable as a steel schizoid armor or one that was not as easily penetrable, fragile, and sensitive as open guts. Skin was a metaphor for a psychic boundary that was open to wounds and hurts but easier to wear than an armor or open guts, and with a considerable capacity for repair. It was an evocative and clinically useful metaphor that Al and I had cocreated.

As he was developing a skin, interestingly and expectedly, Al started bringing things in between the two of us to the session for the first time; his laptop, a bunch of papers and pens. He was creating a transitional space in between the two of us, as an intermediate step to developing his separate sense of self, a psychic skin.

Termination

We were close to our termination, and Al was recognizing the progress we had made with a sense of gratitude. The grandiose wishes of becoming a world-renowned academic and the catastrophic fears of him amounting to nobody had vanished. He had become ordinarily human, expressing his jealousy over my new patients and worried that I may lose interest in him. He had developed friendships in his small community, was visiting Jane in her apartment and occasionally spending the night with her. All of his relations yet seemed tenuous, one foot in, one out.

When a female peer from the hospital invited Al to have dinner, he was confused whether she was sexually interested in him or not, and if so, should he reciprocate her invitation. And the idea of eating the food a friend had prepared was too intrusive and disgusting. He could not imagine eating food that was cooked by someone he was on friendly terms with. He didn't mind eating at restaurants, but eating a dinner prepared by a friend?! . . . He managed to contain his sexual interest in the friend and enjoyed the elegant dinner. It was a significant sublimatory step for a person who confused "eros" and "agape," sexual interest and friendship, some years back.

As our therapeutic field became more humanly complicated, with an array of negative and positive feelings, thoughts on both sides, a shift was occurring in the multiple planes of the hospital where it became relatively easier for Al to relate to people. Instead of a schizoid armor, with very sensitive guts underneath, Al was now recognizing he was an extremely shy person, and could tolerate the friendship of a few people at the most and would probably be like that for the rest of his life.

Around the end of the fourth year, he discharged from the hospital to continue his work with the referring analyst. He was heartbroken and relieved that Jane had decided to stay in her hometown. He still was deeply shy and reserved in human relations, but was interested in living and had found a niche that was populated with others, where he was connected and was able to love and work. He and I had tears in our eyes as he took my extended hand and shook it firmly as he left the office one final time.

REFLECTIONS ON AL

Schizoid Pathology

Salman Akhtar (1987) offered the interesting hypothesis that schizoid individuals were in essence presenting themselves in an "inverse" fashion; they were using their outward appearance as a defensive posture to their inside experiences, an idea reminiscent of the concept of "false self" as we will think about in the case of Barbara, presented in chapter 2. While I agree with Akhtar on his observation, I came to think that schizoid persons may use both aspects of their selves defensively and yet are genuinely capable of being both. It is a split self-representation, and the story of Al is a witness to this. Al was genuinely indifferent and sensitive, sadistic and masochistic all at the same time, despite both presentations being used for purposes of defense. We will see this complicated intrapsychic and interpersonal phenomenon more closely later in the story of Barbara.

Acting Out versus Enactment

During the initial phase of our work, Al's treatment in the hospital was centrally going through actions and evocations. His loquaciousness or somnolence in sessions, flirtatious stance with peers, disappearing from the hospital, and his uncontrollable anger toward me created strong affective evocations and counteractions in me and the peers and staff. These actions and counteractions in the session or outside bring the differential of acting out/in and enactment to the table, an ongoing, important debate in psychoanalytic circles. It is a debate that vacillates between intrapsychic and bipersonal/interpersonal formulations.

Otto Fenichel's (1945, 197) formulation is a good example for an intrapsychic approach, where acting out is seen as an action that unconsciously "relieves inner tension and brings a partial discharge to warded off impulses. . . . The present situation, somehow associatively connected with the repressed content, is used as an occasion for the discharge of repressed energies; the cathexis is displaced from the repressed memories to the present 'derivative,' and this displacement makes the discharge possible."

In contrast to this energic/intrapsychic ego psychological formulation, when working with a population prone to acting out, Johnson noted the parallels between what they coined as "superego lacunae" of the parents of the patient who was acting out and asserted that the child was vicariously gratifying parents' "poorly integrated, forbidden impulses" (Johnson and Szurek 1952). Brian Bird (1957, 630) was in agreement with this observation: "acting out, although personally motivated, is a direct action response to stimulation by another person" that is motivated to "please or to influence another person, or perhaps to do both." He hypothesized that this was an unconsciously initiated process through nonverbal, behavioral channels of communication.

The sessions that were devoted to the topic of acting out at the International Psycho-Analytic Congress of 1968 crystallized the debate. The formulation of Anna Freud (1968) with intrapsychic energic terms was a striking contrast to the assertion of Leon Grinberg (1968) on the importance of a dyad.

Psychoanalysts working with psychotic disorders increased our awareness of the importance of countertransference in the analytic space (Little 1951; Boyer 1979). Similarly, therapists working in psychotherapeutic hospitals had innovative formulations: "Although the basic unit of biological functioning is the individual, the basic unit of psychological functioning seems always to be a twosome. That is, such behavior is always in relation to another person" (Cooperman 1983, 22).

Within mainstream British psychoanalysis there was an earlier appreciation of a two-person psychology. The Kleinians were instrumental in the development of two-person theories with their concepts of splitting, projection, introjection, and projective identification (Feldman 1992; Feldman 1997).

From the British middle group, Donald W. Winnicott's assertion that a baby can be defined only in relation to another person was a reference to the mother–baby twosome as an inseparable unit (Winnicott 1947). Joseph Sandler (1976) foreshadowed the concept of enactment when he suggested the analyst "will, unless he becomes aware of it, tend to comply with the role demanded of him, to integrate it into his mode of responding and relating to the patient. Normally, of course, he can catch this counter-response in himself, particularly if it appears to be in the direction of being inappropriate. However, he may only become aware of it through observing his own behavior, responses and attitudes, after these have been carried over into action" (Sandler 1976, 47).

Over time the field has seen a clear shift toward two-person formulations and toward recognition of the concept of enactment (McLaughlin 1991). And as the initial phase of the treatment of Al demonstrates, I was clearly in it together with him, becoming an actor of his internal object relational scripts, some of which colluded with my own personal scripts. It was not an acting out, but an enactment. A cocreated transference countertransference field based on our mutual histories, conflicts as they colluded with one another (Kayatekin and Plakun 2011).

Reparative Element in Repetition and Enactments

Through his seductive engagement with female patients, Al had tapped into my inhibited adolescent sexuality, and with his relentless, sadistic attacks on me he had recreated my endlessly tolerant "mature boy" image. In other words, he had recreated two main transference plates of his, maternal and paternal, and on my end, he had hooked into conflicted aspects of my adolescent eroticism and aggression.

As we went through the ramifications of these transference-countertransference scripts, Al helped me to become aware of ambivalently held aspects of my self-image. His impact on me had a destructive element; he was refuting some cherished, conflicted images of mine, and he was also being dangerously destructive to our work, thus my therapeutic narcissism. On the other hand, my increased self-awareness offered me a chance for reworking, and recreation of a less conflicted self-object representational scheme, and he toned my therapeutic zeal down.

All of these were an illustration of the patient unwittingly becoming therapist to their therapist in the transference as part of moving toward a healthier adaptation (Searles 1973).

Family

The family dynamics are centrally important in the development of borderline organization (Shapiro et al. 1975). The inability to hold ambivalence or conflict intrapsychically leads to splitting, and this defensive constellation is, as a rule, accompanied with projective identificatory mechanisms (Kernberg 1972). The split aspect has to be put outside of one's self, into someone else. Thus an aspect of the pathology slowly trickles to others, and in time, down the generations.

In this process, we witness the development of simplistic, dichromatic narratives: as an example, at the beginning of the treatment, Al and his parents were reporting their history from the lens of black and white, good and bad. It was a two-dimensional world, and when invited to talk about it, they couldn't expand on their stories beyond a few paragraphs. It was a world of conciseness and simplicity: in Al's eyes, his father was a weakling, his mother was a hysterical nymphomaniac. He thought his parents continued to stay together because a bonus child looked good on their CVs as two successful professionals. On the parents' end, the mother viewed her history as pitch dark; her father was a loser and her mother was a demented person. Al's father, on the other hand, felt his family was good and great. This simplistic family narrative became much more three-dimensional and textured throughout the treatment. We will get into this fascinating process of the complicating of the family narratives through long-term family treatment, in the case of Judy.

Lateral Transferences with Siblings and Peers

Lateral transferences—sibling transferences and transferences that develop from our early peer relations—are a relatively neglected field in psychoanalysis (Blos 1976; Graham 1988; Vivona 2007). Yet the representational scripts that develop from these relations are important motivators and have quite significant influence in our lives, as the treatment of Al demonstrated. A central element in Al's treatment was his increased capacity to develop and work on lateral transferences. Building on the more mature aspects of the central transference/countertransference templates with me, experiencing that I was not threatened by others entering his life as new loves, Al found the freedom to develop relationships outside of the dyad, and form new interpersonal-intrapsychic scripts.

The sibling and peer relations will be expanded on in the stories of Barbara in the next chapter and Henry in chapter 3.

2

PSYCHOANALYTIC PSYCHOTHERAPY IN THE PSYCHOTHERAPEUTIC HOSPITAL

Barbara—The So-Called "False Self"

Barbara was in her mid-forties when we began our work in the psychotherapeutic hospital. She was a college graduate and a housewife. They were married for twenty years and did not have children.

As we will read in detail at the end of this chapter, Barbara came from a family of five. Barbara's mother had significant problems in managing the ordinary chores of family life and needed constant advice from an elderly neighbor or her sister, who were regular presences in the house as supportive maternal figures. Barbara's father had sociopathic tendencies and had a chaotic work life with temporary jobs. It was a disorganized family life; the couple were often intoxicated and would get into heated arguments and physical fights. They had a son and two daughters, Barbara and Liz.

Barbara's brother followed the paths of his mother and father; he dropped out of high school and became a drug addict. During her teens, noticing the discrepancies with other families and feeling deeply ashamed by the lifestyle of her own family, Barbara tried to repair that image. She would clean the house, help her mother cook better. She was also working very hard to be a reasonably good student. Barbara's life took a different path; she became the "good girl" and a central figure in the family's life. She developed a deep bond with Liz, her ten-year-old sister; when Liz was a baby, Barbara would wake up in the middle of the night, change her younger sister's diapers, and bottle feed her. As Liz grew older, Barbara played with her whenever she had time; she was trying to remedy the absences of other family members.

In her early adolescence, as she became more cognizant of her surroundings, Barbara recognized that her father, to her shock, was involved in small-scale drug trafficking. She recognized that this was a well-known fact in the neighborhood, and it became a deep source of shame for her. But she was not even allowed to ask questions or express her embarrassment about it because he would say it was "this business that puts food on the table."

In this traumatic environment, there were some memorable times. Barbara was the lead singer in the school choir, and her parents were extremely proud and supportive of her to the point where she felt they were possessive of her accomplishments; her father wouldn't let Barbara practice with her friends, and would come and watch her practices all the time. The same father who was a drunkard and a drug dealer would treat Barbara like a friend. He would take her on his monthly fishing trips with a buddy of his, where he and his friend would catch fish, get drunk, and ask Barbara to gut the fish that they had caught. She enjoyed the privileged position her father was giving to her and at the same time, she was horrified and disgusted with the chore of gutting the fish that she was forced to do.

Unlike her brother, who was living a clear-cut amoral life, Barbara was getting confused about her parents' contradictory messages. They were living an odd mixture of a psychopathic existence but with terribly rigid moral codes around the appearance of the house, which they had delegated to Barbara's care. It was impossible to make sense of all of these contradictions and reconcile these two split images.

Barbara found an interesting solution to this intolerable confusion of trauma, narcissistic fulfillment and Oedipal victory. As a person who had learned to fend for herself early on, she made up her mind around her early teens: she decided to leave this household as soon as she became a consenting adult. So she secretly began saving money by working on weekends and during summer breaks. Following graduation from high school, with a deep sense of guilt over leaving Liz and her parents behind, she abruptly left the parental household to the shock and intense opposition of her parents. She rented an apartment, bought a car with her secretly saved money, and started working, with the hope of getting Liz under her wing as soon as possible. Barbara, unlike her family, was able to hold on to steady jobs and on the side, she managed to graduate from a community college with a degree in teaching.

Nevertheless, the disowned parts that were dormant for quite some time in Barbara eventually became alive. After her graduation from college, Barbara went through a period where she had multiple affairs, and was smoking pot and drinking regularly. This period ended rather abruptly when Bill came into her life.

Barbara met Bill through a mutual friend. He was coming from the humble background of a blue-collar American family. About ten years older than Barbara, Bill was a hardworking young attorney and a jovial person despite his serious genetic illness. The illness required regular treatments through his early twenties and had caused some serious skeletal deformities in his legs and arms. At some point in his life, he was wheelchair-bound, but he had managed to get out of this horrible state through a series of surgeries that enabled him to walk with crutches.

Barbara knew about being crippled in her soul, and Bill in his body, and they were attracted to one another immediately and began to date. Her relationship with Bill made Barbara feel horribly guilty and ashamed over her recent adventurous years. She felt like she had become an immoral person, acting just like the rest of her family. Bill reawakened a powerful sense of morality in Barbara and in the persona of Bill, she found a chance for repentance. For Bill, Barbara was a joy; he felt like he found a pretty woman who knew about the gutters of life and yet had pulled herself out of that abyss, like he had pulled himself out of the darkness of his severe physical illness.

Once they began living together, Barbara joined Bill's church and developed a strong attachment to the pastor, who was also a counselor. With the pastor's counseling, Barbara developed a formulation; she probably had a dissociative disorder and her altars were the cause of the "bad." They provided an explanation for the years when she was in multiple sexual liaisons and was abusing drugs. She had dislocated and projected her bodily desires, her sexual and aggressive strivings, to the altars in her mind. Thus, such desires, passions, and behaviors were returned back to the turf of her parents and brother. With the help of her pastor, church, and her relationship with Bill, Barbara had again found an internal sense of peace; she was burying her confusing history of trauma, boundary violations, and narcissistic fulfillment. The concept of dissociation gave Barbara a deep sense of relief over what she had done, and the supportive elements of this approach were probably crucial to her psychic survival. After her aunt and the elderly loving neighbor, she felt the pastor and the church was another loving relationship.

Barbara and Bill's mutual attraction developed into a deep attachment and in a year they were married. In the following years, Barbara was instrumental in her husband's developing a very successful law practice and in turn, having a steady income helped Barbara to quit her teaching job and settle into the role of housemaker. Through her husband's successful law practice, they eventually moved into an upper-class lifestyle in their town. They were unable to conceive, so they brought Liz to their family and treated her as their own daughter.

Over the course of the years, Barbara created an image of a selfless person, a perfect mother and wife. They had a beautiful house and an immaculate yard. She was an excellent cook, and doted on her husband and Liz. Furthermore, she was seen as a central maternal figure for her larger family—as they prospered, she took all of the members of her family of origin—her parents and her brother—under her wing.

Barbara took great pride in these accomplishments. In striking contrast to what was not provided during her own upbringing, she became an endless source of supplies—emotional and material—for the people around her. It was a life that was the exact opposite of what she was provided with during her youth.

Around the time of the birth of Liz's daughter, Barbie, who was named after her, Barbara began experiencing what she described as "other selves" in her mind. There was a needy person, like a little baby that needed constant care; and there was a very angry person who was thinking of harming her beloved ones. Barbara was afraid that these, what she and her pastor named as "altars," would take over and make her behave in horrendous ways. Thus, she lived in a state of constant anticipatory fear. She didn't tell anyone about these internal experiences, and from the outside it seemed like she was doing fine. Then came another developmental challenge when Barbie was entering puberty. It was another challenge to Barbara's defensive equilibrium because now Barbie's development had invited others to their interpersonal milieu. Barbie was talking about boys in sexual ways and developing some friendships, and these intrusions and inclusion of sexual, bodily others were well beyond Barbara's ego capacities, triggering tremors in her old intrapsychic fault lines.

No longer capable of holding all of this chaos in, Barbara began displaying some odd behaviors. These lasted for a few days and seemed to come out of the blue: She would become extremely angry, cuss people out, and throw things at her husband. She would mallet her hands to the point where she would suffer some fractures. There were other stretches where she would isolate herself in her room—remaining unkempt, spaced out, eating alone, and refusing to come out. These peculiar periods would clear rapidly after short-term hospitalizations and to the relief of herself and family, Barbara would revert to being her usual happy, energetic, loving, caring self. These states were very perplexing to her family because of their abrupt eruption and equally sudden disappearance.

After repeated breakdowns, it became clear that the image Barbara created with enormous amount of work was crumbling, and she sought help in the hospital.

Barbara in the Hospital

Barbara was deeply sad over her decision to be hospitalized because of what she had to leave behind. She was the cobuilder of a successful business and an adored person in her family and community, and now she was in an asylum. The person, or rather the image of the person, she had worked so hard to build for many decades had collapsed. The first phase of her hospitalization, roughly about a year, was about this transition; mourning the loss of a cherished image and separation from her family. It was also a time of painful adaptation to a new human ecology and thinking about the events of her past that she never had a space and courage to think about.

Barbara referred to me as "Dr. K" or "Sir" in accordance with the morays of the southern gentility that she had risen herself into, a set of behaviors she had adopted with a sense of accomplishment in contrast to her bad-mannered parents. She spoke with a kind and respectful, somewhat infantile, cheerful voice. And unlike any other patient of mine, she refused to use my ottoman to stretch her legs because she was afraid of smearing some dirt on it. Neither would she use my garbage can to dispose of her tissue paper or emptied coffee cups.

In our psychoanalytic work, for several months, she had what one may call an idealizing transference (Kohut and Wolf 1978). Barbara was always pleasant, would come in on time, meticulously dressed, with a heavy makeup, repeatedly expressing gratitude for working with me. In the countertransference, I had the powerful sense that she was trying to occupy a very clean and good space in my mind and in my office. Beyond the genteel admiring affections of a self-made southern lady to a respectable doctor, there was no evidence of a complicated set of ordinary feelings in the office.

As I was treated kindly with admiration and distance, in a parallel fashion, in the larger hospital setting, a generous mother figure was emerging. Barbara would try to console her peers after their intense sessions, take them out for dinner in nearby high-end restaurants, or would buy expensive gifts for them; a generosity she was capable of because of her considerable wealth. As a very active member of the community life, she was joining all the groups that were available and acting as an extremely conscientious member of the community.

There was a mixed sense of appreciation and concern about this "mother of all." Some patients felt uncomfortable with this level of altruism, whereas some younger patients were truly enjoying Barbara's selflessness. Nursing, on the other hand, recognized the unfolding pattern of suffocating altruism and initiated a conversation about why she was taking over so much. The staff had sufficient history of Barbara so that they had a formulation and were able to recognize potential patterns of repetition, and made their therapeutic interventions from that formulation; Barbara was just like the little Barbara, who would be a good student, work, save money, mow the lawn, and clean the house while at the same time be a mother to her baby sister.

In her relations with the staff, there was another element that caught our attention relatively early on. She was quite serious about the rules and would demand that the staff and other patients be the same. Once, she got into a heated argument with a nurse who had given the medication to a patient before Barbara even though she was further in the line, and on another occasion she scolded a senior staff member when she thought he was not leading the group in an efficient way. She was the admired and admiring, loving mother with an enormous capacity for deliverance and a proper citizen with a keen eye on the principle of being equitable and just.

Barbara was creating the imprisoning scripts of her life in the hospital; a prison she did not choose to come into—neither did we, but we were all in it nevertheless.

Partially enjoying the exalted state and at the same time recognizing that it was an unavoidable trap, an enactment, I was trying to get out of this suffocating, pleasurable situation through many therapeutic interventions. To my frustration, what I thought were my efforts in clarification and confrontation of her character defenses that centered on altruism were falling on deaf ears. They were seen as praise by her, and she was not joining me in viewing this as something to explore no matter how many different angles I approached it from.

Instead, to my dismay, she was making statements like, "Yes, I am known as a good mother to many" with some sense of pride. Barbara was telling me that she had no tolerance of any resemblance to her parents and brother, who were immoral, irresponsible as parents, and she wanted to be the exact opposite of them. Making her ego-syntonic character traits ego-dystonic was an impossible therapeutic endeavor at the moment. She treated my thoughts as if they were nonexistent, just like the way she was placing herself in relation to me.

Mourning

Barbara had an argument with her husband about the details of a trip he and Liz and Barbie were planning. Barbara would have done the planning in the past and had asked that he should let her talk with Liz about the details of the vacation. Bill reminded Barbara that she was now in a hospital, and they had to make some decisions on their own. Barbara was heartbroken, infuriated, but reflecting on the facts of their life, felt he was right.

In the session, in tears she remembered that it was the time when they would all go to a nearby beach as a family tradition, and now she was far away from her family, hospitalized in an asylum. Barbie, her husband, and Liz were all taking charge of their own lives. Barbara feared that she had lost her central role in the family. She was deeply sad over being thousands of miles away from her beloved family.

I was noting to myself the lack of a sense of revenge in Barbara when she was hurt and pointed to that.

Barbara: "Yes, it was very hurtful. Feeling excluded and maybe even forgotten, I cried by myself all day long and then decided to close it and move forward. I never felt comfortable with getting even, even when I was a little kid."

I: "I guess we can think about how to understand why that is so difficult for you and maybe find ways of making you more comfortable with the idea of revenge. It may help you."

Barbara kept a keen eye on the family and stayed as the matriarch for several months more. In time, they began living more independently and making decisions on their own, without consulting her on the minutiae of their daily lives. This came as a sad relief to Barbara. She was sad because she was recognizing she was not as needed or important as her family was going on living independently, yet it was a relief because Barbara was claiming her own space and interests.

Her mourning of the loss of a grandiosely held and tiring maternal image was developing in parallel with her deepening reflections on her past. Her parents and brother were beginning to occupy a lot of space in her mind and in her narrative in the analytic space. Her parents had told her that she should never talk to others about their secrets. Even though she had known how troubled her parents were, she had never told it to their face and actually never had talked or thought about that period of her life with anybody, even her husband; it was a forbidden zone of contemplation for her.

The exploration of that era became central to the psychoanalytic work for many months during the first year of work. Barbara was not allowed to cry as a child; her mother had no tolerance for sadness and would threaten to throw her out of the house if she cried. With me she was in tears, as she was thinking about them with anger, missing and hating them at the same time. Despite the brutality of the family life, Barbara was also the apple of her parents' eye and as she reflected on these deeply contradictory stages of love and sadism from her father and mother, Barbara was deepening her mourning.

And while she felt guilty over betraying them as she talked to me, she also felt relieved; she was enjoying the revenge of talking about her parents and was also feeling deeply ashamed of my hearing these stories. She was finally daring to reflect on the "unthought known" (Bollas 1987).

Change

About a year into her treatment, this good and kind patient began showing some other aspects of herself. She was invited to join the treatment team for a regular meeting. As the interviewer asked her to take the chair next to him for a conversation, Barbara began swearing at us and then stormed out of the team meeting before it even started. We were all stunned and at a loss on how to make sense of what had happened.

In the following analytic session, she told me that she was deeply hurt with the demeanor of the interviewer. He had introduced himself to Barbara as "Dr. F." and then used her nickname "Barb" without asking her permission. She immediately felt infantilized and demeaned. She remembered the times when the family would call her the "Pygmy" because of her small stature. The way she was treated by the interviewer felt similar to those times; she was not a respectable person. We were beginning to experience her rage and take a glimpse at the roots of it.

I and You

A week before my vacation, Barbara told me that she was sick and tired of me and was damn glad that I was taking a week off. She bitterly complained that she was coming to our four-times-a-week sessions regularly, attending all the required meetings and felt caged by my and others' expectations from her. It exactly felt like her home. I was taken aback with this sudden onslaught of attack but thought it was a significant moment of self-interpretation and progress in our relatively calm work so far.

In some of her recent dreams, people were leaving her; friends, her mother, and her father. She made another self-interpretation that these dreams were probably related to my upcoming vacation. For a person who for many months had forgiven me about such therapeutic fractures with comments like, "It is your right, you have to take some time off," this was a significant shift in her narrative.

I responded by affirming her self-interpretations with "Hum, uhm."

She remembered how peculiar an experience it was for her to take care of her baby sister at the age of ten while her parents and brother would be out "having fun," and she felt jealous of people who seem to be having fun here. In the hospital, Barbara had partially recreated her teenage life and through that repetition, was now becoming more aware of it.

I: "Hum uhm."

Barbara: "That is not too nice to say but . . ." and paused.

Pointing to her pause, I told her that there seemed to be a side of her that was deeply annoyed and angry but was at the same time hesitant about expressing it, probably because it didn't fit with her self-image.

Barbara agreed and bitterly complained that she felt like she was working all the time here in the hospital and was tired of her pervasive sense of responsibility and a long list of obligations. Then she confessed that even after so many months in the hospital, she had not yet fully unpacked. At home she could not wear some new clothes for many years, would keep them in their original packaging. She ended the session by saying that it was a surprise that she was finding a sense of joy here and had not left the hospital yet. Her deep ambivalence slowly fading, she was settling into the treatment and accepting me and the hospital into her internal world as a new, ambivalently held object.

Surfacing of the Bad

I took a week off, and when I came back I heard that Barbara had a very difficult time and had made a suicide attempt. She was transferred to a local emergency room and was treated overnight. When she came back to the hospital, she was placed in the highest level of care where she was observed very closely. When we reestablished our work she calmed down. We were close to the end of the first year of our work, and she had begun to see me as an important other and developed fears of losing me.

My emergence as an important person in her life also brought the negative transference to the sessions and changed her presentation in the hospital. She stopped buying gifts for others and began skipping sessions, with the excuse that she just simply forgot. Her cautiousness in the hospital was fading away. She was quite frequently tripping, dropping her food trays, shattering plates and glasses, and spilling food on the floor. She tripped and shattered a tall clock. This sloppy woman was such a contrast to the meticulous, careful Barbara we had seen in the early phases of the treatment, a surprise to us and an embarrassment to herself.

Alongside their psychopathic traits, her parents were very peculiar about the cleanliness and tidiness of their house. Thus the clumsiness Barbara was displaying in the hospital would be considered almost a sin in her family of origin, and she would have been punished severely. In the hospital, though, the staff had a more reasonable response to such accidents. They told Barbara that it was not a big deal, she just had to be more careful and to her surprise, life went on without any retributions.

Meanwhile, in the psychoanalytic work, she began having strong responses to ordinary failures of mine like weekend breaks, taking a vacation, being away because of illness, or when she felt like I was not understanding her. We would go through stormy days when she would sulk and pout or get enraged and yell at me. She would tell me that she hated me because I was a man and was abusive like her father. She hated my office because it smelled like her parental home. Her physical appearance shifted. The gentle voice was gone.

She would come to the sessions unkempt, wearing her crumpled and dirty nightgown, spread her feet on my ottoman and create a mess with the muck spilling from the soles of her boots; the sessions were filled with her screaming at the top of her lungs, and she was frequently slamming the door as she stormed out of the office. Her snot filled tissue papers and half-emptied coffee cups would fill my garbage can, spilling dirt out onto my floor. My attempts at initiating a therapeutic conversation were attacked from many different angles; I was unempathic, a man, a foreigner, and lacked the interest and capacity to understand her. Her chaos would spread into my mind; I would lose my therapeutic mind and footing.

Then she would collapse. She wouldn't take care of herself, stay in her bedroom for weeks, eat alone, and hit the wall with her fists to the point where once she needed emergency medical care. She would call and tell me that she couldn't pull herself out of the bed and request that we have the sessions in her room, or at the very least over the phone. These messages were filled with longing to connect, and evoked strong countertransference affects of sadness, suffocation, and sympathy in me and created wishes/impulses to gratify her demands. I was barely managing to contain the temptation to give in to her requests and with a deep sense of guilt would ask her to bring herself to my office where we could try to think together about what was happening. As I managed to contain my wishes, she eventually would drag herself to sessions and tell me how terribly hurt and enraged she was and worst of all, how she felt unimportant to me and powerless over me. With a painful and deep sense of guilt over my refusal to go to her room to talk and using these painful countertransference reactions as a source of data, I offered interpretations of her deep, conflicted dependency needs/wishes. These attempts of mine did not seem to make any impression on Barbara; she continued to talk about how she was terribly hurt that I was not responding to her calls in a way she would respond to me if I needed her help; like the way she mothered her baby sister or her parents in times of need.

Through a suffocating sense of loneliness, sadness, and despair that invaded the hours, she recalled the extreme dependencies of her mother and father, the times when they asked her to take care of the house, the yard, and their baby daughter while they were going on living their intoxicated lives. In a state of deep sadness, she reminisced about the brutal sadism and neglect she suffered in her youth. These enormous losses of her life would move to the here and now, and we recognized my failings in our work in the hospital and her own failings.

The image of good person/patient was destroyed and some disavowed bad, vicious, and dependent sides that she had located in the others around her, were now back in her. During these stormy times, she evoked strong wishes and fantasies in me to defend myself or attack her for being ungrateful or try and rescue her, yet I was able to contain myself and interpret.

In the larger community, the "bad" had emerged with a fierce force. Barbara often got into arguments and severe confrontations with staff and her peers to the point where her suitability for the hospital was being questioned by the community. Nevertheless, she would feel very embarrassed about these incidents and would later try to repair and compensate by being more "good" than usual, offering to taking people out to dinners and buying them expensive gifts. In contrast to her retaliatory family, the hospital staff and peers would not be provoked into fights with her but developed proper boundaries around the level of aggression, and after a point they refused her compensatory "good"-ness symbolized by her attempts to buy dinners or gifts. The staff and patients as a group, the milieu, would respond in a textured way to her aggression and love.

So both in the individual space and in the milieu, these affect storms, the projective/introjective processes, were handled very differently, allowing Barbara to internalize new self-object paradigms to her repertoire. The holding environment (Winnicott 1960; Modell 1976) or container (Bion 1962) as an ever-present element in the hospital was affecting an ongoing treatment well beyond the limits of our individual psychoanalytic work.

Am I Playful or Mean?

Recently, Barbara was calmer, and I was a bit startled when, as she was taking her usual seat in the office, in a teasing tone she said, "Dr. K, if you pay any attention to me, you may recognize that I don't have any makeup on today. And we are planning a girl's night out. We will go out to dinner and the movies. I also have a new hairstyle, as you may have noticed (putting another playful sting in me), and I am trying to tolerate my new hairstyle. I never, ever, in my life had a short haircut."

She was right, I had not recognized it until that moment and suddenly it dawned on me that Barbara was appearing different in the last few weeks; with minimal makeup, a short haircut, and wearing jeans! This was a profound shift from the inhibited or sad or enraged Barbara that I had been used to for some time now. I was listening to this playful narrative and the coy teenager-like woman with a sense of amazement, puzzlement, and delight.

As I was trying to digest these new recognitions of mine, Barbara said that recently she was struggling with a fear that I may transfer her to another therapist. I was baffled by this idea. This countertransference sense of surprise was a moment of heated transference, I thought, and I asked why she thought that I would transfer her to another therapist.

Barbara in turn said that she felt like she was not acting properly in the last few weeks. She was not looking at me with an inner sense of respect and an outer stance of politeness and had caught herself squinting at me. I was well aware of and relieved with the calm that had come back and vaguely aware that she was more spontaneous in the sessions; she was not talking with her usual childish tone, but I had no awareness of her squinting.

When she professed that she was squinting at me, a series of beloved actors of mine flashed through my mind. Amongst them were Marlon Brando, and of course Clint Eastwood, who could squint beautifully, and I had another fleeting thought: that it must be an enjoyable experience to squint at someone who is worthy of receiving your squint as an opponent or maybe even as an enemy worth killing.

With these reveries, split-second thoughts in my mind, and aware that I was bypassing resistance and making a disclosure, I nonetheless told her that her internal experience and mine were quite different; "I have a sense that, following that stormy period, you are allowing yourself to be more playful recently," I said, and pointed to how she may feel like she was in the territory of her brother and parents, having some fun.

Barbara broke into tears as she recalled some early memories. If she was playful, she would be put back in her place, and her parents would give a warning that she should act like a proper girl, not like her wayward brother. Her psychopathic father, her negligent mother, and her brother had the prerogative to be disorganized, playful, and childish but Barbara was not allowed into that turf.

These newly emerging aspects of Barbara, someone who could give an evil eye, have short hair, or go out with the girls and someone who would be enraged with people over ordinary issues and not be just like the good mother, made her confused. She was used to having a psychological makeup all the times just as she was used to wearing a physical makeup.

Barbara had a deeply held belief that she was an unattractive woman. In fact, she felt as if she was so ugly that if she did not very meticulously plan her clothes and makeup, if she were in sporty outwear as she now dared to be in, no man would ever be interested in her. Nursing and peers, on the other hand, were giving her surprising feedback that in her natural state she was coming across as a more interesting and attractive woman.

The "Barbie Stuff"

Barbara was presenting herself as a more complicated human being, with a wide range of capabilities from extremes of caring for others, to an enraged vengeful woman who would fracture her hands with a mallet, to a playful person, just like an adolescent experimenting with different sides of herself. She had an interesting coinage to this phase; she was telling me that she needed to "do the Barbie stuff." She and I noted that the coinage was not about just the famous doll but was also her dear niece Barbie—a girl she loved dearly and probably envied; because of what she had and Barbara did not.

Around about a year and a half into treatment, as she was cautiously experimenting with the "Barbie stuff," rages that pushed her to the edge of dissociation continued to resurface. With continual exploration and reexploration of these incidents, the subtle narcissistic injuries that triggered these very unusual presentations became clearer to Barbara and me. When she sensed any disrespect or lack of affirmation of her "good"-ness, she would become very hurt but would suppress it. After a series of such injuries, she would, all of a sudden, fly into a semidissociated rage. The moments of hurt were hard to locate because Barbara had made herself relatively numb to such injuries. Thus, as we were trying to locate such moments as injurious for Barbara, we were trying to lower her psychic pain threshold.

In time, Barbara developed a capacity to experience these injuries without suppressing them, responded with expressing her hurt or retaliating with proper aggression when needed, and began owning all of these internal experiences and reactions as belonging to her. She was changing the narrative and was now capable of omitting the "because" clause of "dissociation." She got into passionate arguments and fights with staff and patients, and the lack of severe retaliation from the others she was fighting with helped her to understand that not every disagreement was about life and death, there were gradations. Barbara, through these interactions within the therapeutic community, developed a modified sense of "bad" ness.

The last year was a period when Barbara vacillated between different presentations; good, bad, and playful. By this time though, she and I had witnessed these patterns several times, so Barbara and I were developing a capacity to observe her in these modes of being and acting. Thus she was more amenable to analytic/interpretative exploration in the here and now. In a staccato fashion, the therapeutic field began to change; these vacillations became less frequent, lost their intensity and in between these good and bad modes of being, a different presentation began to emerge. Barbara became more forgiving of others and herself. She toned down her altruism and vengefulness. She was not treating her life as a constant project/work of repairing herself. She began having some stretches of fun.

The Final Crisis and Termination

As we mutually agreed on a termination date, we went through our most intense crisis. She had told us that she was going to discharge and visit her beloved old neighbor, who was developing dementia and was now moving to a nursing home. I got a phone message from one of her peers in the community who reported that Barbara had told her that she would commit suicide upon discharge—which was in about a week. After almost three years of what felt like a very successful work, just before termination, she had shocked us. Upon hearing this, with some ideas on how this unexpected threat had come about, we asked Barbara what she thought was going on that made her to threaten us with suicide.

Barbara said that she had made those comments to her peer in a state of extreme anger after an argument with her husband and didn't think that way now. She was asking that we grant her discharge home despite what she said.

I firmly told Barbara that we could not, in good conscience, approve her planned discharge. Both I and the hospital were taking her comments about suicide very seriously. When she pointed to the context and said maybe those were words uttered out of exasperation, I told her that talking about suicide is similar to threatening the life of the president of the United States, or talking about a bomb at an airport. These words had no contextual relevance and would always be taken literally. She was enraged and accused me of being as sadistic as her father. She had just made a silly comment and how dare we interfere with this important trip. I reiterated that we as a team recommend that she stay with us for some weeks before leaving us for good.

It was a time when I/we as a team owned our limitations and boundaries in the face of such a brutal, murderous attack coming from her. Her deeply disidentified parts were back again and were coming out with full force; she was retesting an archaic script with new others.

After some heated days with ongoing discussions in therapy and with family work, nursing, and community involvement, this crisis calmed down. She agreed to stay and leave the hospital when she felt she was in a safer state of mind. She was contained, her murderous aggression was metabolized and returned to her without an equally strong retaliation but with protection of ourselves and her. It was a termination regression (LaFarge 2014) that necessitated the involvement of her team and the community.

The following few weeks were a smooth process of grief and exhilaration; mourning the loss of me and the hospital, celebrating and consolidating her gains, and enjoying the sense of getting out of the hospital. She said, "These were like the teenage years that I didn't have." She confessed to having some erotic fantasies about me and felt terribly guilty over these. I pointed to how I was the closest man to her in the last three years, and that it ordinarily would come with some erotic fantasies.

Barbara was feeling guilty that now she was in a much better space than her brother who was struggling mightily with his substance abuse; she was sad and relieved that she was not the "mother of all" anymore, and she was looking forward to a more ordinary but content life back in her hometown.

I met Barbara in an alumnus meeting some years later. She seemed quite pleased with her life.

REFLECTIONS ON BARBARA

What Happened to Barbara?

As psychoanalytic clinicians, we are accustomed to a certain cluster of behaviors; when a patient cuts herself, restricts, binges/purges, threatens/attempts suicide, we feel like we are in familiar territory. And we have clinical theories about such action patterns that guide us in our interventions. Yet as the story of Barbara illustrates, there is another category of pathological actions that we are at a loss on how to think about. These pathological presentations occur in persons who appear as well-adapted, high-functioning individuals. The dramatic changes in their behavior are sudden, without any obvious precipitant. And perhaps the most confusing aspect of the clinical presentation is the fact that these patients have a remarkable capacity to recover and go back to their functioning in their old, usual ways.

These patients deny feeling depressed or being amnesic about these peculiar events but report that they had "lost their sense of self" and have no understanding of how they behaved in the way they did. Barbara's was closer to the spectrum of dissociative pathology (Loewenstein and Ross 1992), but building on the inner experience of these patients, on how they define these odd patches, leads me to prefer to think of these episodes as a collapse of the sense of self, a moment when their intrapsychic and interpersonal economy imploded. This interesting phenomenon is closely tied to another concept, the "false self."

False Self

With the idea of "good boy," Robert Tyson offered an evocative phrase that partially fits the clinical presentation of Barbara. He described a clinical syndrome of "compliant boys [who] have a history of good behavior and high academic performance but unexpectedly run into apparently benign school difficulties; only later does the more malignant character of the problem become manifest. . . . These good boys mature into productive adults who do what they are told, achieving the goals that are set out for them. Near midlife, some gradually feel a sense of inner emptiness, resulting in a puzzling contrast with their often impressive achievements" (Tyson 1996, 386).

Reporting on the transference patterns of some "hysterical patients" in analysis, Elizabeth Zetzel (1968, 259) pointed to a similar phenomenon. She stated that these patients are "not only passive; they also feel helpless. . . . Despite these handicaps they are often attractive, gifted women whose depression is hidden by laughter and flirtation. Their manifest symptoms may be obviously hysterical. . . . It may therefore prove difficult to recognize depressive characters at the time of initial evaluation." Zetzel (p. 260) ascribed the problem to developmental failures in the ego functioning of these patients. She stated that the development is traumatic with absent or psychologically troubled parents, unhappy and/or broken marriages, serious and prolonged illnesses. "They seldom present a history which includes a genuine period of latency in respect of either achievement or peer relationships."

The classical reference to the phenomenon that Barbara reminds us is the concept of "false self" as it was popularized by Donald W. Winnicott (1960), where the patient, after many decades of what looked like stellar functioning from the outside, collapses into a regressed state and turns into the opposite of the self-image she has managed to preserve for many years. Margaret Little beautifully describes the concept through her own analysis with Winnicott (Little 1985, 1987).

Winnicott suggests that false self is a defense against and the protector of the true self. Through my experience with primitive pathology, I came to believe that false/true self is not a precise dichotomy and needs to be reevaluated and redefined. The dynamics/genetics of Barbara as well as the evolution of her treatment suggests to me that neither of these presentations of Barbara can be conceptualized as a true self being defended against/protected by a false self. Rather, these two core systems were closely connected, almost bound together. Neither was a defensive formation in origin, even though they served some defensive functions for one another. The dormant system of a dependent, vengeful Barbara had a propensity to surface with vehemence and then give way to the presentation of her usual loving, caring self. And most importantly, with treatment, one system did not replace the other—instead, central elements of both systems lost intensity and coalesced to form a more cohesive, ordinarily conflicted representational system.

Building on my experience with this pattern of psychopathology, I am inclined to formulate these patients in the more clinically relevant language of "good and bad self." On the surface, it may appear as if this is more of an issue of semantics, but this formulation provides a different stance in our clinical work, where one approaches different aspects of the patient equivalently instead of labeling them as true or false, as authentic or as a facade.

It seems to me that these split, good/bad aspects of the representational system have a capacity to vacillate, as the story of Barbara suggests. And both are powerful motivating systems, even though one is owned and the other is disavowed. A relevant shorthand for this genre of pathology can be coined as "good self" versus "bad self." Good corresponding to the classical false self, and bad corresponding to classical true self.

The Self and the Object

Furthermore, following the paradigm of "there is no such thing as a baby" (Winnicott 1947), I will propose that this phenomenon can be better understood not in terms of a "self" as it is highlighted in the self-psychological approach (Kohut 1978), but in terms of internalized "self and object representations" (Modell 1976; Kernberg 2001).

The Self and Object Representation and the Other

And the last point: when we have splitting as a central defense, as a rule, it is accompanied by projective identificatory processes. The patient is in need of placing/evoking these disowned parts in others around him and thus an aspect of the representational world is created on the outside, be it in the ordinary relations of the patient or as a transference repetition in the treatment settings.

The transference patterns of Barbara in the hospital are good evidence for this hypothesis. During the process of psychoanalytic hospital treatment, Barbara had the capacity to evoke her self and object representations in the person of the therapist, in other clinicians, and in the therapeutic community—that is, in the multiple therapeutic analytic fields of the hospital.

These were not exact replicas or repetitions of the old scripts, but partial revocations. The objects who were the recipient of the dislocated aspects of Barbara's internal world were attempted to be encrypted as pure good and bad, sadistic, immoral, or selflessly altruistic; whereas the objects and the groups in the hospital were "good enough" and thus "bad enough."

This differential, "the partial evocation of the scripts," provided Barbara with numerous opportunities of reparation as she was generating cycles of enactments and gave her the opportunity of getting out of the yoke of these representational systems. As these good/bad enough objects partially fell into the roles of the old scripts and then moved out of them, Barbara slowly moved away from extremes of goodness and badness—moved away from templates of powerful altruistic and aggressive traits. The availability of peers in the hospital, in noninterpretative ways, provided other significant arenas within which she developed significant capacities to be playful—an experience that was sorely missing in her latency and adolescence.

Family—The Developmental Context

In contrast to the plentitude of theories of individual development in psychoanalysis (Fonagy and Target 2003), there is a conspicuous lack of interest in the development of families. Yet, through our work in the hospital, we are reminded that the development of the individual patient has to be conceptualized in the larger context of her parents' level of differentiation within their own families of origin. In severe pathologies, the patient's parents' are not fully differentiated from their own families, and through the well-defined defense maneuvers of splitting and projective/introjective identification the uncontained conflicts/deficits of previous generations accumulate in the index patient. A similar observation was made by Murray Bowen (1978) and object relational family researchers (Shapiro et al. 1975) and was probably swept to the sidelines of psychoanalytic thinking.

I will take you back to the details of the developmental history of Barbara's family to demonstrate the fascinating phenomenon of the lack of a triadic family structure surrounding the hospitalized patient and the parallel transgenerational transmission of pathology. This is a section on pathogenesis. How I approach the family therapy in treatment, the technical aspects of family work, as I understand and practice it, is provided in the section on Judy in chapter 4.

Family History of Barbara—An Interpretative Synopsis

Barbara's maternal grandparents were from upper-middle-class backgrounds in a major Latin American city. They immigrated to the United States during the Great Depression and in the process, lost almost all of their belongings and even worse, all of their sense of belonging. They had an excruciatingly difficult time in creating a meaningful way of living in the relieving and traumatic experience of a new country and managed to form a sense of stability through dedication to one another. For a few years, they worked in farms, and in time they opened a small grocery store. They had three daughters, and with their slowly developing mom-and-pop store, they were able to provide a decent lifestyle for their children. Two of their daughters graduated from college, got married, and eventually created successful middle-class lifestyles. Their youngest, Sarah, who was to become the mother of Barbara, had a different course in life.

Sarah was the apple of her parents' eye. A charming little girl, she stood out as a different person from her sisters and peers. She was deeply empathetic from an early age; she was keenly aware of the pervasive sense of grief in the family, worried about her sad mother and father, and brought stray animals to the house and took care of them. This nice little girl, to the chagrin of her parents, had a nervous breakdown during her late adolescence, and became a slightly awkward person from that point on. She had grave academic difficulties, dropped out of college, and then lost interest in furthering her education and worse, she took an interest in drugs and alcohol.

Barbara's maternal grandparents never fully processed what had happened to them through the cataclysm of their immigration. They moved from upper-middle-class echelons in their hometown to being farmhands and then to small business owners in a new country that had greeted them with both considerable opportunities and hostility. There was a deep subtext of grief in their household; Barbara would recall how her grandmother would listen to the music of her country in tears and switch to Spanish when talking about intimate subjects. Sarah was carrying the unmet dependency needs and painful grief of her parents and was developing the split image of a caretaker and a cripple. As a person intensely attuned to others' vulnerabilities, later she became a vulnerable, crippled person that would be in need of others' help for the rest of her life.

Barbara's paternal lineage was from Central America. Barbara's father had crossed the border illegally to a Southwestern town with an older cousin. He had left his parents and five brothers behind with the hope that in time he would bring them to the United States. Once in the United States, a country on the edge of World War II, Jorge—George by now—worked on farms for a few years, and when the war erupted, he enlisted in the army with his cousin to obtain citizenship. He saw active combat and during the horrific battles lost a leg, his cousin, and many budding friendships in this newly adopted country. Having lost his family to immigration and his leg and cousin and friendships, he came back from the war severely traumatized. He was described as "hell on wheels" by people around him, a young and strong man ready to fight with anybody over a minor disagreement, probably suffering from posttraumatic stress disorder. Now all alone, he tried to reestablish a life on his own. George had dropped out of high school in his pursuit of coming to the United States; he had no means or language capabilities to continue his education, so he went back to working as a farmhand.

After a few years of working at the farms, George met Sarah. They both were carrying the irreconcilable deposits from their families: paradoxical senses of fierce independence and endless dependence, selfless altruism and selfish sociopathy. They were soul mates; uneducated mavericks, crippled persons, misfits in their families, lost in the wilderness of Southwestern farmlands. Feeling the kinship, they fell in love and began living together. George was ten years older than Sarah, and when he got her pregnant, he felt terribly guilty and proposed. Sarah accepted, they got married and decided to move to a different place with the hope of opening a new chapter in their lives. The newlywed couple settled at the outskirts of a big city. George began to work in a small-town store while Sarah, besides fulfilling the duties of a housewife, had some temporary jobs—delivering newspapers, cleaning houses, and working on farms during the harvesting season. The couple had a son and two daughters, Barbara and Liz.

Sarah had significant problems in managing the ordinary chores of family life; she would get anxious over ordinary maternal roles like shopping for her family, helping her children with homework, and cooking healthy meals. She would rely on the advice of her sister and an elderly neighbor. In the young eyes of Barbara, her mother was an enigma; it was not clear whether she was incompetent or was simply uninterested. Her aunt and the elderly neighbor became the mother figures that she could depend on.

The parents lived the life of severe addicts, and yet there was another peculiar aspect to them: in contrast to their internal chaos, they were very strict on the appearance of their house. They allocated the care of the exterior of the house to Barbara, and inside the house, they would not allow the children to disturb an obsessively organized orderliness and cleanliness. The dining room would be locked, opened only for occasional visitors; the couches and sofas in the living area would be covered with furniture throws, again to be uncovered for visitors, and the kids were not allowed to sit on them. So the children would sit on some pillows thrown on the floor, have their meals, and do their homework in this awkward way. What appeared like a paradox was, in fact, in congruence with their "psychopathically lax and obsessively harsh" split sense of morality as it had evolved through their own traumatic developments.

Barbara was consciously disidentifying with the "bad" in her family. But at the same time, she was unconsciously introjecting and identifying with the "good" that was projected into her. As a projectee and as a projector, she located the bad in her mother, father, and brother, and she became a person devoid of overt aggression, an endless supply for the dependent needs of others.

She took her parents and her brother under her wing in their later years. Liz and her baby daughter were like a daughter and granddaughter to Barbara, and everyone was calling her "mommy." She was very proud of this side of herself. This process had created a three-generational structure that was distorted; chronological hierarchy was reversed, and the nuclear family of Barbara was unformed.

As Barbara was becoming the "mother of all," Barbara's parents' obsessive-psychopathic lifestyle died out. They became deeply religious and remorseful of their past lives. Now they were admiring the accomplishments of their daughter; her mother would openly admit that she was amazed about how competent a mother and wife Barbara had become, and her father would tell her that he was always proud of her. Barbara's parents had transformed so much that Barbara's husband was surprised when she told him about their chaotic past. He had come to know them as two very nice, loving, and caring old people!

Now Barbara was faced with the impossible intrapsychic task of re-introjecting the bad that her parents carried for so many decades and keeping it side by side with the good, some of which she had to give back to her parents. This intrapsychic/interpersonal economy was coming to exhaustion, and around the time Liz's daughter inserted herself as an autonomous, sexual being into her life, Barbara crumbled.

3

THE TEAM AND THE MILIEU IN THE PSYCHOTHERAPEUTIC HOSPITAL

Z. E. Kayatekin, MD and M. S. Kayatekin, MD

So far we have discussed the dyadic relationship of the patient with the individual therapist and then with the patient's omnipresent family. Now we will focus on how the patient in the hospital unfolds into the human ecologies of her peers and staff in the unusual environment of the psychotherapeutic hospital.

The psychotherapeutic hospitals that we worked in were either fully open, like Riggs, or semiopen with some privilege systems, like Hacettepe and Menninger, where the patients are free to move in and out of the unit depending on their safety assessment. The patients stay in these hospitals on the average for many months and sometimes up to several years. They are treated in psychoanalytically informed therapeutic modalities ranging from intensive individual therapy to psychoanalytic group work, couples and/or family therapy, intensive therapeutic nursing, and milieu involvement, as well as state-of-the-art psychopharmacological treatments and cognitive behavioral, dialectical, behavioral approaches.

Once admitted to these systems, the patient is assigned to a "team" that comprises a psychiatrist, therapist, psychologist, social worker, primary nurse, and several other mental health professionals such as a substance abuse counselor or eating disorder specialist. Another significant group is the natural group of the patient, his family. The members of the family are in a neighborhood relationship and are an integral part of the treatment through the family work. And a fascinating concept named as "milieu," or the "therapeutic community," envelopes the whole approach.

The treatment environment gives due weight to the intrapsychic and interpersonal world as well as the group phenomena as these continually impact and shape one another.

Over the course of his stay in the hospital, the patient naturally develops intense and unique individual relationships and is involved in a complicated set of group relationships. These venues of individual and group relatedness serve many functions, such as a sense of security, belonging, sharing, responsibility, and citizenship (Munich and Green 2009). These are all well-known aspects of the hospital treatment. But in our opinion, they do not provide an adequate explanation of the efficacy of the hospital treatment because they bypass the central psychoanalytic concepts of resistance, defense, repetition, transference, and such. And this is where we would like to share a few hypotheses through the work with Henry.

HENRY—THE VILLAGE THAT RAISES THE PATIENT

After a series of failed inpatient treatments, Henry had finally found some solace in the therapeutic animal farm where he was working for almost a year. His coworkers were well aware of his toying with the idea of suicide, which was, after all, not an uncommon topic amongst these marginalized young men and women who had found a safe haven at the farm. In the evenings, after a long day of work, as they gathered around a camp fire they would have long conversations about the central themes of life, such as conflicts with their parents, drugs, sex, and politics and suicide; none were bothered by the thoughts about life and death. Henry and his friends at the farm had taken a break from life; they were in a moratorium, as they were searching their souls and their "identity confusions" in the Eriksonian sense (Erikson 1970).

However, one hot summer night as they were preparing for sleep, finding Henry hanging from a tree limb was not something any of them had anticipated. They managed to cut the rope and pull him down, and were relieved that Henry was still breathing and had a pulse. Paramedics arrived, and Henry was transferred to a local emergency room. After he was medically stabilized, he was referred to the psychotherapeutic hospital.

Development

In his parents' eyes, Henry had an unremarkable early childhood. He was a bit late to start talking, but then became surprisingly articulate. His early family environment seemed happy and secure. His parents were getting along well, earning decent incomes, living a comfortable upper-middle-class life.

Around the age of six, Henry's sense of safety was shattered. As he was going through the excitement and fear of starting the elementary school, his parents got divorced in a matter of a few months. Henry didn't show a strong reaction to this tumultuous phase, but from that point on, he had difficulties tolerating being away from his mother.

As he was adapting to living the fragmented life of a child with divorced parents, he was hit by another trauma: his mother was diagnosed with cancer. She survived the cancer but the recovery process was agonizing for both her and Henry. It was a time when his mother was lost for Henry, as she was fighting for her life. Henry's father, who had remarried, tried to help. Henry spent his weekends, holidays, and summers at his dad's new home, where he felt a misfit, despite all the good intentions of his stepmother. He was feeling profoundly lonely, scared for his mother's life, and unable to share his internal turmoil with anyone.

After the scare of the cancer subsided, Henry's mother got into a new relationship with the hope of establishing a new family. Henry's relationship with his mother's boyfriend proved to be difficult from the very beginning; Henry was rebellious and also felt threatened. The relationship between his mother and her boyfriend was also shaky; they had frequent arguments leading to occasional physical altercations.

With the lack of a cohesive family on both maternal and paternal sides, Henry had a very difficult time at the elementary school. He was irritable, depressed, and oppositional; his academic performance was poor; and he was unable to fit into any of his peer groups. He was evaluated by numerous psychiatrists and was given a plethora of diagnoses, prescribed stimulants, mood stabilizers, and antidepressant medications, none of which was of any help. His teachers thought that regular schools were not a good fit for him, so he was sent to a school for special education.

As he was entering puberty, Henry was at a loss; he was feeling defeated as a student, with some psychiatric diagnoses stuck on him.

Unable to find a way of defining himself as a person amongst his peers, Henry found a niche in basketball. He had considerable talent in this sport; he spent all of his spare time practicing the basics, jump shots, hooks, and dribbling and became superbly skilled in all the individual skills of a team game. He was accepted to the junior varsity team and became a star and moved to senior varsity. However, his height remained quite short relative to the telescoping growth of his peers. And, despite his impressive athletic skills, he was a terrible team player. He would get paralyzed when he was in the role of a "team maker" where he had to lead the group, and thus failed miserably as he was reaching the top of his high school sports career. Another path was blocked. Now he felt "stupid" in his classes, and like a "loser" in his favorite sport.

Painfully lacking a sense of belonging at school and feeling deeply lonely at home, Henry joined a group of neighborhood misfit kids who had taken to skateboarding as their defining characteristic. Relieved from the catastrophic sense of loneliness, he took to skateboarding, drinking, and using drugs with these new friends. Euphoria of alcohol/drugs and a sense of belonging to a group provided some relief.

In his senior year, Henry fell in love with a classmate. They had a year-long, on-and-off relationship, and then she precipitously left Henry. This pushed Henry over the edge and he crumbled. It was a repetition of a familiar theme: first his father, then his mother, and now his first love abandoning him. He became very depressed, his drug and alcohol use got out of control, and he made several suicide attempts, which led to extended rehab treatments with no significant benefits. The therapeutic farm seemed to be a good solution to his unending troubles.

When he made a very serious suicide attempt after a year at the farm, Henry's parents were emotionally and financially exhausted. What was going on with Henry was a mystery, and everyone was at a loss on how to help him.

Henry in the Hospital

Once in the hospital, Henry was deeply pessimistic. He believed that no one could help him, as his previous multiple treatment failures had proven. So far, he had found some relief only with street drugs, which led him to believe that he must have some kind of "biological/chemical imbalance" that could only be rectified by other drugs. He felt suicide was the only other option.

During the first week of hospitalization, Henry had an unusual array of somatic complaints. He would panic about any physical sensation, from a vague abdominal pain to a mild headache, any mild skin lesion would evoke intense anxiety, and he would demand that the internist be called urgently. The internist would examine him frequently, sometimes more than once a day, a lot more than his peers in the unit that comprised young adults who had minimal risk for serious medical illness. The internist and his colleagues were a team of competent clinicians, used to sailing the unique waters of the psychotherapeutic wards. They would reassure and console him, to be called again after a short while.

Henry was talking through his body. This unusual presentation made sense in the context of the life-threatening ordeal of his mother that made her body the center of attention while Henry was in his early teens. And his later attachment to animals, who could only speak through their bodies, was probably a continuation of this theme of being at a loss for words when one's body was facing such a deadly threat. In the hospital, he was probably enacting his old traumatic relation with his mother's body, his still-developing, confusing, late-adolescent body, and his reparative relation with the animals.

As his bodily concerns were addressed by the medical team, Henry developed a different presentation. He began to have frequent angry outbursts that seemed to come out of nowhere. It was very difficult to soothe him when he was upset. He had a deeply held conviction that nobody cared for him. If the staff did not pay attention to his outbursts, he complained that he was ignored. If the staff attended to him and he was asked to go to a quiet place, in his mind, the staff didn't want to be bothered; "They only care about their own comfort," he would say. He would get even more upset if the staff tried to calm him down, because he felt they were "infantilizing" him. And they were "terribly ineffective" in either case, a paradox that is rather common in the life of the hospital.

These episodes were initially formulated by the staff in impersonal, generic narratives as "low frustration tolerance" and "anger management problems." As his psychiatrist, I was somewhat disturbed by these formulations but kept the perspective in mind that we were beginning to understand Henry, thus we would all be starting with generic formulations, and hopefully, eventually, we would develop a personal understanding of him.

Henry was easily getting unsettled in groups. He would blow his top with a comment made by a peer or a facilitator and impulsively leave the group. Some staff perceived him as rash, prone to acting out, and some thought he was outright hostile. The staff was wondering whether we could help him, pointing to his previous multiple treatment failures and his current lack of engagement in treatment with us. It was not an unusual initial countertransference response of staff, who were trying to adjust to yet another troubled soul in a unit of twenty-eight such patients.

A central struggle was perhaps Henry's inability to reflect on what was going on. He showed no curiosity for his or others' minds; he believed no one could understand him, neither could he understand himself or others. And we were not in a better position as his team; we only had a primordial understanding of the workings of his mind that barely went beyond generic formulations.

When I had the occasional serenity of my mind during the ordinary confusion and craziness of the hospital work, I was capable of thinking that Henry was probably engaging with the treatment as best as he could, moving between the extremes of infantile dependence and counterdependence, and during my frequent therapeutic conversations with Henry, I was trying to introduce a new vocabulary to facilitate this process.

Therapeutic Conversations with Henry

My therapeutic conversations with Henry were not psychotherapy sessions per se, but were an invitation for a psychotherapeutic exploration where we would try to understand what had happened to him, what was going on now, and "why"; I was attempting to help him think about his role, how he might have contributed to his story, without turning myself to a psychodynamic therapist.

For Henry, figuring out "why it happened" and what his contributions were, be it conscious or unconscious, was both the most difficult aspect of the therapeutic conversations and the most important one. If he recognized that he had contributed to the problem, he would feel terribly embarrassed and guilty. And yet these were also the prerequisites of feeling good and proud of himself and his actions. Furthermore, I thought that the recognition of these moments of guilt, shame, and pride would lead to the diminution of their affective intensities and could potentially expand the willful capabilities of his mind, his "conflict free zones," his "agency" or his "authority," depending on what psychoanalytic school you articulate from.

With this therapeutic formulation in mind, we, as his team, recognized some central themes in the historical material: Henry's father "abandoning" the family, his mother fighting for her life, Henry fearing his mother dying on him, his challenging relationship with his mother's boyfriend, his ambivalent feelings over his half-sisters and his stepmother, and his nonambivalent attachment to the animal farm. The farm was becoming an important, organizing metaphor as the compromise Henry found for the dilemmas of his life. It was a place where he had unconditional acceptance, where he wouldn't be abandoned but rather surrounded by a group of friends and animals with whom he felt a deep sense of kinship. If one were to forget the phenomenon of negative therapeutic reaction, it was therefore more of an enigma why he attempted to take his life in that comfortable, safe place, as he was developing new friendships.

The Increasing Sophistication of the Narrative

Even though his formulations were different than ours, Henry was slowly expanding on and complicating his initial formulation of himself from "I have a problem with emotional dysregulation" toward building a more complicated series of sentences. We, as the team, were trying to develop a mutual language as it was emerging from both ends. Henry started to recognize a context for his tantrums, including other people in his narrative, even though he was not naming any specific persons at the moment. And there was a budding sense of temporality; he was not a person fixed in time, a simplified generalization. He had a past and a future.

As Henry was developing more sophisticated narratives of his personal history, I was cognizant of the defensive elements in regard to his dependent sides. As he reflected on what was happening, it was striking that he still was deeply ambivalent about getting help from others. When offered some opinions or help, he would loudly state that there was nothing anyone could do for him.

On the other side of the ambivalence, as expected, Henry was often getting quite upset with his clinical team. He was complaining that some of the team members were not reaching out to him when he needed them to. He felt like a wild horse trapped in a stable, just like the ones he had tended in the farm. The analogy was pertinent; he felt like a horse, and we were the ones who were trying to tame and then ride him. He was running and kicking, unyielding to being tamed. As staff, we felt the same way as we wondered who the horse and who the cowboy was, in the rodeo of the hospital.

Henry was refusing to accept the importance of others, especially the members of his team as persons who might have an impact on him. Instead of being other minds that could think together with him, we were still functions for him—as it is called in the psychoanalytic jargon, "part objects"; men and women, doctor or nurse, people who were around, who just needed to wait for him to calm down, give him medications, and listen to him because we were paid to do that.

As a team, we tried to make sense of what was going on by taking another look at Henry's history and how it might be an unfolding of his life anew in the microcosm of the hospital. His social worker, who was a witness to his work in the process groups and in family therapy, was telling us that Henry felt like "he got the raw end of the deal in life." During the process groups, Henry was talking about being depressed since the age of ten, when his mother was diagnosed with cancer—an illness that was to hover over their lives for many years. He was also telling poignant stories about physical/emotional abuse he endured from his mother's boyfriend. The peers were deeply sympathetic and supportive of the idea that his depression might be related to these traumatic experiences of cancer and abuse.

The Milieu and the Team

As his hostility toward the team was peaking, Henry was developing friendships with some of his peers. It was a pattern that seemed similar to his history in adolescence; bitterly conflicted with his parents, yet appearing as kind and nice in his relations with friends. It was also of note that Henry was struggling with making connections at an intimate level with any particular peer or member of the staff, someone with whom he could identify with concordantly or complementarily (Racker 1968), someone who looked like him or someone who looked like a significant other from his past. His one-on-one relationships as well as his group relationships were still tentative, premature, and exhausting for Henry. And thus, he would regularly isolate himself in his room and revert to reading books to recuperate.

At this new stage in his interactions with staff, Henry fluctuated between being placidly pleasant and bitterly discontent. At times, he would say he was glad that he was admitted to this great hospital, then would shift to declaring that the same hospital was a huge waste of time and money. Henry's ongoing acting out was evoking intense responses from the staff. Nursing complained about being at a loss on how to deal with him. Frustrated, angry messages from the various staff members flooded our emails and we would hold endless discussions about him during our team meetings.

As we were desperately trying to make a sense out of his outbursts, we recognized that these tantrums were primarily happening during the evening shifts or weekends, which was a time when there was less of a structure and when none of his primary team members were around. And as we became aware of this pattern, came a turning point.

Abigail—The First Transference Person in the Hospital

Abigail was a competent and compassionate senior nurse. Her relationship with Henry soured during a rather ordinary exchange; while delivering medications during one of the evening shifts, Abigail got suspicious and asked Henry if he was cheeking his medication. Henry became furious and accused Abigail of treating him like his mother. Abigail, on her end, tried to defend her routine clinical inquiry. Henry, in his typical way of responding, vacillated between denying the event altogether and assigning a number of causes to what had happened; his recent "anxiety about taking medications," "having a bad day," "not having heard from his girlfriend." It was hard for him to admit and own the fact that he had tried to find a way of not taking his medication; instead he developed a deep resentment toward Abigail. Finally, Henry had found a specific person. Abigail, his primary nurse, was his first transference object.

The Power of the Milieu

In the third week of Henry's hospitalization, a maelstrom unfolded that shifted the transference heat from the confines of the hospital to the outside. During a phone conversation, his girlfriend told Henry that she was breaking up with him and added insult to this unexpected injury by confessing that she had been cheating on him all through his hospitalization.

Henry was enraged, he was screaming at the top of his lungs, cursing at his girlfriend and threatening to kill himself. His rage escalated; he threw tables and chairs around and punched holes in the walls. He was mightily out of control, scaring the staff and patients to the point where we called a code; the security and the staff from other units poured in for support. This amassing of staff around him calmed Henry down. He said he had gotten "emotionally dysregulated," "felt triggered," and then apologized as he headed toward his room.

It was a critical moment. The team held an urgent meeting where the current situation and Henry's overall treatment were discussed. The clinical staff were quite pessimistic about his progress; there were some who suggested that we were not a good fit for him and he had to be transferred to our subacute care unit. Some team members thought we should transfer Henry to a locked facility. There were passionate disagreements on which route to follow, as often happens in hospital work. The substance abuse counselor, who had the most intimate connection with Henry, was able to calm down the flaring passions in the team, and with his help, despite the dramatic nature of the events, we decided to "slow it down."

A community meeting was held with Henry present. There was a lively discussion about Henry's recent outburst. A wide range of responses from peers were expressed; some empathized with him, while others expressed their anger at him or fear of him. The staff openly expressed their concerns about his unacceptable level of aggression. It was a moment when the community, without acting rashly, was nevertheless showing firm boundaries to the extremes of aggression. Henry was confused, deeply hurt, angry, and embarrassed over what happened to him and over what he did to others. All of this was too much for him; he requested to be discharged.

Then we faced a tsunami. Some peers came to us, supportive of Henry, pointing to his apology, to his history of sufferings, to his budding relationships with peers. They were passionately telling us that he was here for a reason and that we couldn't give up on him. Other peers, however, were cornering us in the unit and expressing their disappointments that we did not discharge him immediately. They were quite critical of our inaction because they thought Henry's extreme aggression was unacceptable; he needed to express his feelings, not act on them. Worse yet, some patients expressed concerns about their safety and threatened to discharge if Henry were allowed to stay. Henry's parents bombarded the team and the administration with phone messages and emails. We felt under siege, with contradictory requests coming from different parts of the hospital. Meanwhile, Henry was still very angry and unable to engage in any therapeutic dialogue. He was enraged with his parents' indecision on discharge and felt controlled by his family and by the entire hospital.

As the storm calmed down, the team met with Henry and offered an alternative formulation of what had transpired: "Terribly hurt and confused, Henry had gone into a tailspin of sadness, anger, wishes for revenge, as any such trauma would engender. And then he responded with such intensity that he ended up shooting himself in the foot by being physically threatening. It was understandable and yet unacceptable, so Henry had to do something to repair his relationships, if he was interested in staying in the hospital."

Henry and the hospital community agreed with this formulation and with the reparative solution it offered. Henry initiated a series of dialogues with the members of the team and his peers about what had transpired in order to make sense of how he had contributed to this explosion. As a therapeutic system, the hospital was in full motion, interpreting verbally in individual sessions, interpreting through action in the larger community, responding to the unacceptable aspects of his aggression, yet not retaliating, and helping him to reinternalize a modified form of aggression.

As he initiated a series of conversations, Henry regressed and went through a period in which his attention focused back on his body on a quasipsychotic level; he was terrified about having a sexually transmitted disease and repetitively wanted to be tested for it. And then a plethora of bodily complaints piled up on one another, gastrointestinal complaints, then knee pain, then shoulder pain. After his aggressive explosion, Henry was again back to talking via his body.

In the meantime, his family therapist, individual therapist, and primary nurse were unanimously discontent with their work with Henry. They were getting tired of his ongoing emotional outbursts, the lack of therapeutic alliance, his unwillingness to be curious about his mind—in sum, his inability to participate in a therapeutic endeavor.

It was probably telling that even his insurance company was approving his treatment in the hospital. It was an extraordinarily rare event; the insurance reviewer was suggesting that this was "a complicated case" and recommending that we should give him time to settle in treatment as he might not tolerate changes well.

Everyone, from his treatment team to the insurance company, felt helpless, as did Henry.

The Turning Point—The New and Good-Enough Object

Within this pervasive sense of defeat, Henry was still complaining about his primary nurse, Abigail, who was also expressing a deep sense of frustration over her inability to help him no matter how hard she tried, which sounded just like Henry's mother. Some nurses commented that Henry was perceiving his primary nurse as hovering over him, which, again sounded like him talking about his mother. He was at a stalemate with his primary nurse, a negative transference that neither was able to understand and resolve. After a thorough review of the case that included an outside consultation on the therapeutic stalemate, the team decided to assign Henry to a younger nurse, Emily, with whom he seemed to be more comfortable in their occasional conversations.

Emily was an easygoing person but also had a reputation for being straightforward and tough when needed. She liked Henry and had more tolerance than most of the staff toward his irritating sides. She would talk about him as if she was talking about her troubled child: "I think he is a jerk, but I can see he is hurt. He wants help but at the same time rejects any help you offer." She had the capacity to listen and hear Henry, and made sure she followed up on his concerns. She did not get easily frustrated when Henry was upset, and used humor, to which Henry responded well.

Emily had an intuitive sense of gaging Henry's needs around the dialectical tension of intimacy and private space: "Henry is initially irritable when we talk, but he tends to open up when I allow him to do so. I let him know that I want to check in with him when he has a minute, and then make sure I follow through even if he doesn't come up to me. I believe, he wants to feel like you care but not be overly pushy in how you show it. I touch base with him briefly throughout the shift. Over time he began to approach me and let me know how he's doing. . . . When he gets upset, I don't insist. I let him know that I will be available when he is ready; he usually comes later on, apologizes and talks."

Emily intuitively knew how to be "good enough" for Henry, thus had the capacity to become a "new object" (Winnicott 1960; Loewald 1960).

In the background, another figure was emerging as a new object—Sam, the addiction counselor. Sam was a little older than Henry and was able to establish a friendly relationship with him from the very early days of his hospitalization. Sam would meet with him casually but regularly, out in the main lounge. They would chat about their mutual interests such as football, and they would play ping pong, rather rambunctiously, like two young men in a playful competition. And they would "shoot the shit," as Sam would say.

Henry gradually started talking to Sam about himself, expressing anger, resentment, and sadness over many aspects of his young life. As a person familiar with the rough aspects of life, Sam would listen and make some empathic comments, and, once in a while, add a different point of view on his story. For example, he would point to Henry's anger and how it had often been self-defeating. Sam was wisely and patiently building a working therapeutic relationship on the foundation of a chumship, similar to the initial phases of the work with Al. His benevolent and inviting paternalistic attitude was helping Henry to understand that he had a mind and so did others (Allen et al. 2008), and thus he was capable of initiating actions as much as others. And having a mind and a capacity to think and initiate actions had some consequences, some of which were not pleasant.

On the other hand, Emily and Sam were providing a new template of relating to an adult man and to an adult woman. It was a triadic structure Henry had lacked for most of his life, and he was creating it in the hospital.

Peer Transferences

As he became more open and less confrontational with staff, in parallel, Henry started to relate more intimately to some peers. His buddy relation with Jack, a peer in the unit, was especially important for him. They spent hours on the porch, smoking cigarettes, drinking coffee, and talking intimately about many aspects of their lives.

Jack was a young man with a comparable background to Henry's and initially had a very similar attitude toward treatment. However, to Henry's envy, Jack was now talking about how well his treatment was going; he was steadily improving, and he had full trust in the treatment team. Interestingly, Jack's treatment team was the same as Henry's!

Through his trial identifications with Jack, Henry became more comfortable with the prospect of connecting with the team and the larger community and began reaching out to other peers. His primary nurse, Emily, summarized this transition well: "At the beginning of his treatment, I don't think Henry realized he was giving off a vibe of 'don't mess with me.' Therefore none of his peers felt comfortable approaching him, but he read this as 'they don't give a shit about me.' Over time, he softened and started seeing that others were struggling as well. We were all in agreement with Emily that Henry was developing a sense of commonality and belonging, yet we could not help but recognize that, to keep his narcissism intact, Henry was quick to add a qualifier: "No one struggles as much I do."

What Do You Think About Me?

About six weeks into his hospitalization came another critical moment in Henry's treatment, the "diagnostic conference"; the time when Henry would hear about what the team was thinking about him. The diagnostic conference, as it was couched in the colloquialism of the hospital, was a moment for a change in the patient's narrative. The treatment team integrates its observations of several weeks and provides a new formulation, thus offering Henry an opportunity to contemplate changing the way he formulated himself through this new lens.

Henry, who had come to the hospital with the view of himself as a drug addict, "loser," and "stupid," was fantasizing that the treatment team would pass a similar judgment on him, and it would be a time of shameful exposure. To his surprise, none of his fearful anticipations came true. Henry fully agreed with the narrative provided by the team. He felt understood.

Then came the next step; the diagnostic feedback conference that included the parents. This second step was a chance to offer the new hypotheses that were developed through our intense work with Henry to the family. Henry actively participated in the family feedback. Amongst many other themes, he talked about his loneliness and how much he suffered in the hands of his mother's boyfriend, whom, he felt had no tolerance for him. He expressed anger at his mother for doing nothing, not protecting him despite being a witness to all that he suffered. We talked about the similar helplessness his mother might have experienced during those difficult times. Henry's mother, who initially appeared irritable, angry, and rather rigid, was in tears, blaming herself that she "should have helped him more." We reminded her of the horrendous saga of cancer hovering over her as Henry was struggling with what looked like insurmountable problems with alcohol/drugs and depression. We suggested to review the idea of "blame," of herself and others, and maybe tone it down in a way in which the members of the family were formulating their contributions to the problems. It was a crucial element of the formulation; a moment where we were helping them to develop a healthier stance of agency instead of vacillating from omnipotence to impotence, from taking a grandiose sense of responsibility to abandoning any sense of responsibility.

When Henry, with a deep sense of shame, talked about his failures in school, his father shared his own painful experiences while growing up about how he felt stupid, struggled socially, and how he tried to compensate for these perceived deficits. His father's revelations seemed to make it easier for Henry to talk about his own struggles. We also talked about the existential difficulties the parents were facing at that time, including the divorce, major health problems, and the problematic relations afterward. As the team was holding each member of the family, each of them were able to deepen the conversation within themselves.

After the conference, Henry seemed relieved. He continued to talk with the team members about his life story and the challenges he had faced. He spent an enjoyable weekend with his parents, who were very satisfied with the current state of the treatment. As a team, we had managed to provide a narrative where all the members of the family felt understood, were held accountable, yet were not blamed.

Consolidation of the New Narrative

After this important juncture in the treatment, Henry's outbursts disappeared. Even though he continued to get easily frustrated, he was able to approach staff and apologize if he had a rather strong reaction. Most significantly, he was willing to initiate a conversation to explore what had happened that had led to the explosion, allowing us and himself to develop a mutual analytic/reflective space.

In the milieu, Henry consolidated friendships with several peers. He was telling his nurse, Emily, that, for the first time in his life, he was feeling like he had friends amongst whom he felt accepted and respected. Besides his chumship with Jack, Henry was finally able to have a sense of belonging to a group without using alcohol or drugs.

During the last few weeks of his hospitalization, Henry had another series of somatic concerns, and was often asking to see the internist. Unlike earlier times, however, he was now able to notice how his somatic symptoms increased in proportion to his overall anxiety. Instead of acting out, he frequently wanted to talk with the team and the staff about his concerns. He was certain, for example, that his parents would decide on his aftercare on his behalf, without getting his input. The staff and the team listened patiently, but questioned his sense of certainty since neither of his parents had expressed any opinion on this subject and they seemed to be respectful of the process. To Henry's surprise, the family meetings went smoothly; his parents followed the family therapist's guidance and recommendations despite Henry's provocative comments. Henry eventually calmed down.

A parallel development was observed in groups; Henry became more tolerant of differing views in the groups, instead of rashly leaving the group. He had become the most senior member in these groups, as several patients were discharged. He was able to empathize with and reflect on others' stories and make wise comments in groups, gaining the respect of the newcomers.

His pessimistic certainty seemed to be softening as the staff approached him with humor, support, and patience, avoiding addressing his narcissism head on but still challenging it. He became more appreciative of staff's efforts in helping him.

Henry's individual therapist, Samantha, reported dramatic changes on how Henry was now able to reflect on his actions and the workings of his mind. He was allowing Samantha to make some comments about him, and agreeing with some of them. They explored how he now was able to express his emotions, after numbing them with drugs for so long. They also discussed his capacity for self-sabotage and his tendency to stuff his feelings until he exploded.

Henry shared with Samantha his feelings of betrayal, rage, and shame with regard to his girlfriend breaking up with him while he was in the hospital and his sense of abandonment while growing up. The other themes that often came up were his sense of being controlled by his parents and the dynamics of how that process was mutually created. They talked about how Henry's fear of rejection and his deep sense of shame made him lead by anger, thus pushing people away when he was actually seeking a connection. This dynamic seemed to repeat itself through the individual therapy as well but grew less pronounced over time.

Henry gradually became much more reflective even when he was angry, as Samantha observed. She noted that her "willingness to stay with him, welcome him back, call him when he was late, and also insist on having a final session, might have reinforced that he mattered and was important, when he struggled with feelings that he was less than what he seemed." Finally the therapy had gained traction.

With his addiction counselor, Sam, Henry started talking directly about his drug use as a maladaptive way to manage his feelings. Sam educated him on the biology of addiction, the risks of relapse, and how he could maintain his recovery.

At the end of our work, Henry was expressing interest and excitement about developing a life that was worth living—he had developed more awareness about his parents and their struggles, and the consequences of his drug use.

After these intense several months in the medium-term, time-limited inpatient program, Henry stayed about a year in our stepdown program where he consolidated the gains he made and also graduated from high school.

REFLECTIONS ON HENRY

Changing the Narrative Through the Formulation as a Team

One important aspect of psychoanalytically informed work in the hospital is an attempt to change the narrative of the patient from a simple, one-dimensional person, living in a vacuum, to a complicated, multidimensional person who has temporal continuity and lives in the context of important others. The conferences regarding Henry were a synoptic summary of these efforts and teamwork was central to this effort (Krikorian and Fowler 2011). By integrating the pieces of information gathered from various venues of therapies, the team offered a different, complicated, multidimensional narrative to Henry and his family.

It was an attempt to formulate how everyone was right, that they all tried their best, and yet this approach did not preclude the necessity of a critique, but in fact it required it, addressing the fact that they could have done things differently in certain areas and probably needed to do better in the future. It was a process of recognition of the interrelatedness of the family members, a process of owning and forgiveness.

In technical terms, the central stance was being equidistant to all family members, and the central theme was helping them move from positions that vacillate between omnipotence and impotence to a reasonable sense of agency, which, by definition, carries the risk of making mistakes.

The Milieu

Henry's story was a testament to the importance of the milieu, or the therapeutic community. The concept of therapeutic community had a few foci of creation—from the experiments in United Kingdom to the grand American experiment of Menninger (Jones 1953; Main 1957; Menninger 1939/1982). Over the course of years, it has become one of the most powerful aspects of psychotherapeutic hospital treatment (Munich and Green 2009). In fact, a significant majority of the patients treated in the psychotherapeutic hospital would report that it was the most important element of their treatment, an observation proven to be valid by some studies (Heede et al. 2009).

The therapeutic community is an overarching concept that allows us to think in terms of the staff and the patients living under the same roof with a sense of commonality and citizenship. In this small village, we display our ordinary sides, transferences, and countertransferences in addition to our defined roles as staff. And likewise, the patients join the hospital as ordinary persons beyond their roles as patients.

The concept of "therapeutic community" or "milieu," without necessarily erasing the staff/patient gradient, equalizes all of the members under the roof of the hospital, and this interesting dialectic between the treatment relationships on the one hand, and of citizenship on the other, facilitates the re-creation of the patient's object relational scripts.

Most importantly, these are not just dyadic maternal/paternal scripts, but scripts of the person in the family and in the extended family, and history of object relationships as they were internalized in layers in the ordinary human ecologies that we all live in, like school, neighborhood, and such. Thus the psychotherapeutic hospital provides the best possible replica of our real lives where we are free to recreate our internal worlds, notice, examine, and add new, more adaptive scripts.

The Power of Noninterpretative Change in the Milieu

In the psychoanalytic dyadic space, we cherish speech. However there is solid evidence that some other important elements are operative beyond the speech. (Scott 1998; Gabbard and Westen 2003; Gilmore 2005; Boston Change Process Study Group 2010). As the brief story of Jane illustrates, the village of the psychotherapeutic hospital is a testament to the immense power of noninterpretative change through peer relations and group processes.

Jane

Jane was a single woman, in her mid-fifties, a prosperous business owner. She presented herself to the hospital with the chief complaint of needing help in translating "insight into action."

It was a thought-provoking formulation; she had gained considerable insight into herself over the course of a decade-long psychoanalysis, and she felt this treatment had saved her life. With psychoanalysis, she had cleared out of a pervasive sense of hopelessness, put her life in perspective, and gotten back to a productive work life. Nevertheless, after so many years of beneficial work with her analyst, recently she felt stuck in her life—in her charity work, in her love life, and in analysis. Jane had long feared that her fate would be similar to that of her father: when Jane was in her mid-twenties, her father had made a serious suicide attempt that left him hemiplegic for the rest of his life. Her analyst recommended admission to a psychotherapeutic hospital.

Jane had a history of neglect and physical abuse, as well as significant achievements. She believed in supporting disadvantaged youth, a cause to which she gave considerable time and money.

In the hospital, Jane was paired with a cognitive behavioral therapist who actively guided her in exploring what she really wanted out of her life, and then helped her commit to living by those values. Part of this work included examining what got in the way of living the life she really wanted, and problem-solving around those issues. The therapist was serving some ego functions for her and was actively engaging with the action of her indecision through obsessive ruminations. Jane was also attending several psychoanalytically informed group therapies and was in a larger system, a therapeutic milieu.

This milieu was comprised of successful professionals like Jane who were going through similar crises that necessitated a thorough and painful exploration of their lives. The milieu gave her the opportunity to share her experiences with professionally identifiable peers of similar age, and this process helped reverse her tendencies toward isolation. Furthermore, by being in the inpatient unit and having the provisions of meals as well as access to the nursing staff who attended to her body and provided twenty-four-hour comfort, and having many others "minding" her, Jane found refuge. She had finally allowed herself to be one of those sick, troubled teenagers that once she was, and one of the people that she committed her charity work to in her mature years.

Once she allowed this regression, Jane also allowed herself to unfold multiple transference potentialities within the rich interpersonal ecology of the peers who were being treated in the hospital. One poignant example was the following: in a psychoanalytically informed group on suicide, a patient graphically described her wishes to shoot herself in the head. Since Jane was the person to find her father in the basement of their house gravely wounded, this brought in vivid memories of the scene. Living through this horrific scene allowed her to recognize the traumatic nature of the event more viscerally, and her intense anger at her father surfaced.

Jane had many times worked on the aggressive sides of her father in the transference with her beloved analyst and had a good understanding of different aspects of it. In the psychoanalytic group, she recognized the patient who was talking about shooting herself had striking resemblances to her father, whom she was talking about for many years with her analyst. In the person of this patient, now she "got it in her guts." She was then able to "shoot down" this very aggressive, somewhat sociopathic patient with her capacity for impressively articulate speech. Once this happened, she was no longer afraid of the aggressive peer. This gender ambiguous transference to her peer that was developing in the transitional Oedipal play space (Ogden 1989; Gabbard 1994), in contrast to what she had experienced with her male analyst, was much more vivid and real. This young woman fit the script of the role of her murderous father much better than her gentle, caring, older male analyst.

Jane was in a somewhat friendly, erotic, flirtatious relationship with her psychiatrist in the hospital, a doctor who was little older than her but much younger than her current boyfriend. Being her reflective, courageous, eloquent self, she admitted, with some hesitation, to some fantasies about her psychiatrist and connected this to her deeply ambivalent attachment to her partner. Her partner had been enormously helpful to her for almost a decade, but he was now becoming quite feeble, both physically and mentally. Jane, on the other hand, with a deep sense of guilt, was recognizing her unsatisfied sexuality and her somewhat obliterated youthfulness and wished to find a younger partner.

The hospital, with the help of therapeutic regression, provided better actors for her representational scripts, and Jane was able to connect her insights to action.

4

PSYCHOANALYTIC WORK WITH FAMILIES

Working with families in the psychotherapeutic treatment of young adults is probably a "sine qua non" for the achievement of a good therapeutic outcome (Shapiro 1987; Schwartz 2011). The patient whom I discuss in this chapter was treated partly in the hospital and mostly in my private practice. So I focus on the family here, keeping the hospital on the side. There is no section on detailed theoretical discussions. Instead, I spread out the internal workings of my mind as theoretical constructions, reveries, countertransference feelings, and formulations in between the clinical material.

JUDY—THE BODY AS THE ROSETTA STONE OF THE PSYCHE

Judy was a junior in college when we met. She had been suffering from anorexia nervosa and bulimia since her mid-teens. Her parents were physicians in their early forties who had divorced after a twenty-year marriage, a few years before we started working, and they were still on friendly terms. Judy had a sister, Donna, who was in junior high school. In accordance with their parents' divorce decree, Judy and Donna were living with their father and were visiting their mother every other weekend. Judy had a relatively uneventful developmental history in her comfortable middle-class family, so the development of the eating disorder had come as a surprise to her parents.

Before she was admitted to the hospital, a colleague of mine was working with Judy in psychoanalytic psychotherapy three times a week and managing her psychopharmacologic treatment. After about a year of helpful treatment, for unclear reasons, Judy rapidly deteriorated in a matter of a few months and was hospitalized for secondary to severe weight loss and metabolic imbalance.

Following her admission to the hospital, we developed a new plan; I would be working as the team leader and family therapist, meeting with the family once a week for extended, ninety-minute family sessions, and her individual therapist would be working with Judy in twice-weekly psychoanalytic psychotherapy sessions and managing her medications. A cognitive behavioral therapist, as a member of the team, would be actively engaging Judy at the level of her behavior (bulimia, restricting, and excessive exercising), and her primary nurse would be involved in Judy's daily life in the hospital. And as an inpatient, Judy would naturally be a part of an active milieu and groups program of the psychotherapeutic hospital.

During my first attempts to gather a family history, I recognized that Judy's mother and father had an unusual aspect to their relationship. As left-wing liberals, they had gone to a Latin American country in the early 1970s with the Peace Corps and were then caught in the maelstrom of the toppling of the elected regime by a military junta. Labeled as communists, both were detained, tortured, and imprisoned for a few months by the totalitarian and corrupt military dictatorship. They were released after enormous political pressure from their influential families and managed to get back to the United States. The camaraderie they displayed under the terrible conditions of their imprisonment had added a powerful level of mutual respect and loyalty to the couple. Their children were named after two of their best friends who perished in the prisons of the autocratic military regime. And thus their divorce, the idea of leaving one another and going their own ways, had become a very difficult task.

First Meeting

During our first family session, Judy, after all of her defensive-adaptive attempts had failed and now in the hospital, was talking about her deep sense of guilt over hurting her parents by causing so much trouble. She said she didn't know how to exist and wanted to remain silent for a while.

Meeting with her daughter in the hospital, the mother was terribly sad. When I asked her to articulate what was going on inside of her mind, she said she can't talk. She was sobbing uncontrollably. After calming down, she relayed the following story: before Judy was hospitalized, Judy's illness was suffocating her mother. On a weekend visit just before hospitalization, when she went to a café with Judy, she felt terribly frustrated and helpless over Judy's gobbling of teas, coffees, and pastries one after another and then running to the bathroom to purge. She couldn't figure out whether Judy was simply out of control because of her illness or she was trying to send a message through her actions. In either case, Judy's mother was exhausted by all of this.

Judy's father was composed but said it was a horrendous week for him too. After holding it in for so many months, in a rather unusual fashion for him, just prior to her hospitalization he had expressed his deep frustration with Judy's relentless anorexic rituals. He was getting terribly tired of Judy cooking odd food in the middle of the night and hearing her devour it with gurgling sounds, and then going on with her bulimic rituals in the bathroom. The noises of vomiting and flushing the toilet were audible to him and Judy's sister. He was cat-napping in the last year and a half, keeping a close eye and ear on what his daughter was doing without uttering a word about it. He had finally exploded and asked his daughter to stop what she was doing in the kitchen and in the bathroom. He felt terribly guilty afterward.

I was noticing that the mother and father were polar opposites as far as what Judy was capable of evoking in them, a ripe fault line for borderline pathology to grow on.

Judy's sister Donna, somewhat in a daze, was listening to Judy and her parents, trying to understand what was going on with her dear sister who was now in a hospital and for whom they were meeting in a doctor's office. Judy was afraid that she may have a negative impact on her sister by this dramatic shift of events. Judy had fantasies that she may get her sister sick and that Donna may also develop an eating disorder. If that happened, Judy thought, she couldn't forgive herself.

The family members were all at a loss, exhausted; it was a tragic and painful but an opportune moment for effective therapy and change.

After the stories of Judy's impact on them, the father in passing made a slight reference to a heart problem that immediately caught my attention. It was a potential moment of decentralizing Judy as a projective focus, so I actively inquired as to what he was referring to. He said he had a cardiac spasm. As I opened this line of inquiry, Judy told us that right before she was hospitalized, she had recognized that there was something wrong with her father; he looked more tired than usual, and she became vigilant about his health.

With the intention of exploring, and thus interfering with the more apparent projective-introjective cycles focused on Judy as projectee and highlighting some other less obvious cycles where she was the projector, I pointed to how they both were vigilant about each other—the father over Judy's eating rituals and Judy over her father's vague heart complaints. They said that watching each other was a well-known habit for both of them.

The father then started talking about how his illness wasn't that big of a deal; he could take care of it if he wanted to. I told them that the father's approach reminded me of the similar stance of Judy's about her own illness, as I had heard during our initial interviews. They were both provocative in the way they dealt with their illnesses, giving some subtle but noticeable hints, and at the same time would be acting as if they were omnipotent about their capabilities to control it and were denying their effect on each other. Judy's mother agreed with this observation.

I turned to the father and asked whether it was true that he would run five stairs of flights to his apartment and kept on smoking forty cigarettes every day, despite his heart condition. "Yes," he said, "I never get tired and never think about myself." I commented on how, in certain ways, he was worse than Judy in the way he treated his body. The mother joined the conversation and said her ex-mother-in-law was very similar to her husband. Neither of them talked about their problems but would act in semisecret, self-destructive ways that were maddening to the others around them. We were finding some red threads to Judy's modus operandi.

When we got together as a team and brought our bits of information together, it became clear that the father's cardiac event had occurred right after he had learned that Judy was in a romantic relation with a classmate; it was the first time that Judy developed an interest in a man. Her father was deeply attached to Judy; with a deeply confused sense of their relationship, he had once told Judy that they may as well die together because, in the event of her death, he couldn't tolerate carrying her coffin. He was now facing an enormous developmental challenge with the appearance of another man in Judy's life that was pushing him out of the orbit of his daughter.

And in the midst of this plethora of confusing information, I was developing the hypothesis that Judy and her father and the whole family were actually regressing together in the face of Judy's attempt to form a new love relation with a man, and possibly also due to her intensifying transference love with her psychoanalytic psychotherapist.

Session

Judy's sister Donna opened the session, associating to a recent traumatic event; a teacher of hers had died of cardiac arrest in the gym. Witnessing the collapse and death of a revered teacher was a harrowing event. The trauma though was not just because of the death of the teacher, but it also reminded Donna of her father's mysterious cardiac condition and her grandfather's funeral. A year ago, when she had heard about the sudden death of her beloved grandfather, she had chosen to go to a basketball game to avoid attending the funeral, and now she was feeling terribly guilty.

As Donna was talking about these losses, Judy immediately tried to interfere and suppress Donna's unfolding mourning. When I asked Judy to expand on the motives for her intervention, she said she always felt guilty and never wanted Donna to suffer from those feelings or mourning. It seemed like Donna was ready to explore and articulate the experience, and as I was trying to understand and interrupt Judy's defensive intervention, the father came to the rescue. He suggested that maybe we should talk about some other incident.

I was surprised with the dual interference, first by Judy and then by her father, of Donna's attempt to process her grief. Yet I reminded myself that this probably was an unbearably painful set of experiences for the members of the family at the moment. As it happens regularly in family work, I was noticing the roots of the defensive operations of the ego and was in a juncture where I had to decide on making a defense interpretation or letting the process unfold, respecting its adaptive sides. I decided not to pursue further clarification of these interpersonal interventions.

I Am Noticed

Over the course of some months, the father became increasingly angry with me. Upon my invitation to expand on his obvious anger, he said that after beginning the family sessions, Judy wasn't talking with him as much as she did in the past and this was hurtful. And he felt like I was hurting Judy. This brought another interesting theme, the third person. Father was never comfortable with, and in fact hated it when there was a third person. As I was trying to formulate what the idea of a third person meant, Judy came to my help. She said her father was unable to use the pronoun "I," instead he preferred "we." The third person in this instance was myself as an "I" outside of the dyad of "we." Mother joined the discussion stating that it was always like that.

I: "In this family, saying something like 'I want this' is a taboo."

Father: "Yes, 'I' is a selfish word. I believe in 'we,'; it should be a democracy. I am in favor of asking the opinion of others before I make any decision. It may sound odd, but if I was to remarry, I would ask the permission of my daughters and even my ex-wife."

Following these significant series of clarifications, the members of the family talked about how they could not forget each other, how their minds were always preoccupied with one other.

As the family members were talking amongst themselves, I was on the fly trying to formulate my impressions. Judy's father was never able to say I/me; Judy and her father were enslaving each other but what was the role of Donna and the mother in this intricate set of dynamics? I was pondering the enormous space occupied by others in the minds of this family. And it appeared as if in this family, there were private spaces that were destroyed, such as when the father and daughter didn't mind walking around the house in their underwear. And then, there were semisecrecies in the eating disorder and heart condition. The family system had a semantic confusion about what was public, private, and secret. The central affects that we build our individualities around—pride, shame, guilt—and the affects that we use to differentiate ourselves from others—envy and jealousy—were banished and defended against or experienced in agonizing ways.

Keeping these disorganized thoughts to myself, I interpreted my intrusion into the family system that was passionately protected by the father and suggested that his anger was related to my attempt to be included. I recognized the complicit nodding of the mother as an affirmation of this idea when the father exploded: "You will never get my love, Dr. K!"

The Father's Open Hostility and Love

A few months into the family work, Judy's father was openly discontent with the treatment; he was coming late to our sessions and attempting to leave early. He was questioning the validity of our approach and requesting we end these therapy sessions. At the same time, the mother and the father were pointing to some subtle but significant changes. They were not feeling as excluded in each other's presence and were recognizing an increased capacity to move apart from one another and develop new interests without feeling guilty. Some secret aspects of their lives were becoming open. The father was making peace with his recently refound belief in God in contrast to his fervent atheism of early youth, whereas the mother was talking about feeling more comfortable in openly admitting how she had moved from left-wing radicalism toward an environmentalist/LGBT activism. This was a significant shift for a once-Marxist/atheist couple who had been tortured in a South American country and had deep loyalties to those horrendous times and identities.

Feeling like I was trying to swallow and digest the familiar yet exhausting ambivalence of the parents, I was recommending that the father and all the rest of us tolerate the process. It felt as if I was also tolerating the incorporation and keeping it in. For me, Judy's eating disorder symptoms were becoming a symbolic, metaphorical condensation of thinking about the dynamics of the family.

Sporadically and slowly, members of the family were acknowledging that they all were feeling well. Judy and her mother had spent two weeks during Judy's winter break and the mother was delighted over the fact that she had not surrendered to Judy's obsessive wishes to eat certain types of food in certain portions. Judy, on her end, was both glad and infuriated that her mother had not given in to her demands. The father had taken some time off from the troubles of Judy, and Donna was enjoying a basketball camp.

As they were talking about this general sense of contentment in the session, I was recognizing some countertransference feelings; an irritating feeling that my ideas, words, sentences were being mocked by Judy and her mother, unlike previous times when I felt understood and maybe idealized by that part of the family. The father seemed a bit removed from the enmeshment with his daughter and now maybe it was time for the mother/daughter dyad to surface more clearly in the negative transference.

Session

Donna seemed irritated at the beginning of the session. She was five minutes late and was angry that we had started the session without her. Her irritation seemed to continue through the initial phase of our meeting, so I asked about that.

Donna: "Yes, I am angry nowadays."

Judy had an explanation for what was happening: "My dad and I are finding new personal interests. I am enjoying my time with my new boyfriend, and my father is contemplating the idea of running for political office in the state elections. Donna, on the other hand, is lacking any such outlets."

Donna said she was not aware of being hurt by these developments but was clearly recognizing that she was angry.

The father too seemed like he was hurt; he was sitting alone, in a corner of the room. He said he was troubled by Judy's changes and felt like all of those years when he tried to be a perfect, available father were a waste. The mother said maybe they made some mistakes raising their children!

Judy Discharged from the Hospital

Judy was medically stable, her eating disorder symptoms were under control, and there was enough traction gained in her individual and family work. So after six months of intensive hospital work, Judy was discharged from the hospital. In contrast to the times prior to the deterioration that prompted the hospitalization, now she was quite active in her daily life, in a stable relation with her boyfriend, attending college, and had plans to move to her own place sometime in the near future.

As Judy was taking these steps with an ordinary degree of ambivalence, her father was worried that she was developing a lot of secrets and was probably running away from him, and in parallel, Judy thought that she was being abandoned by her father. The idea of secrecy versus privacy was becoming a central theme for the family members. Judy, and in parallel, her family members, were developing private spaces, claiming them in the ordinary developmental sense and yet were worried that these were secret spaces where they were banishing the other.

With the intent of a therapeutic exploration, I asked the father about his impression of Judy "running away from him."

The father: "She is never at home. These family therapy sessions became the only space where we have a chance to talk with one another. We used to share so many things in the past. Now it is all gone. I think she is going too fast."

I asked Judy whether there was a kernel of truth in her father's observation, that maybe she was going too fast.

Judy said: "That is absolutely true, Dr. K. Last night he said 'good night, I love you' four times, which bothered the hell out of me. I am becoming aware of how close our relationship is and want to develop a different way of relating but that is the only way to do it. He has great difficulty letting me grow."

As a counter argument, the father noted the mixed messages Judy and Donna were giving. The father said "they both talk about growing, becoming father and children, not friends, but then act as if they were not ready." To prove the point, he said Donna still comes back to him and initiates a conversation on some themes as if he was her friend.

It was a par-for-the-course developmental scheme with ambivalent actions, feelings, and thoughts in every member of the family, yet there was an intensity of the irrationality/ambivalence and lack of some perspective in the father that was disconcerting to me. I was having difficulty in empathically relating to or rationally following his narrative and was wondering whether underneath the obsessive, composed appearance, he may actually be prone to disorganized prepsychotic thinking.

I asked the mother, who was silent, about what was going on in her mind.

She said she knew these sides of her kids. They had no sense of boundaries. They would leave their belongings and clothes all around the house. Donna's bedroom was a pigsty and Judy was even worse; she would start peeling her clothes off like a snake skin as she entered the house on her way to her bedroom, and would leave almost everything other than her underwear in the living area. The mother had tried hard for a long while to bring some order to this mess but her husband was extremely tolerant. "I believe now he is coming to his senses," she concluded.

The father: "I agree, now that is over. I have no intention of carrying on with that attitude."

Fascinated with this wealth of dynamically significant minutiae of their lives and yet sensing the lack of sadness and mourning over the differentiation of all members, I told Judy that it appeared as if she was struggling with saying goodbye to her father, and to the ways in which they related to one another. No one was interested in my idea.

At this juncture, the mother said, "Sorry to say this but as long as Judy stays with her dad, she may remain sick and may not be able to separate for the rest of her life." From the usual, rather peripheral, listening/silent presence of Judy's mother, these words dropped into the session like a bolt of lightning that struck out of the blue skies.

The father became enraged and started yelling, "It is all because of me, right? You are doing the same infuriating thing. You are staying passive, on the fence all the time and then putting all the blame on me!" And he countered with his own lightning bolt: "I am going to say this for the first time in my life but maybe I should have left this house six years ago!"

Somewhat overwhelmed with this unexpected explosion, I regained my composure when I made the formulation that these were some ordinary, passionate, but delayed fights between this long-divorced couple. I brought back the theme of the lack of mourning about their separation. They had divorced some years ago and acted as if it did not happen. When they decided to separate their lives, they probably felt like they betrayed their comrade in arms with whom they went through unthinkable suffering in torture chambers. Again, my interpretations fell on deaf ears. The family was avoiding my words.

Then the mother gave a hopeful therapeutic opening to the treatment from her genetic/historical end: she recounted how she was brought up in a family with very strict rules and wanted to raise their kids with no such rules with the hope of making them feel "happy and free." Now she wondered maybe she was wrong in her thinking at the time.

I: "Hum uhm."

Despite the mother's attempt to focus on herself, the father focused the session on an interesting theme by stating that he felt angry over the fact that he was being interpreted without anyone asking him what was going on inside of his mind. Donna suggested that maybe he should be open about his feelings. This brought a muddled narrative from the father: he was not going to play these games and give up his privacy for Dr. K. No one had asked about his feelings and all of this was confusing for him.

It was an agonizing sight to watch, evoking strong countertransference feelings and reminiscences of proud and confused men in my life. In a parallel fashion to his daughter's anorexia/bulimia, the father was hungry, wishing to be fed, and then would hate someone who is like the food that he would have to internalize and then would have to vomit out. I told him that he was right, that he was exposed, put in a terrible spot, and yet I didn't know any other way of working.

He continued to get further disorganized and rambled in passing about he and his ex-wife getting remarried in order to help Judy. Still unable to follow his discourse, I was puzzled about this particular remark and with the hope of finding some rational thread, I asked what he meant by remarrying, and I was surprised by his response. Apparently, before we started our work, the father had told his ex-wife that if the doctor recommended getting remarried to help Judy, he would do it but would eventually die!!

Our time was up, and as I was trying to end the session he was going on with a very loud, irrational tirade about how no one had a right to his privacy and how he would never come to these sessions anymore. As everyone slowly shrank in their chairs in the face of what felt like a ruminative, irrational discourse of the father, to my surprise, I exploded.

With a tense, trembling voice, I told him that I had no personal interest in his life and neither I had any professional wish to remarry them and continued: "Your daughter was almost dying and I am, we are trying to sort things out here. You cannot quit at this moment; we can review our format and revise it, but I find it unacceptable that you are calling it quits." He was stunned, as was I. As they were leaving the office, he said that my remarks were very heavy handed.

Session

At the beginning of the next session, the father said he was pleased with my strong reaction. They had been wondering whether I had the capacity to be involved in their work in an emotional way and my reaction made the whole family realize that I was on their side. I was surprised but thanked them for their help in recognizing my relative absence in the heat of things. This was one of my familiar characteristics, a side of my character neurosis that had also surfaced in the case of Al and many others. It had come back again: the good boy who is a great listener but who may come across as uninterested. I would absorb the micro trauma without responding, and would therefore appear very tolerant or numb, and then explode with some ferocity, just like my father.

In the script of Judy's life, I was repeating a central theme of the family; being numb or endlessly tolerant. Just like when Donna was trying to sooth her father with the common family term of "no tears" when she recognized that her father was getting sad, or when Judy's parents tried to ignore her unfolding eating disorder. We had all allowed our fragilities to surface.

It was also one of those rare treatments where for extended periods of time I felt unheard; to use Judy's anorexia as a metaphor, my interpretative food, my mind and thoughts were refused by the family. And then it was as if I had forcefully pushed myself into their minds, similar to Judy's struggles around food with her mother.

After this blowout of mine, albeit with considerable reluctance, the foursome began discussing their feelings, which I thought also meant their subtle, barely recognized thoughts about one another. In this search, they were all trying to understand what was private, what was secret, and what was public. I put this hypothesis on the table and asked for their ideas.

The father: "I do not say anything about what I am capable of doing, for example, how many computer languages I can use (it was pre-Windows times). Those, in my opinion, are all private. On the other hand, my personal relationships are out in the open."

The mother's stance was the exact opposite. In her opinion, her relationships were private and her work and skills could be totally out in the open. It was again telling how the mother and the father, as it is so common in many borderline pathologies that get located in an index patient, were defining themselves in contrast to one another.

As we were having these discussions, Judy was in her corner, covering her face with her books and was mumbling about how horrible it was to hurt other people. She wished that there was a way she could live without impacting others negatively. I told her that she wanted to live an impossible life.

Body as an Evocateur, Provocateur

As Judy became more cognizant of her ability to have an effect on others, her eating disorder stabilized. She was less tortured by restricting/binging rituals and surprisingly, she began worrying about her body. She wanted to have a physical exam but was shying away from it because she was afraid that she had caused irreversible damage to her reproductive organs through her anorexia. When I therapeutically confronted her on the issue, Judy told all of us that it was her body and we didn't have any say over it. It was an interesting argument: Judy was making a statement that she had a right to treat her body in any way she wanted and thought this had no impact on the other people around her. She was undermining the communicative capacity of her body.

I: "You are back to hurting your parents through your body. This time around though, not through the powerful impact of your eating disorder on your appearance, but through the damage you might have caused inside of your body, specifically, to your fertility."

She was curious to hear why I thought that way. I found myself struggling over whether I should divulge how she impacted me, and I decided to disclose it nevertheless. I said when I heard that her menses were still missing, I felt like it had an impact on me too, not just on her parents.

Clearly stunned with my response, Judy asked why I was cornering her. In return, I said that I may be cornering her but I felt like she was also cornering me and her mother, father, and sister. The lumpenproletariat of my country of origin, Turkey, was swirling in the back of my mind. These were people who were, when they were threatened, would not hesitate to counter the threat in a way that seemed inconceivable to me. I had read stories and seen pictures of men holding terror-stricken little children in their arms, with a knife pointed at the child's throat, threatening to cut the throat of their own children, if the police were to come and evacuate them from their illegally built shacks. In a similar vein, Judy was telling me that I was responsible for some of the actions that were initiated by her.

The father developed an interesting series of associations on this theme. He thought that recently Judy was making an attempt to connect with him and Donna. As an example that illustrated his point, Judy had offered to play cards with them on the weekends; this had both shocked and deeply pleased him and Donna. Judy vehemently opposed her father's interpretation. She had no intention of making her father and Donna happy; there was nobody else around so she had no choice but to play with them. She stated that she was a selfish person and had no interest in pleasing her father and sister, she just wanted to please herself. The mother agreed with Judy's formulation. In her opinion Judy was not interested in others, she was very selfish as she had stated before. It was just a coincidence that she had her father and sister as objects available for the card game.

This was the other aspect of Judy formulating herself as a person existing in a vacuum: a way of experiencing herself in what seemed like empty space devoid of other humans as we had witnessed in the story of Al. Others who had their own autonomous minds, others who Judy would cathect in and relate to as unique persons, were missing. The others were just functions in her mind's eye, part objects that were needed for fulfillment of her needs. In Judy's case, it clearly was a defensive regression, and it was not too difficult to help her move up with therapeutic interventions, unlike the profound stickiness of Al's position.

With this formulation in the back of my mind, I commented on how difficult it was for Judy to say that she specifically wanted to play with her father and sister and enjoyed it. The father joined me and to further facilitate the therapeutic confrontation I had initiated, pointed to another change. In the past, he and Judy would share a lot of things but this would only happen at his work place; she would visit him at work where they would talk about many different topics. And in striking contrast, in the evenings or on weekends, when they were at home, she would be totally silent, immersed in her own interests. Now, she had dropped the habit of visiting him and was initiating conversations at home, in their leisure time, and both seemed to be enjoying it.

For me, it was a moment of reflection. I was trying to formulate the change and strategize my interventions. On the one hand, it was significant that the father developed the pattern of adding a positive whenever I made a comment on Judy, Donna, or himself, as if I was attacking them, so he was providing a protective image. On the other hand, I had a fantasy that Judy and her father were scared of being engulfed or engulfing in the past, thus needed dad's work space, a place with other people around. And that helped both to be together with and converse with one another. With therapy, the primitive psychotic anxieties had lost their intensity and decreased toward more neurotic anxieties, enabling them to face each other without the need for some external anchors or scaffolding. Judy and her father were clearly moving out of a need for objects that would provide scaffolding in between or around them and were becoming ready to face each other as persons with no intermediaries.

As I was absorbed in these reverie-like formulations, Judy contested my interpretation: "I have no loving/caring sides." Mother immediately agreed with this. I asked the mother whether she was similar to Judy in this regard, wondering about underlying identificatory processes. The mother refuted this: "Not at all, I help my friends when they need me. Judy is terribly egotistical." The father then gave some examples to counter this solidly engrained simplistic image of Judy in her mother's mind. Judy was turning beet red with embarrassment as she heard her father's story about her self-image, a story that was complicating the stick figure images she and her mother were providing, adding shades of grey to the black-and-white image.

I was contemplating what was transpiring at the moment and came up with a hypothesis that maybe Judy was struggling between two deeply, murderously jealous, split maternal and paternal identifications of hers. And I articulated this as a hypothesis in a rather convoluted narrative.

I: "I am thinking to myself that maybe you, Judy, are struggling between two loves: your love for your mother and your love for your father. Maybe you have always found it terribly difficult to reconcile these two loves of yours, when in reality your mother and father have always been in deeply entrenched conflicts.

Judy: "Yes. They have a way of pinning on me all the things they do not like about me as coming from the other person. 'Now you act like your mom' my dad would say, and 'now you are acting like your dad' would be the counterpart coming from my mother."

As we were exploring these aspects of their relating to one another, the father intervened and pointed to another change in Judy: she was not asking for money recently. He was happy and also worried about this change. This brought up another theme on the split stances of the mother and the father. Judy never had a clear amount of allowance from her father. She would determine what she needed for clothing, school fees, and so on and then would try to come up with ways of getting this money. The mother, on the other end, was a strict budgeter and would give a certain amount of money to Judy, and then Judy would get the extras secretly from her father. This was a striking contrast and had a significant similarity to Judy's eating disorder, a bulimic paternal and a restricting maternal identification.

Eating Disorder Resurfacing

A year and a half into our work, Judy became acutely symptomatic again. She was devouring all the food available to her, from chocolates to pastry, to cheese, vegetables and meat, and leftovers and then vomiting them.

This brought another fascinating aspect of the dynamics of their relationship. When Judy was severely symptomatic, rummaging the refrigerator for food, gorging on what she found, and then vomiting all that she consumed in the bathroom, she was also leaving her marks around the kitchen. The father and Donna were deeply troubled about finding pieces of cheese, bread, and butter that Judy had taken bites off and left in the refrigerator and on the countertops. It drove them insane, and they felt like Judy was sending them a message. They were at a total loss on how to help Judy stay away from her favorite foods in the refrigerator, so her father bought a second refrigerator and put it in his bedroom. And this was where Judy's huge stock of carrots, apples, and juices were stored. But Donna was approaching this dilemma differently, insisting that she was getting sick and tired of Judy's eating disorder and maybe she should pay for the food she was wasting through her binges and purges. The mother lived in a different city, so she was not as emotionally involved but she was protecting Judy on her reluctance to explore what was causing her recent decompensation, claiming that Judy had a right to her privacy.

As we were passionately working on the boundaries around the resurgence of Judy's symptomatic eating, another interesting piece of information emerged. The father's family was in the habit of getting Judy whatever she wanted; her uncle had bought her an expensive perfume recently, and grandmother was giving her handsome allowances. The father told us that they were much worse with their boundaries than him, and he was fighting them too!

It was of note that the father was occasionally becoming critical of Judy, and then he would apologize immediately for getting angry. Being angry with or critical of his children was a taboo for the father. He had an ingrained image of himself: if his anger would come out, it would be once and for good, and he would sever his ties with them forever. Thus he always treated Judy and Donna with endless patience, as equals, with the hope that they could be strong persons, capable of defending themselves. That absolutist script was now softening.

Session

Judy was silent and so were her parents.

I: "You are quite angry about the last session Judy?"

Judy: "I sure am. You all, and especially you, Dr. K, you made it sound like I am a horrific bitch. I am a nuisance for all of you. I will go out and create a life for myself where I won't be a bother to anyone. I am not interested in talking with you, and these sessions are not going anywhere."

The father: "I think we are all going through an interesting phase. Judy is distressed with her body, which is something new for us, recognizing that maybe there is a significant damage to her body. She is recognizing it as such and also giving me a punishment."

I: "Can you expand on that?"

The father: "She has not been talking with us for many days now. She is eating on her own and cooking her own food. And there seems to be a tension developing between Donna and Judy.

Judy: "If I found someone on the streets, I wouldn't come here probably."

The mother: "You are bluffing."

I was surprised with the mother's anger, then Judy pitched in.

Judy: "You, again, especially you, Dr. K, make me look like I have a sinister plan of hurting my family through my anorexia. You portray me as a selfish, imperialistic devourer of my parents and my sister."

I: "Judy, I think you are trying to understand that you are not living in a vacuum but have effects on your loved ones."

Judy: "What if I disappear, immigrate to another continent?"

I: "That will make everybody's worries worse."

After this intense discussion, Judy, the father, and I had a conversation where we agreed that treatment was going well, and we all recognized that Judy was not just draining others but was also giving enormous amounts to others by swallowing her wishes around buying new books, a new bike, or maybe living on her own. She was restricting her pleasures in her relationships.

It was a moment of enlightenment for me, too. I said that I was aware that Judy was not just sadistic toward herself but she was also just as sadistic toward others. On the other hand, even though it seemed like a paradox, I was recognizing a different aspect of hers; she would pamper herself, indulge in food, and at the same time be very caring and giving to others. And it appeared as if she did not know how to bring these two sides, the sadistic and loving, together. I connected these split sides of herself to similar, but less intense, conflicted aspects of her parents. Judy was listening intently; it was one of those moments where you as the therapist recognize that she is taking it in by her look, attention, and interest. She was finally eating my interpretative food.

Judy: "That is the first time someone ever told that to me." And she made a fascinating self-interpretation that it was very hard for her to be criticized and/or praised. They were both recognitions of her, and she could not tolerate that.

After these series of interactions, the mother and the father, with some sense of shyness and pride, talked about how they saw themselves in certain aspects of Judy! It was an important moment of acknowledgement.

Developing a Loving Relationship with Her Body

Judy was developing a tender relationship with her body—a capacity to feel sorry for her body and feel helpless over its workings. As she was coming to terms with her limitations, she was going through phases of hope and hopelessness where she was ready to give up on herself.

As we were focusing on the troubles Judy was going through in our sessions, the mother made an interesting observation. She said there was clear progress in the family, and she thought that maybe Judy was inviting the focus back on herself because Donna had recently graduated from junior high. And instead of paying attention to Donna's achievement, we were again suffocated with Judy's anorexia. Maybe she was jealous of her sister getting some space and attention from us!

Judy became infuriated with what she heard and accused the mother with her articulate deprecatory narrative, but the mother was not fazed and defended her position in the face of Judy's vicious attack.

The father pitched in on the idea of Judy's uncontrollable jealousy. Several days ago she had come back to the apartment and found that her father was not there! She had thrown a fit when her dad was not where he was supposed to be! How dare, in her mind, could her father not be at home when Judy came back? Where was he and with whom? As we delved into what had happened, Judy said she felt very alone when she couldn't find out where her dad was. When she called him and the father said he was lobbying for his political interests, she felt terribly hurt and alone and that had led to her blowing a gasket.

When she was struggling with these issues of potency and jealousy, her anorexia flared up and Judy came close to another hospitalization. She also began inflicting burns on her arms with cigarettes, in front of her dad. This was the final straw. It broke both her mother and father down, they were both hopeless about this illness, and were crying their eyes out in agony. Thankfully, these acts of self-destruction stopped relatively quickly. Paradoxically, as she was regressing with scary self-destructive acts, Judy was at the same time becoming more feminine in the ordinary sense. She was maintaining her weight, tolerating the fat tissue around her waist and breasts, and ambivalently tolerating her menses that had finally resumed after so many years.

Psychic Structure Encoded in Anorexia

The mother ecstatically told us that Judy ate a piece of salmon! Judy corrected her mother. In fact she had had a few pieces of salmon. For Judy it was a big ordeal; it felt as if she was fed like an infant by her mother, or maybe it was like having sex. And salmon was oily, tasty, and disgusting all at the same time. She had added a piece of cheese to neutralize this odd mixture of feelings.

As we went on with the conversation about Judy having some salmon, an interesting detail emerged. Judy had initially declined the fish, but in an unusual fashion, her mother had insisted that she taste it. This gentle insistence had made a huge difference for Judy. In the past, the mother had a peculiar attitude around feeding Judy. She would meticulously prepare healthy food in well-planned caloric proportions and would bring them to the table. As a rule, Judy would adamantly refuse to eat them and then the mother would either back down or she would try and force Judy to eat them. And they would have a tremendous, painful struggle over food. This time around, Judy felt that her mother was not ambivalent about the food she was offering; what she offered was not a well-prepared "healthy" food. And she was not insisting but inviting.

Thus, the mother had altered her approach to food at the age of forty-something, and at the age of twenty-two, Judy had accepted her mother's loving maternal insistence to eat the smoked salmon and had managed to eat it and keep it in. These series of interactions between her mother and Judy symbolized the identification process that was evolving. The mother was more content with her food-self and Judy thus was eager to incorporate it.

Further along in the session, another series of stunning material emerged. Judy and her parents would go on binges of drinking and eating after they had restricted themselves for many months on a calorie-counted diet. I pointed to what was now an obvious parallel, that their relations had the quality of an eating disorder, vacillating from one extreme of restricting to the other extreme of binging. Judy found this an interesting insight and again began listening attentively. I stated that perhaps she did not know how to hold her mother and father in; she either refrained from taking them in, or gorged on them and then purged them out. It made sense to me and I was trying to convey it to them; the father was telling Judy that he loved her five times a day whereas the mother never told this. The father was a binge lover and the mother was a restricting anorexic lover.

Even though it appeared to me somewhat overly dramatic, the family was fascinated with this interpretation. The father said he tried to be a father, a mother, and a friend to Judy and recognized that it was deeply confusing and probably suffocating, and it didn't work. The mother said she wanted to give some space to Judy but ended up abandoning her. Now she thought it probably was a huge mistake. They were recognizing the antagonistic stances they had mutually created.

Judy: "If I could help them resolve this odd togetherness, I would, for celebration, eat a pound of cheesecake and wouldn't purge it!"

The mother was pleased that Judy was having her menses, and for a change she was coming to stay with her. There was a sense of joy in the family. The illness was letting go of Judy; the symptoms of anorexia and bulimia were receding and more importantly, Judy was moving herself out of the center of projective/introjective cycle. We ended the family work after just about two years, and Judy continued with intensive psychoanalytic therapy for some more years.

REFLECTIONS ON JUDY—THE BODY AS THE ROSETTA STONE TO THE PSYCHE

The work with Al gave some clues on how our bodies are an important avenue of communication. Early on, Al chose to deposit the skin he peeled off of his fingertips in his coffee cup. As he became more capable of allowing me as an object into his scripts, he was able to peel his skin and fling it to the floor of my office, depositing it in me.

These were rather subtle messages conveyed through Al's body, but when we come to the work with Judy, the centrality of the body as a proto-script with iconic-hieroglyphic qualities becomes more noticeable. Through Judy, we understand how themes of the representational and interpersonal world of our patients may be synoptically condensed into one's core, proximate, bodily self, and how one uses the body as a communicator.

With this accentuation of our awareness of the symbolic and communicator function of the body in Judy, we can go back to Barbara and see some commonalities on how, as products of our creation, our bodies, like our dreams, may be another road to the unconscious, to be translated over the course of psychoanalysis.

All through her life, Barbara's body had felt like another person residing in her. During her childhood and teens she was tiny and suffered from asthma. As she grew older, she had serious medical problems and multiple abdominal surgeries. Obesity, arthritis, infections, and recurrent fractures in her feet piled up on her. With inexhaustible patience, she attended to the endless problems that her body caused. She bought her body the best, freshest of produce, milk, fruits, and fruit juices. She had elaborate, almost ritualistic ways of bathing, washing and drying her hair, putting on her makeup, going to the hair dresser, having a manicure/pedicure and massages to repair/soothe a needy/ugly body. In sum, her body was severely restraining her, and on the other hand, this same body was severely restrained by Barbara. She never allowed herself to play with her body, or her body to play with her—just like the sad fact that she never played with any of her peers.

During her three-year hospitalization, without any direct interpretative work in this area, she spontaneously liberated herself from the imprisonment by her body, and her body from the imprisonment by her. She became more playful, authentic, and comfortable in the way she related to her body and in the ways in which her body related to her. She cut her hair short for the first time in her life, she tolerated wearing no makeup, and engaged in some erotic fantasies about me.

As the stories of Judy and Barbara exemplify, the way in which one relates to one's body is a synopsis of our internal object relations world, a representational set of scripts that have substantial influence on the way one's external interpersonal world is organized.

5

FROM THE HOSPITAL TO THE OFFICE

Kate—Less Is More

Judy was a gateway from the hospital to the couch. In this chapter, I focus on the work I conduct in my office.

My psychoanalytic office work and hospitalist work were two different but neighboring frameworks that provided an interesting tension throughout my career. The modes of being with the individual patient within these two different contexts needed a significant degree of flexibility. The shift in my approach from one to another occasionally caused some confusion, but I believe it was overall a very helpful dialectic for me and my patients.

In psychoanalytic work, we have some cherished traditions. Our sessions are forty-five to fifty minutes long, and we are attentive to the protection of that time bracket, we prefer to see the patient more frequently than once or twice a week (Stern 2009), respect the free associative process, work with whatever is presented to us in the associative material, listen to the transference, and so on. There are exceptions to these generally accepted routines; the shortened sessions of Lacanians (Roudinesco 2002), single-session psychoanalysis of Owen Renik (2001), banishing of some associative content as suggested by Thomas Ogden (2005) to a supervisee, and even Freud's imposing the termination on the Wolf Man (Freud 1918). Salman Akhtar summarized these alterations of the frame wonderfully in his recent book (Akhtar 2011). These well-tested rules need periodic reflection to make sure we treat them as valuable traditions, not like dogmas. Kate was one such patient who made me to reflect on, but not necessarily change, some of our valued, basic psychoanalytic traditions and techniques.

My Surprisingly Strong Reaction

Feeling content with my work of what seemed like a long week, I was waiting for my last appointment. A tired-looking young woman entered my office and said she had heard good things about me and was not interested in treatment, but wanted to get my opinion on some psychological issues like self-hypnosis.

It was an odd request; I was expecting a patient whereas this young woman had come in for what felt like an intellectual discussion. And this shift irritated me. But when I learned that she was an undergraduate student at a local prestigious liberal arts college where I had many esteemed colleagues and some analytic patients, my initial irritation dampened. Instead of a patient, I had a young woman asking for a consultation, I thought. Maybe after all, it was a nice way to end the tiring week—no diagnostic dilemmas, no treatment recommendations. My anxiety withered away, and my grandiosity flattered, I agreed to her request.

To my amazement, as she began talking, she rapidly began evoking strong negative affects and fantasies in me. Kate, as I learned her name was, looked spaced out, and her narrative was very vague. There was a set of barely comprehensible themes articulated in a foggy way: she had "excessive energy inside herself," she was "being affected by others," and she was "indifferent to many things, but the real stuff."

In my effort to decipher these foggy sentences, I recognized that I had switched from the mode of a consultant to that of the wary doctor. Using my general psychiatrist's lens, I was thinking about an incipient psychosis. As I began responding to her inquiry, profoundly surprising myself as I spoke, I further shifted the frame, and instead of answering her questions, I forcefully told Kate that she was probably psychotic and needed treatment, and I would be interested in treating her if she had any interest in that. I ended the session in a daze—she had asked for a consultation, and instead I had offered to become a therapist without her soliciting and authorizing such a request!

Kate, who was going to become my patient for the following two years, found me the next day during my lunch break. As I was munching on a sandwich in my office, she forcefully placed herself into my space, thanked me for giving her a tentative diagnosis of psychosis and offering help and told me that she decided to work with me in psychotherapy. One of the reasons why she decided to work with me was that I had surprised her for the first time in many years, by saying something she couldn't predict—that she was sick. That moment of surprise was something she had not experienced for a long while. She also made some vague comments about an energy she felt after our meeting, and said she would like to give some of it back to me. After a few minutes of this surprising monologue, she abruptly terminated her unexpected visit. As she walked out of my office, I was left behind, confused, still trying to finish my lunch.

Psychotherapy with Kate

As we began our first psychotherapy session, for a few seconds Kate stalled at the doorstep of my office. It was if she couldn't decide whether she should come in or not. I invited her in, rather enthusiastically as I had done with Al, and she came in. It felt as if I was holding, containing, and acting on behalf of this amalgam of an odd-looking, dried out, young, perplexing, intelligent, troubled soul who was at the edge of precatatonia.

When I invited her to talk about what she had in her mind, Kate said she did not know where to begin. She had difficulty in choosing one of the many themes that were circling in her mind. With my hard-to-contain therapeutic eagerness and my wish to think and act on her behalf, I told Kate that at the moment it may be extremely difficult for her to make choices, but that we might, nevertheless, try to start with what is at the top of her list. It felt as if she was pulling me into an active stance where I was trying to pull her out of her den.

Kate countered my invitation with a fascinating story. During the last ten years of her relatively young twenty-four-year life, she had taken care of many people. She considered most of these individuals to be friends but there were some others who just floundered through her house and she did not feel connected to them at all. These young men and women, friends or not, would end up spending endless hours talking with her while they were squatting in her home. Even after they left, most would call her at any time of the day, sometimes in the middle of the night, waking Kate from her deep sleep. They would be asking for her advice on a plethora of issues from academic or relationship problems to their contemplation of suicide. Kate would end up spending large amounts of time with them until she felt they no longer needed her counsel.

As I was listening to this unusual saga, intuitively I asked whether she was tired. Kate said she was exhausted. It was a moment of therapeutic hope for me; I thought she was ready to think and talk about her character structure.

Noting her extreme capacity for love and thus, I surmised, for aggression, I told Kate that taking and giving were important for her. She was not interested in my comment and told me that she felt like the conversations between the two of us were rather superficial. There were so many things to talk about, and she just touched on a few today. I told her that it appeared as if she had a hatred of limitations—in this instance, about time. She said that she could talk with me and to me for many years. I told her that I thought I understood her.

Then Kate said there was something different in my office and she was not comfortable with it. I suggested that she might have recognized that there was somebody sitting in her chair in the previous session. She thought about it for a while and told me that it is probably right and now she felt better. She reminded me that she is deeply attuned to others, even to their smell.

It seemed like we were developing a plain, straightforward psychotherapeutic conversation between a doctor and a patient without too many defensive distortions. And thus began our work.

Synopsis of the Central Dilemma

A few weeks into treatment Kate told me that she had disturbing, recurrent dreams in which her insides—her guts, spleen, and liver, all of the contents of her belly—would be spilling out. To her amazement, her insides were pathetically small. Horrified that they had all spilled out and with a sense of terror, Kate tried to tuck them back into her belly and was relieved when she was able to put her insides back in. This repetitive visceral dream was a straightforward and creative analogy to the analytic task that was awaiting us.

As it happens quite often in any psychoanalytic conversation, Kate defensively and adaptively switched from the images of her insides to talking about some aspects of her relationships with her parents. Kate, as an adolescent wishing to go out with her friends, would ask for limits; she would ask her parents when it would be a good time for her to come back home. Her parents would say: "Whenever you choose to." They were very lenient and would assure her that it was up to her: she should come back home whenever she thought it was the right time. It was confusing and liberating at the same time.

Then she gave a synoptic summary of her family that was again related to the themes of spilling and containment in the poignant dream. Kate's mother had several nervous breakdowns around her late twenties. These would last for weeks—she would lie in the bed in a catatonic, depressive stupor for many days in a row, and then would go into states of agitated crying spells where she would take Kate and Kate's baby brother to her bed, cuddle with them to help her calm down, and then fall asleep. Not knowing what to do with her psychotic mother, these states would leave Kate feeling agonizingly helpless and deeply scared.

As these horrendous episodes continued through Kate's preteen years, Kate felt sadistically attacked and constrained by her mother's illness, but she also was omnipotently holding and containing her mother's psychotic agitation through allowing her to cuddle with herself and her brother. Kate's father was working in an industry that would take him away from home for a month or two, several times a year. He initially didn't recognize the intensity of these episodes but once he did, he moved to a job that allowed him to stay at home where he was able to be a steady figure and sought appropriate psychiatric help for his wife.

Outside of this painful psychotic drama, Kate's parents behaved as genuinely altruistic people toward their kids most of the time and always toward outsiders. Kate's friends loved her parents because of their generosity. Her home was like a second home to all of her friends; they would come and stay whenever they wanted, for as long as they wanted, while being fed and parented by Kate's parents.

It was the end of the session, and I felt like she had worked wonderfully on the dream without my prompting, and I thought spilling her guts in therapy could be deadly for Kate, and maybe for her family. But the fact that she had managed to tuck them back in was a sign of hope.

Interpersonal Ecology Rattled

The early connection that I felt with Kate, and her reciprocal early attachment to me in the space of psychotherapy, was also felt by other people around Kate; her father and mother were recognizing some significant differences in the way she behaved after she began working with me. As our therapy deepened, I began receiving disturbing calls from her brother and mother, both of whom felt enormous anxiety about the process of my psychotherapeutic work with Kate. I clearly was interfering with and impacting a tightly knit pathological system.

Kate became deeply distressed with the news when I brought these out-of-session events to our work. I asked why she was so distressed about it. She had no clear response beyond surmising that "maybe they noticed our weekly sessions and called." When I invited her to think aloud, she said: "I don't want to do that because I like to think on my own and about myself." She felt angry when someone helped her. "When you offer the idea of my parents and brother as causative elements in my problems, I am deeply uncomfortable with that idea. I want neither to be affected by them nor affect them myself." I pointed out that she had a very interesting sense of self, ahistorical on the one hand, and on the other hand, with a monstrous sense of agency—almost God-like. Without a pre- or postcursor.

Soon after the session, I got a call from Kate's lesbian partner, who was very worried about Kate, who was talking about her imminent death in a few weeks. I thought this was one of those moments where the patient, due to the nature of her internal object relational scripts and actual attachments, needed much more than the two-person space of psychotherapy. So I decided to shift the frame.

I offered hospitalization but Kate was averse to it, saying that the hospital where I worked was a very expensive place that she couldn't afford anyway. I recommended a second plan by offering that her family join our work for some family therapy sessions. This idea did not get any traction either, so as the third choice I suggested that her partner could join some sessions. To my relief, they accepted this plan. Now I had the opportunity to work with a regressed dyad in situ, and thus would have a better chance for therapeutic impact. I carried this couples' work sporadically for some months, keeping the option of hospitalization in my mind all the time.

As we shifted our work to couples, it became clear that Kate's lover and her therapeutic litter—all of whom were deeply dependent on her and some of whom were sexually attracted to her—were resentful of her psychotherapy with me. They wanted her back. As I heard this dramatic story, a story that put her life in perspective for me as her analyst, I developed a conjecture in my mind and articulated it, offering it to both of us as an interpretation: "For the first time in a long while, you wanted something for yourself by coming to psychotherapy with me." Kate paused for some minutes and then agreed that it was a plausible hypothesis.

Our First Separation

When I came back from a two-week vacation, she told me that she had been relieved that we had not been meeting and enjoyed her time off. She felt liberated, had visited friends on the West Coast and had a great time.

It was a relief for me too. It was roughly half a year into our work, and I had developed a pervasive sense of dread whenever I thought about Kate. When I reflected on our work, I was fascinated with this peculiar person and our work, yet at the same time wanted her out of my life. I was getting calls at my home from her friends and brother expressing their worries, while Kate was also occasionally calling me, asking how I was doing. I patiently asked them to contact me at my office. Despite my fascination and immense learning, I was getting deeply annoyed with the treatment I had initiated and was now hoping that it would come to an end.

This powerful negative countertransference was not an unusual experience for me. It had emerged a little too fast this time, but I knew well that it was a necessary part of the treatment. Nevertheless, it was one thing to have the knowledge about the ordinariness of the experience and something totally different to feel it, again, in one's own flesh.

Session

Kate entered the office with brusque steps, wearing high-heeled shoes, and dressed rather colorfully. I had the fleeting fantasy that the dried-out or the old person that I would usually associate with her was not present in the session today.

Kate said she didn't understand my motives. She knew I was trying to do something—maybe I was trying to get her to become dependent on me or make her acknowledge that she may have missed me. She said she felt annoyed when she noticed the possibility of these feelings.

I said she was probably allowing me to enter into her private life, her mind, and her thoughts, and therefore I was probably becoming a person she could not avoid thinking about.

She continued: she perceived two different sides of me and she did not know what to do with them. One side was somewhat loving, caring, and empathetic whereas the other was indifferent and maybe even sadistically hateful—ending the sessions after fifty minutes, taking time off, and not responding to her calls. I acted very differently than the way she treated her "patients." It was a terrifying dichotomy for her, and she couldn't bring the two sides together.

As I was following this discourse with some sense of therapeutic fulfillment, she suddenly asked me whether I was ready to handle some surprising developments.

It was a moment of confusion for me, and I tried to make some attempts toward a theoretical formulation. I thought that she was attempting to working upward from a split transference. To help this upward move, I thought that she would vehemently defend against such interpretations such as dependent feelings toward me. I uttered these, what I considered as quasideveloped intrapsychic defense formulations in the transference, with the approving images of my analyst and supervisors in the back of mind.

To my disappointment, they made no sense to her. Kate said she thought I did not know what I was getting into. I had again forgotten that the appearance of theory and my teachers in the session was a sign that I was probably lost. With no guidance, I felt embarrassingly lost, sailing in thick fog. And time would prove she was right; what was happening at the periphery of our work was indeed quite scary as the subsequent developments would prove.

Session

There was silence. Recognizing my recent pattern of increased activity in the sessions, I maintained the silence for a while. I thought that she too had to participate. I was attempting to be less fearful and not anxious to do something this time, unlike many times before, when I would initiate the therapeutic conversation.

> Kate: "What a nice change. We are talking through the silence."

> I: "Seems like you enjoy it."

> Kate: "Yes, I enjoy the silence. Silence can be of two types. One is a tired silence and the other one is a joyful, creative silence." Then she stood up and started looking out of my window and said she was also recognizing that I was vacillating in my approach; active in some sessions and then coming up with a silence that felt quite inauthentic for her.

She said, "Maybe it's time for me to go." And she left. I was losing my footing.

The Limitations

Kate told me that she found this place unhelpful because of my therapeutic time frames, my walls, and my door, that I began the session on time and ended in fifty minutes. She had a very rich life and putting all of it into words in a limited amount of time is a way of losing the richness of her inner world.

As I was playing in my mind with the paradox of how one loses the richness of images, fantasies, and reveries when one tries to put things into words, I invited her to expand on her ideas: "Kate, in your opinion, how much time do you think you need here, in our work, within the confines of this office?"

> Kate: "I am not so sure. It may be a mere fifteen minutes or it may turn out that on that specific day, I may need many hours. After I leave this place, sometimes I muse on our session for the rest of the week, and sometimes the session is over once it is over."

> I: "Am I present in the reflections that may go on for a week?"

> Kate: "Yes your thoughts, my thoughts . . . I mull over them again and again."

We were finally talking with one another. It continued as a warm and lively session. Evoking my curiosity in her story, Kate talked about how people got attracted to her, would call her any time of the day to talk about themselves, and she would listen to them as long as they needed. That's what she wished we had, and I was not providing it. I agreed with a "hum uhm."

I thought I had an understanding of her deep ambivalence; wishing to have me in a limitless fashion and at the same time being terrified that I may surrender to that wish. She was coming here for the "bad," that I fail her wishes. And if she were to find the "good," a doctor who was limitless, she would fly off.

I put these instantaneous, poorly articulated ideas in between us: "Tell me what is good and what is bad for you?

Kate supported my hypothesis: "What is good for me is bad, and vice versa."

It was a huge relief to work with a person who—at least intellectually—understood the simple motto of working with serious psychopathology: "good may be bad and bad may be good." I supported Kate's self-interpretation with an empathetic "hum uhm."

While I was enjoying the decent, mutually created interpretation, she made some comments on my seeming to be too sure of myself. She thought that my stance could be a risky one and warned that I had to be very careful about seeming so confident. She was attacking the good that had come out of me and her.

> I: "I'm sure of myself and think I'm doing a good job and I'm a good doctor, but I also take my work very seriously, and I'm ready to listen to what you think we may be doing wrong."
>
> Kate: "That you are a good doctor is obvious, but your self-assuredness can be very dangerous. You may be prone to making mistakes." And the session ended.

After a session where I thought a therapeutic conversation was unfolding, she had left me alone again, with some vague but frightening thoughts.

The impact of our work on Kate's psyche and her interpersonal milieu was intensifying. Kate's lover visited with me again. She was very concerned about what she was witnessing, and she induced a fearful concern in me through what she described. Kate was spending a lot of time in a scary silence and immobility. She had withdrawn to a state of utter absence, thinking and whispering to herself, appearing as if she had become psychotic. These episodes would specifically happen around the perimeter of our psychotherapeutic work, on the days preceding or following the session.

As I thought about this worrisome young woman, I recognized the paradoxical impact Kate had on me as the therapy unfolded. I felt quite fulfilled with and proud of my work with what I thought was a person with severe pathology. At the same time, I had horrifying fantasies and fears that Kate or her family or friends may do something terrible—kill me in a violent way or blow my brains out with a shotgun or stab me to death. These deeply contradictory fantasies probably had their parallels in Kate's mind.

Countertransference Fascination

My increasing countertransference fascination and excitement got me worried. I had learned to interpret this countertransference feeling as a bad prognostic sign many times before, so I asked Kate what was in this work for her.

Kate: "I don't want anything in particular. I live in the moment and don't have any expectations about the future. I never had any dreams, because I was idealized all my life. I was the best in everything; as a student in high school and college, as a good girl in my family, as a great friend—in everything one could imagine."

Building on the idea that there were primitive regressed relationships in her family, I told her that I had a hypothesis: "Being good may have also pushed you to the position of not having a full, complicated, fulfilling life for your own self but abandoning some aspects of your mind, interests, capacities, in short, a portion of your life, to your brother. And probably vice versa."

It was an interesting moment in the session. Kate became animated and talked about how her brother was the exact opposite of her. Sometimes she wanted to have the same attitude that her brother had. He was invested in "minor" things in life; he decorated his bedroom with the pictures of basketball stars, always talked about mundane matters of his daily life with others, and lived a care-free life. Kate's brother, in her mind's eye, always followed his own dreams, was very selfish, and would use people and then throw them away. Yet Kate was the only person her brother respected. He would be scared of people whom he felt were far superior to him. And Kate would help him to protect his self-esteem in such relations. She hesitatingly acknowledged that she hated some aspects of her relationship with her brother.

I listened to her thoughts and supported them. I was pleased with her narrative as I perceived that she was developing a self-analytic capability. After that long, heated story, Kate started trembling and said, "Oh my God, I'm sick and tired of talking about my family." She elaborated: even when she thinks about them, her mother and brother drain her; the only person who gives her a sense of relief is her father.

Session

Kate came to the session with a friend who had a black lab puppy in her arms, and asked whether she could bring her friend's puppy to the session because her friend had a doctor's appointment. For some unknown reason she was arousing intense fear and anger in me.

I: "I don't know whether bringing the puppy to the session is similar to handing me a gun and asking me to shoot you." Because I was so fond of dogs and had a black puppy and some other dogs myself, at the time it seemed like an odd formulation, but in time, I was to be proven right.

After my refusal to let the puppy into our psychotherapy session, she brought up the issue of my recent refusals: first my refusal to listen to what she had to say. A few sessions ago, I had interrupted her wish to talk about the common theme of "there is something odd in this session." It was an active intervention on her associations, a contradictory stance to the basic psychoanalytic attitude of respecting the associations of the patient, but I felt imprisoned and attacked by this repetitive theme. As James T. McLaughlin (1991) and Ogden (2005) poignantly demonstrated, words and speech do become actions. And if the aggressive element is intolerable, one may go beyond the ordinary tolerant stance and simply ask for the cessation of aggression. I had limited her aggressive repetitive inquiry. And now I was putting a limit on her request to get her friend's cute puppy into the session.

I: "Kate, I am always worried when you say something is 'good.' I constantly evaluate your comments, narrative, and requests from the perspective of what you claim to be good, may actually be murderously bad for you. And further, I am always on the edge about whenever you want to give something to me. I immediately wonder to myself whether that is an attack on me or it is an act of me stealing from you."

I had to treat Kate's idiosyncratic language as if it was like dream work that needed to be translated. It was full of inversions and displacements; good was bad, generous could be selfish, giving could be taking, and love could be hate, and so on and so forth.

How Does One Live with a Dog?

Kate had recently adopted Kara, the lovely black lab puppy she wanted to bring to our session from her friend who had moved out of town. Kara had put a significant strain on Kate's meager budget because of her need for proper food, a dog bed, toys, and veterinary care. Yet for Kate, the most difficult aspect of having Kara in her life was not the monetary burden, but her mere presence.

Kara had no sense of a rhyme and a rhythm, of time and order; she would get up in the middle of the night and would need to be taken out for her natural needs. She would bounce all around Kate's small house, and then she would fall dead asleep for many hours. With no guidance on how to relate to this lovely and maddening creature, Kate would mirror her. She would bounce around with her when the puppy felt like doing it, and then would freeze and lay by her side as Kara slept, so she wouldn't disturb the puppy's sleep. This frisky puppy was making Kate's life miserable by creating deep confusions in Kate about how she should treat her.

As she talked about her adventures with Kara, I couldn't help but wonder aloud whether Kate saw some similarities between herself, Kara, and me.

Kate smiled and said "You are probably right."

Kate switched from Kara and in the rest of the session talked about me in a way that made me feel uncomfortable. She said: "You want to hide it, but your eyes and your face show that your soul is strained." I fully concurred with her.

"All of this is displayed on the wrinkles on your forehead," she continued. To my amazement and dismay, she again was accurate in her perception and interpretation. With a slight sense of discomfort over being seen and understood, I supported her analysis with a "hum, uhm." She continued with her cutting analysis: "Otherwise, your face is young. You may have a sick person in your family or you may have suffered from sickness yourself." Both were true.

Wishing that this inquiry would come to an end but masochistically curious about it at the same time, somewhat reluctantly, I told her that these were very fascinating thoughts, and I invited her to talk further about her impressions. Both to my relief and my disappointment, she said: "I will stop. It is becoming very dangerous." I wondered whether I had taken away her exploration, or intruded into her creative space—in this instance playing with my image—as she had complained about a while ago.

Session

Kate started the session with a comment about there being something odd about me. She felt as if I was not present. Her perceptiveness was again, stunning. The weight of the grief of the sudden death of my father some years ago was slowly lifting; I was not as overwhelmed or scared by his absence and was getting used to the idea of living without him. I was slowly getting back on my feet, finding some patches of happiness permeating back into my life, accompanied with a throbbing sense of guilt.

I: "I think I am less scared of you, that's true. Having said that, I am waiting for you to get less scary too. You vacillate between being surprisingly open and honest, wonderfully interested and loving in our sessions on the one hand, and on the other hand scarily secretive and threatening, all at the same time. It seems to me as if you do know how to put all of these fragmented experiences together."

Kate responded that I was trying to do something very dangerous. It was like the silence before the storm. She warned me that she might not come back for therapy: "My body may want to stay at home, and you may be relieved if I don't come." A few days later she called and said she did not want to come to the session because she is in agonizing pain. She was deeply hurt when she heard that I was not afraid of her anymore.

Major Fracture—I Will Be Leaving

About a year and a half into our work, I was recruited by a hospital in a different state and decided to leave my hospital in some months. When she heard this news, Kate wanted to stop working with me immediately but agreed with my recommendation to set up a termination date in the coming year and work toward it.

After this declaration, I was anticipating grief and anger, but instead Kate opened up a different set of themes in our work. She was curious about my past and asked many questions about my training, some of which I answered. She complimented me on my skills and told me that I would be an established person in about ten years. It was fascinating to see that she had an access to my fantasy of being an established doctor by that time. She left the session in an unusually chirpy mood, even saying "bye" for the first time. I had the fantasy that she was letting go of me.

I was wrong. In the next session she said that she loved me very much. I was surprised but thanked her for her affection. I had the fantasy that this was more of an infantile attachment but in the following session she said it is actually what is meant by adult love. As a lesbian, it was the first time, she said, that she told a man that she loved him.

I: "It's new to see that side of you. I was only aware of the side that is deeply curious, and also aware a bit about the side that can get angry but almost about nothing else. So this comes as a surprise—that you have some other ordinary sides."

The word "ordinary" didn't sit well with Kate. "I have many different sides to myself, but you are not aware of those."

I: "Maybe I want to hear them, not just to try and guess or to be aware of them."

Then she surprised me with another query: "Do I look good and okay."

When I asked what she meant by good and okay, Kate insisted that it was what it meant.

I told her that I don't have any clear meanings here, especially around good and bad, right and wrong, ugly and beautiful.

I was right in not answering her question. Kate was feeling miserable. Her relationship with Bobbie, her lover and best friend, was going south; Bobbie was insisting that they move to another city to get out of the orbit of Kate's parents and me, and her parents had banished Kate.

I: "My news then, added insult to your injuries."

Kate: "Yes, very much so." And she told me that she had seen my son the day before, and it added to her hurt. My hospital was in a small town so it was not uncommon for my patients to see me or the members of my family at a restaurant or at a grocery store or in many other public places. When Kate unexpectedly caught the sight of my son in the local mall, he looked sad to Kate. Kate felt like he needed more attention and time from me and felt sorry for my son.

It was a touching perception that probably reflected something about herself, but had a grain of truth about my relationship with my son as a busy therapist working long hours. I had the sad spontaneous association to how love is about tolerating being away from, or losing your loved ones as I had fully understood the depths of my love to my father after he had departed forever some years ago. Kate had become more aware of her affection for me when I declared my impending disappearance.

I revealed part of these thoughts to Kate. She was in tears.

Then All Hell Broke Loose

As I was anticipating that we were entering the familiar territory of an unfolding erotic, dependent transference, all hell broke loose. On a weekend, as I was having dinner with my family, I got a call from Kate. She was inviting me and my wife for a coffee at the bookstore where she worked part time. I thanked her but made it clear that I wouldn't do that. After a while a friend of Kate called requesting an explanation as to why I had turned Kate's invitation down. I reiterated my unwillingness to come for a coffee or for a chat and hung up. After several more calls from this friend, who insisted on talking with me, I told her that I would call the police if they called me one more time. I was stunned with this invasion of my privacy and stayed awake the whole night.

When Kate came to session the next day, I told her, with a palpable anger and without mincing my words, that her actions were unacceptable, that I could not work in this way, and that she had to protect the treatment.

Kate: "You don't know how to protect yourself because you are afraid."

I, still simmering with anger: "Of course I'm afraid. It is no different than someone appearing at your doorstep, breaking into your house, and attacking you."

As I talked, it suddenly dawned on me that that fear was an alien concept for Kate. She was very surprised with my sense of fear; she had delegated the function of experiencing and containing fear to me. "She has recognized that I no longer had intense fear in the countertransference, so she is coming at me through her unconscious provocation of others' aggression, in the hope of understanding it herself," I thought to myself. Yet this accurate self-interpretation did not have any impact on the intensity of my dread.

Kate's Termination with Her "Friends"

Kate appeared exhausted and shut down. She told me that her friends were slowly disappearing, leaving Kate with both a sense of relief and a hurtful sense of abandonment. It was a difficult transition, but one that would be to her benefit, I thought. Kate agreed.

She asked me a series of poignant questions within this new territory of her suicidal friends leaving her. What if they decided to take their lives and acted on it? What if it was actually Kate who had pushed them to suicide? Would her mother have succumbed to one such horrifying act if Kate was not around? With some loose associations, she was conveying the idea that perhaps her only gracious way out was becoming psychotic and locked away in an asylum for the rest of her life, or maybe disappearing from the face of the earth by running away to an unannounced island, or maybe suicide.

As I became more cognizant of these grave thoughts and fantasies, I told her that I thought there was a substantial risk of death when she wanted something for herself because of the way her life had shaped up and the way she had built it. Some may need to be dead, psychically, if others were to survive in that relationship. And that if she would dare to leave that relationship, then there was the risk of someone literally dying; either Kate or a loved one.

To my surprise, Kate took the risk of death, be it psychic or real, of hers or others and managed to send a friend to another city and a second one was preparing to leave her soon. She was still taking their phone calls but was responding briefly, in a way that conveyed her wish to terminate their relationship in the near future. Kate had identified with my more clearly defined limitations and boundaries, and as I took the lead to further her differentiation through our work and ultimately through my termination, she was feeling comfortable in implementing these new skills of boundary formation, where the differentiation of the self and other occurs.

Separation Is Death

I took a month-long sabbatical break from the hospital work and visited Turkey, my country of origin. When we initiated our work upon my return, Kate came to the first session appearing like she was terminally ill; she had lost weight, was unkempt, depleted, and detached. And worse, she couldn't remember how we used to work together, she had forgotten everything.

The past month was a catastrophic time for her: her father had a heart attack and emergency bypass surgery, and Kate had suffered from serious gastric bleeding that necessitated a short hospital stay. With a deep sense of sympathy, I told her I was terribly sorry for her father's predicament and her illness and said that I remembered her and our work quite well.

Kate: "Well that's good, I sure hope that you will help me remember what we were thinking about before you disappeared."

Coming Back Alive with Fury

Kate came to the next session furiously alive. She said that I was inaccurate in my interpretation of her thoughts and my interpretations made her look like a soft and helpless person. And that during the sessions before my month-long vacation, I had simplified the richness of the fabric of her family. My returning had rekindled her memory about our intense work! I was surprised with this sudden turn of events as she was making rich connections to where we had left off.

It was a short-lived pleasure. The psychotherapeutic momentum that was building in our therapy sessions quickly turned sour when, to my chagrin, she again told me about some threats coming my way. When I asked her to clarify what she was talking about, she was very vague for a few sessions, and by then, her cryptic narrative had begun to exhaust me.

Eventually, with no therapeutic coating, I asked her, "what the hell she was taking about," and I wanted an immediate clarification.

Shocked with my vehemence, Kate made it sound like her parents were planning something, and she also made a stunning comment: she recommended that I should stop doing individual therapy because it was a very dangerous method. Realizing that I wouldn't get any further clarification from Kate, my frustration increased to a level where I angrily told her that I was sick and tired of her threats. She immediately stood up and left the session without uttering a single word. She left me in the office, stunned over my anger and her sudden departure.

Many patients of mine had expressed their anger and frustration passionately to me, and I had occasionally expressed similar feelings toward them. They occasionally would slam the door as they left the office, yelling and swearing. I had never done that myself, but often yearned for that opportunity. However, this felt like an exceptional moment. She had abruptly left the session, while in fantasy, it felt like I had slammed the door at her face and had kicked her out. And I wondered in retrospect whether I would ever be able or willing to do this again.

I tried to understand and recover from this unexpected series of interactions, intellectualizing the events and wondering about the possibility of defense against an unfolding erotic transference. I recalled that she had become more flirtatiously alive and was wearing seductive clothes to the sessions. I had fears about my safety and hers and had worries about my capabilities as a therapist and was recognizing that I was also enjoying the deep sense of relief that she was finally gone.

She called me several months later and asked whether we could talk for twenty minutes. I agreed and we had a brief consultation. Kate was feeling agonizingly alone and sad and was wondering whether there was any chance I would work with her again. In a tone that felt cold and indifferent to me, I told her that if she wanted to reinitiate the work and agree on a reasonable termination date, then she had to protect the work, put an end to her threats and those coming from her loved ones.

Kate promised that she would be very cautious in protecting our work. She made a statement that was eye-opening. Kate's mother was becoming depressed, and her father and her brother were telling Kate that our work was destabilizing the family and wanted to know what we were talking about. With these pressures coming from her family, she had been sharing all the details of our work with her family. Now she promised that she would keep everything to herself!

Back to Termination

In the first session after the rupture, Kate talked about the horrific fears she was experiencing at her parental home. She had started noticing a new side of her usually docile and soft-spoken father. Kate now thought he was a person with a potential for violence. He had started talking about how Kate needed to be "gone" or how maybe it was a good idea that he disappear. These vague comments were evoking strong fears of suicide/homicide in Kate. I recalled that I had similar fantasies and fears many months ago and now I was witnessing one major source of the aggression that was initially projected into me. Sympathizing with the danger of the situation, I pointed to her new experience of fear. "Kate," I said, "fear can sometimes be very helpful even though it is an unpleasant emotion." She nodded.

She then put a difficult question on the table, in between the two of us: she asked whether I had accepted her back willingly. Painfully aware of my ambivalence, I said: "I am not so sure. Working with you is very difficult due to your deep allegiances. Yet I find you reasonably sane considering your circumstances and have invested in you and in this work, so I want to have a decent closure." At the end of that session, she made another interesting remark: "You were trying to bring the transference to my awareness for many months. It was there on the first day; it took me many long months to get out of it!" Thus she continued to seductively surprise me about the intricate workings of her unusual mind.

Pointing to her friends' continual disappearances from her orbit, I made an interpretation that I felt was quite appropriate; I commented on how she was treated by others as if she only performed a function for them. She was like the watering hole for an animal in the desert, irreplaceable but at the same time very impersonal. If she were not to provide the water, then they would seek it in some other oases. As I talked about this theme, my mind was recognizing a parallel; it felt like I also had found a therapeutic oasis in my work with her. I was going to leave her in a few months, with a "victorious treatment of prepsychotic psychopathology" in my CV. I felt quite strongly that there was something in Kate that allowed others to use her as an object. She was not a subject; she was someone who was not worth the sympathy and empathy of the other.

Kate's thoughts went to her father. He was on a fast track in the oil industry when his wife crumbled. The family myth, which no doubt carried a huge kernel of truth, was that despite being very close to being promoted to a senior managerial level, he had quit that promising job, returned home, and focused on helping his beloved, depressed, psychotic wife. After several years of this intense attention, with ongoing psychiatric treatment, he had saved his wife from suicide. Once she was out of the pit of several suicide attempts and a few short-term hospitalizations, her pathology calmed down and in a few years, in her early thirties, she graduated from college. Her demons had disappeared and she was able to pursue graduate studies, and in time she became a successful professor in her field. Whereas Kate's father was stuck, working in a meager job, and probably was deeply resentful with some aspects of his life.

I pointed to the stunning similarity between Kate and her father. She acknowledged this interpretative observation of mine and said that he was known as a wise man, the "professor"; many of Kate's friends would come and talk with her father, sometimes until early morning hours. After many hours of friendly, heated, and passionate conversations that sounded like political debates at times, Kate's father would regularly "win." He would convince his younger rivals about the validity of his own arguments. He would give them advice on their personal problems and lend them money; he had developed a reputation as a beloved elder in the community that was surrounding Kate.

Destruction of Kate's Creativity

As she delved into the stories of her mother and father, Kate remembered a central theme around her creative endeavors such as painting or writing that bothered her all her life. She would paint a picture or write a piece of poetry, usually spontaneously, in a matter of minutes. Every single person, without exception, would become fascinated by her creation. Then they would either literally snatch away the picture or poetry or offer an interpretation of them. Both actions were disturbing to Kate but especially the latter kind; she felt that the interpretation of a painting or poetry was a complicated task by its nature, but the commentators would be so certain of their simplistic interpretations. This would make Kate furious.

I now was making internal notes to myself on how I had been repeating the script. Deeply fascinated by her story and our work, I had not been sparing my self-assured interpretations. Despite these internal conversations, I made an interpretation about how her soul, her sense of self, was stolen.

She agreed and associated to how people had recently shifted the way they were relating to her. Instead of displaying an envious-aggressive interest in her creations, people nowadays felt sorry for her, and she in turn felt like she hurt people when they felt sorry for her.

As she came to recognize what belonged to her and what belonged to others, Kate was facing painful aspects of human condition: being hurt by others and hurting others, being scared of others and scaring others, experiencing many such dilemmas around impacting others and being impacted by them, in pleasurable and painful ways. It was the wonderfully described and awkwardly named Kleinian world of "depressive position." The recognition of these dilemmas was so painful for Kate that she was afraid that her body might not tolerate it and might die.

I felt genuinely sorry. When I expressed this to Kate she said, "Oh no, not another one!" and confessed that for a change, she actually felt sorry for herself too.

Then she started talking about her life in rich and evocative ways and gave me a number of details I had previously not been made aware of: she had changed her lifestyle about four years ago to protect and save Bobbie, who became her lover. Before that change, she had been an active, bisexual woman interested in music, writing, dancing, drinking, and drugs, and had had a series of intimate affairs with men and women. But after meeting Bobbie, something had changed in her, and she had devoted herself to protecting her, just like Kate's father dealt with her mother's predicament. And in the process, many other "patients," most of whom were friends, had accumulated in her litter. Now her story was making sense, and I was becoming aware of the regression that had led her to my office.

Body

As Kate began having more access to her affective states, she began experiencing multiple bodily complaints from irregular heartbeat to stomach disturbances. Occasionally, as she was talking with Bobbie about her traumatic past, she would regress to excruciatingly sad states when she would start sobbing uncontrollably and would start vomiting, and once to her deep embarrassment had soiled herself. The fact that she could not control her body was deeply troubling for her. Her mind's hypertrophied interest in others was already a burden for Kate for many years and now the surge of her body felt to Kate like her burden was doubled.

> Kate: "It's painful to see my soul awakening and my body is getting out of control."
>
> I: "Hum uhm."
>
> Kate: "Is there a chance that I can become schizophrenic?"
>
> I: "Earlier in our work I had some suspicions that you were being schizophrenic but now I think you don't have a chance of becoming one, even though you are capable of going through a horrible, psychotic-like patch."
>
> Kate: "I can act like one?"
>
> I: "That's possible, your creativity is quite remarkable. You may choose to look like a psychotic person, but you may find a better way of living, I think, if you can tolerate becoming an ordinary person."

Then Kate asked whether I was relieved that my meetings with her would be coming to an end. I said that, I probably did feel a sense of relief but that there were always different aspects to leaving people and relationships behind and that I would miss her. She replied that she never misses anybody; she never felt separate from anyone and does not know how to experience those feelings.

I asked about her bodily complaints and she replied that she was considering going to a doctor. It was a sad and frightening place for me to be. Fantasies of her losing our work or me or herself were in my mind. She looked like a fatigued, terminally ill patient.

The termination of our work on the horizon, Kate was becoming very sad and did not want to go through the process of mourning. "I do not want to do those things; they will happen anyhow," she said. As she tried to move away from the separation in her thoughts, I was gently trying to keep us in the here and now. It was difficult for her and for me.

Throughout the course of the therapy, she had implemented some very significant changes and now there was no one around her, or for her to be around. Kate was sick and tired of Bobbie's ongoing complaints and the endless questioning of her parents and brother. These were new thoughts in her narrative. She started stating that she had limits and that she could get exhausted. Kate was moving out of the grandiosity of endless toleration toward the ordinary experience of having limits.

Kate as a Therapist

In the session, I pointed to how she's feeling tired and reminded her that in the past she would pull many sick people toward her sphere of influence without recognizing what she was doing. She reminded me that I had a similar tendency. Somewhat surprised with this accurate observation, I acknowledged her insightful comment but tried to rebut it.

> I: "What you are insinuating may have a grain of truth in it, but in the final analysis, assuming we are both therapists, you have twenty such deeply dependent patients around you, whereas I have just you."

> Kate: "Well, if you have someone like me, who has a litter of twenty around herself, then, when you have me as a patient, by definition you will end up having twenty other persons, most of whom are in far worse condition than I am."

To my admiration and envy, what Kate just said was so true, as her other observations had been so many times.

The Last Session

As she came into another one of what seemed like an endless series of termination sessions, I was unusually anxious and scared. It was a rare state of mind for me and my inability to make any sense of it increased my anxiety. To my astonishment, as we started the session, Kate told me that this would be our last one. She said that she did not want to drive me any crazier. It appeared to her as if I was close to losing my mind and kicking her out of the office, or even worse, being seduced by her lustful wishes of love. She said that she would have gone mad by now if she were in my shoes.

Then she recounted a long list of mistakes she thought I had made throughout the course of our work and was wondering whether I made those intentionally or not.

When I pointed to her fury, Kate said: "Yes I'm furious, but I want you to be in my place and understand that if you make fatal mistakes, then the outcome will be terrible." The first month of our work had been an especially terrible, painful time for her. She had been shredded to pieces by others and was torn apart within herself.

After two years of my surviving and continuing to work as her doctor in an unusually intense psychotherapy—a process that seemed to have an acrimonious, adversarial undertone most of the time—I was perceiving a stunning, hurtful attitude, a conspicuous lack of gratitude. With the last bit of therapist space left in my mind, I managed to acknowledge her right to anger and said that I greatly prefer her rage directed at me to rage indirectly coming from her family and friends. I also said that to her credit, from what I had learned through our work together, I may handle things better with my other patients.

As I became calmer, I told her that I hoped she would continue critiquing our work and find the mistakes I and she might have made and that learning from those mistakes indeed would help her. I added that I hoped she could keep her capacity for vengeance and anger alive, which would help her tremendously. Kate said that her capacity for vengeance already did help, because she had passed two courses in college that she had been procrastinating about for months, and she was now closer to graduation.

As she was leaving my office, she turned back and said, "Thanks anyways," with a wry smile. I felt as if it was a moment of forgiveness on both ends. "You're welcome and good luck," was my rather dry last comment.

I sporadically heard from Kate. She and Bobbie immigrated to a European country that was much more tolerant of gay marriages, and it appeared like they were content with their lives.

REFLECTIONS ON KATE

Less Is More

My decision to see Kate only once a week was a significant deviation from my general approach in working with patients who have serious pathology, but proved to be very helpful in Kate's case. The lower frequency of the sessions with Kate was a striking contrast to her endless availability to her "patients," and unbeknownst to me had therefore provided an action interpretation right from the start. As I later found out, a study out of Cassell hospital demonstrated that reducing the time of inpatient stay in the hospital proved to be a more effective way of dealing with severe pathology (Chiesa et al. 2003). This is in support of my experience with Kate.

Impact on the Interpersonal World of the Patient

As the story of Kate amply demonstrates, finding a good enough, new object in the person of the analyst requires massive reshufflings in the internal representational world and the external interpersonal dynamics of the patient. This is a relatively unexplored area in our literature but is present to a degree in every analytic intervention (Paniagua 2012; Simmel 1929). Kate's case was rather intense, and Kate and I somewhat surprisingly managed to do this only through her individual therapy and with only patchy couples work. But quite often this critical problem requires a shift in the frame, and bringing the "central objects," not just in the transference/countertransference scripts, but as real persons, into the consulting room becomes a necessity in order to avoid therapeutic failures.

This is a technical approach that I strongly believe in. Yet some clinicians take a diametrically opposite stance and recommend that the patient be seen solely in individual therapy with their regular frequency of four to five times a week. They even recommend that the couch be used (Boyer 1986; Vamik Volkan, personal communication). I do not know how to resolve these differences theoretically. I strongly believe that "personal style" and "technique proper" is sometimes a foggy differentiation in psychoanalysis, and our espousal of certain techniques may in fact reflect differences in our personalities, and our own transferences to the patients.

Either way, Kate's treatment turned out to be successful. However, as I had acknowledged to myself and to her at the very end of our two-year-long work, I thought that it could have been less painful for her, her immediate family, and for me if I had insisted on the inclusion of couples and family work in the treatment. Building on Kate's treatment and some others, in time I became much more comfortable in making couples and family work a part of my treatment contracts, and I generally did get good results. In the next chapter, I give brief vignettes on how I work with the bipersonal defenses and bipersonal/family resistances when a person with severe pathology is brought to my clinical attention as the patient.

6

FROM THE HOSPITAL TO THE OFFICE

Pauline—I Will Go to the Doctor If We All Go Together

I received a call from a man who sounded desperate to get help for his daughter, who seemed to be suffering from psychosis. She was hospitalized for several months due to severe isolation and neglect of self-care. She was isolating in the basement of their house, sleeping all day long and staying awake all night, surfing the Internet. She was also showing mild suspiciousness; she would pay great attention to the bodily gestures of the people around her and interpret them as meaningful signals directed toward her.

I told the anxious father that I would be interested in providing a consultation to see whether I would be able to work with his daughter, and asked that he inform her about this conversation, as well as any other conversations that may take between the two of us thereafter. Several weeks later, I received a second call from the father of my prospective patient. He told me that despite every effort by him and his wife, his daughter was not interested in coming to my office.

I recommended that we start the work with family therapy. He was perplexed: he did not understand the rationale behind my recommendation that they come as a family, because in his opinion, his daughter was the patient. Nevertheless, out of desperation he agreed to give it a try. To the surprise of his parents, my prospective patient, Pauline, agreed to join her parents for a trial visit to my office.

In my mind, it was not too much of a mystery: I was acting on the basis of the time-proven hypothesis that whatever the nature and the causes of the patient's psychopathology, the whole family system had fallen into a vortex after the unfolding of the patient's psychotic episode, so they all were in a web of enmeshed regressed relationships. And thus the leverage was either to hospitalize the patient or bring the whole system to the treatment, to address the secondary regressions after the eruption of psychosis.

I presumed that Pauline, as did many other patients of mine, understood this formulation intuitively and felt an unconscious relief from my rapid intervention with the projective-introjective cycle that made her the sole focus, "the problem," and found some hope in my invitation.

Brief History of Pauline

Pauline was a high-school teacher in her early thirties. Her father was an international businessman who spent most of his time traveling or living in different countries for extended stretches and her mother was a housewife. She was their only child and was described as a universally liked, pleasant, and jovial kid. People who met Pauline would praise the parents on her intelligence, good looks, and sociability. She was also known for her kind-heartedness; she would help younger kids and elders around her.

After graduating from college, Pauline started working as a high-school teacher, a profession she loved. In the high school where she worked, Pauline fell in love with a fellow teacher. They had an intimate relationship for a few years, got engaged, and moved in together. Around her late twenties, Pauline began displaying some subtle behavioral changes. She was becoming more suspicious, and was thinking that people were making gestures that were poking fun at her and sometimes conveying signals that they may come after her. To calm her anxiety down, she began drinking excessively. In time, her behavioral changes and alcohol usage intensified to a level where she ended up losing interest in work; she would spend her days drinking in her apartment, and was eventually fired from her position. Right around this time, her boyfriend left her.

Devastated by the simultaneous loss of her love and her job, and with the pressure of family, Pauline agreed to an extended hospitalization where she was detoxified and underwent a psychiatric evaluation. After this treatment she managed to maintain her sobriety but stopped taking her medications and regressed to a level where she was spending all her time isolating in the basement of her parental home when her father contacted me. When I evaluated her, I thought she still was clearing from psychosis and was organizing at a lower borderline level. I initiated twice weekly therapy and once every other week family work.

Session

Pauline came with her mother. The mother talked about how she missed the old "good" Pauline. When I asked about what she meant by that, she gave a lively account of the daughter she longed for. Pauline was her golden girl, adored by the rest of the family and close friends, as the following poignant memory demonstrated. They were at the family winter house in the snowy mountains of a neighboring state where the extended family would often spend a week together. During the week, the relatives would approach the mother and comment on how Pauline was such a pleasant young woman with a most affectionate smile and a beautiful gaze. She would look you in the eye, greet you with a gentle handshake, and ask how you were doing. She would engage you in a most pleasant conversation making you feel like she knew you as a person. These accolades would thrill her mother. Then, as her peers would go out with other girls and boys, skiing, snow-boarding, and having fun, Pauline would instead go and take care of young kids who were trying to learn how to ski on the bunny hill, and all of the families would feel indebted to her. Pauline was also a star back at home. She was as an outstanding student at an elite high school. She was a star swimmer, made superb academic grades, and was also dating one of the most popular boys in her class.

The shiny image of Pauline at school and within her family was like a dream come true for Pauline's mother; what more she could ask for in her quite sad life? Her husband had embarked on a career that brought a lot of money to the young family but had left her all alone because of his extended absences due to the demands of his work, thus she had to raise Pauline alone.

When I invited Pauline to expand on how she experienced the world during her teens and adolescence, she came up with a shockingly different story. To her, it felt as if she was acting all the time and serving some functions for others. The stellar student at school, the scenes at their winter resort where others saw her as an "intelligent and beautiful young woman who was invested in taking care of young kids," for her, was a tiring set of obligations where she felt like she needed to act in certain ways; it never felt authentic. She was exhausted with what she felt like was a facade.

For Pauline's mother, these clarifications were deeply surprising new narratives. The reality as the mother perceived it from outside appearances was the opposite of what Pauline felt on the inside. Her mother was not aware of what actually was going on in Pauline's mind. Pauline was talking about a false-self formation that we touched on earlier, in the case of Barbara.

This was a relatively easy technical moment where the resistance was minimal. When I invited her to expand on her experience, without too much of a resistance she painted a very different picture from what was observed on the outside.

There were many instances when Pauline shut off my therapeutic invitations. She would adamantly refuse to relay the content of her internal experiences nor would she explain her reluctance to talk about them. She would defeat my efforts, stating these were "off topic." When I found that insisting on resistance analysis in these areas would be extremely painful for Pauline, I simply deferred the exploration to the coming months and sometimes years. Through my individual work with Pauline, I came to understand in time that these deep pockets of resistance contained painfully embarrassing memories about aspects of herself or her parents. She was mortified at the prospect of hurting her parents or initiating a massive attack from them if she were to delve into these memories.

Session

Pauline and her mother were working on a vacation plan.

The mother: "I want to take a brief vacation, and Pauline wants to join me in that. So I occasionally call to see where things are with her. I need to buy a ticket as soon as possible because it is getting more expensive by the day."

Pauline, who was taking some graduate courses, said, "I do not have any control over my school schedule; they will call me with a date on my oral exam but so far they haven't. So I do not know anything about whether I will be able to go at the time you are planning. And I also feel like I am mostly responding to your demands that I come with you."

I thought we were at a juncture that would provide some grist for the psychoanalytic mill. Here were the elements of the intrapsychic and interpersonal conflict as I rapidly bullet-pointed in my mind:

The mother wanted to go on this trip.

She wanted Pauline to come with her.

She was in a rush to book in order to get a reasonable fare.

Pauline seemed reluctant to respond to her queries about whether she would join her on the trip and seemed unsure of when she could.

The mother did not want to go ahead and purchase a ticket, as she felt that would hurt Pauline.

Pauline was not getting a clear response from her school on the date of her make-up exam.

She was interested in going but thought the wish for the trip was mostly located in the mother, who wanted her to come along.

Mother and Pauline were both annoyed with each other over the pressures they were generating on one another through these assumptions.

I also surmised that on a deeper level the mother was struggling with a central question: was Pauline incapable of making a decision because of her psychiatric illness, or was she trying to manipulate her around the buying of tickets? It was a common, if not universal confusion about the ego capacities of a patient who is struggling with borderline or psychotic level of organization, wondering whether the person is omnipotent or impotent.

With these rapid formulations in the back of my mind, I invited further exploration.

> I: "Pauline, you made it sound like she wants you there for her own self. Can you expand on that?"

> Pauline: "Don't get me wrong, I like going to this family villa in that beautiful setting for our reunions, but I also feel I serve my mother some sort of a function there. She is usually not interested in me, as she gets lost in her conversations with her extended family. But when there is intense heat in the discussions, which is not an uncommon occurrence, or rather the norm I may say, then she comes to me for support."

I: "How so?"

Pauline: "I don't fully understand, but I think I become important for her."

I, to the mother: "This ties to our previous conversations. I think one of the things that is sorely missing in your life is your husband. You always had the financial support of your husband, but he was and still is absent from home for long stretches of time. Some of these pretty ordinary daily decisions are much easier if they are shared with another mind. So in his absence, Pauline probably filled that gap for you."

The mother: "I agree a hundred percent. My in-laws were willing to live in our house and help me to compensate for the absences of my husband. But I found that arrangement very difficult and so decided to raise Pauline by myself. I did not even hire a nanny or a housekeeper, partly because I felt that I just had one child, and should be able to take care of her by myself and shouldn't act like a spoiled and incompetent woman. Those years felt deeply alone for me. I am a person who has great difficulties in making decisions to begin with, and I used Pauline as a sounding board in many of my decisions."

I: "That is very clear, and I think, on the other side of the coin, Pauline is used to pulling you into her decision making. In this instance, Pauline is not telling you whether or when she can come. That is partly due to the scheduling of her examination, but it is also significant that she is not letting go of you with a statement like 'Why don't you go ahead and book the plane, I can come some other time.' Instead she states she wants to come, for you and for herself, but doesn't give you a time frame, leaving you in limbo."

Pauline then stated that she was feeling very sorry for her mother and would feel guilty if she were to go alone. Yet she was torn between a wish to go and visit the extended family or just stay in town and have some time off and be just with herself, without thinking about her mother all the time.

Now I was working from the end of the projectee, that is, Pauline, and was exploring, highlighting her active psychological stance in keeping the projector/projectee cycle alive, and in this instance, on how she was creating a similar but a reverse cycle where her mother was the one who needed her help. In other words, she was reversing the natural maturational asymmetry of a mother and a daughter and was becoming the projector.

The potential reversal of the natural asymmetry is an understudied aspect of the fascinating phenomena of projective identificatory processes. We are tempted to think of the chronologically mature person: the mother, the father as the nidus where the process starts. But as the young child grows, he or she can easily become an active center, reversing the maturity scale. Barbara, in the way she related to her parents, was a good example of this phenomenon. One way to think about her is that as she was developing as the good girl in her teens, the foundation of seeing her parents as helpless, defective persons was already being laid as an internal script in her and this became very apparent in her mature years.

This potential for reversal is an important point to keep in mind because it leads to a formulation where both persons are active participants in the projective-introjective process at the same time and so the clinician needs to work on their mutual resistances in the family work.

CHRISTINE—HOW SICK ARE YOU?

Christine was in her late twenties, and during the past ten years she had had several episodes of psychosis that lasted for a few months and required brief hospital treatments. Fortunately, she would compensate to a level of reasonable functioning as long as she took her medications properly and continued with her psychotherapy. Once the psychosis cleared, she would become perfectly able to take good care of herself: she had a decent life socializing with a few old friends, was dating a young man in her town, and was attending graduate studies in art in a local college.

When I took over her treatment, she was living with her mother, an African American woman who had immigrated to this exclusively white, small mill town after marrying Christine's father in her country of origin in Africa. The father had severed all the ties with his family when Christine was five years old and had moved to a different state. Christine had an older sister who was living in a nearby city.

After her first breakdown, Christine developed some peculiar habits. When she was at home, she would isolate in her room and communicate with her mother or sister with just a few words such as "I do not know," "yes," "no," and "maybe." However, she was active in her community and was quite talkative with nonrelated persons such as her boyfriend and his family. This contradictory attitude evoked confusion and resentment in her mother and sister. Furthermore, there was an ongoing serious conflict with the mother about Christine's lack of interest in helping her; in the house, on their farm, and with some real estate that they rented out. Again, this was in stark contrast to Christine's enthusiastically offering of help when anybody else asked for it.

I thought that, quite similar to Pauline, Christine was clearly suffering from psychosis, and a secondary regression evoked by this severe illness had pulled all of her family members in. Yet in contrast to Pauline, Christine was functioning very close to a psychotic level of personality organization.

I was well versed on the controversies around the role of the family dynamics in the pathogenesis of the primary regression, that is, the psychosis. But at the moment, I was focusing on the secondary, "postpsychotic" regression within the family in order to help all the members clear out of this vicious cycle. And during this work, we could also get some ideas on how the family dynamics may have been a fuel to the fire of psychosis.

I invited the family to regular twice-weekly sessions side by side having twice-weekly individual sessions with Christine.

Here I will report, close to verbatim, from a few sessions in order to use them as vignettes on the powerful projective/introjective cycles that were operative in the regressed, symbiotic relatedness that the family had fallen into. As they were desperately trying to make some sense of and get some traction out of this vicious deadlock, they were sliding deeper into it. To help all of the participants observe together and then reflect on it, I tried to let the process unfold for a while, then point to moments of defensive interventions made by the family members, and invited an exploration of the roots of these defensive interventions.

Session

Christine: "I have nothing to talk about."

The mother then took the lead and said that the previous day was Christine's birthday, and Christine came across as more polite than usual. They all went out to dinner with Christine's boyfriend joining them. During the dinner, the boyfriend asked questions about Christine's mother's heritage and made comments about her ancient African religion and local African dialect. He was talking about the differences between African Americans who were recent immigrants from Africa like Christine's mother and the African Americans who had been in America for many generations. Christine's mother was infuriated by his impolite and uninformed comments. As the discussion on this unexpected topic continued, Christine was silently eating her dinner.

I asked Christine what she experienced during that dinner. She said she remembered the conversation but didn't recall having any particular response to what was being discussed at the table.

The mother went on talking about how the boyfriend was trying to impress her with his knowledge and was instead offending her with the topic he had brought up. And when she did not understand some American colloquialisms and asked for an explanation, his sarcastic responses added insult to the injury. Nevertheless she tolerated him; she was known as a good listener in her relationships with the townspeople and would never counter their ideas or give advice unless she was asked for it.

Christine was rather sullen so I asked her what she was thinking about.

Christine: "Not so sure."

The mother became infuriated and asked her to "wake up and act like a lady, not like a retarded person."

Christine: "I don't remember what transpired . . . really."

The mother: "Then maybe you are overmedicated. Talk with Dr. K right now so he may change your medications."

I: "What exactly worries you?"

The mother: "She can easily turn into a character like the 'stooges,' an infant, retarded in relationships with men." Then she recounted the story of how Christine had fallen for another man, a relative of her husband—and had ended up spending thousands of dollars, nearly exhausting all of her trust money.

Christine made a feeble attempt to defend her actions but the mother immediately took over and chastised her about the damage she had incurred. At the end of her monologue, she said, “Do you hear me?”

Christine did not respond.

I asked the mother whether she ever got a response from her daughter. She said she had not.

Then came an abrupt shift in the narrative of the mother; she stated that Christine was a “catch for any boy.” I was appalled with this sudden shift from a “retarded” person to a “catch.”

Christine: “I don’t know whether I am a catch or not.”

The mother: “Are you educated?”

Christine: “Yes.”

The mother: “Do you have a graduate degree?”

Christine: “I am working for one.”

The mother: “Did you work in the Peace Corps?”

Christine: “Yes.”

The mother: “Are you blind, deaf, or neutered?”

Christine: “No.”

The mother: “Do you have goals in life?”

Christine: “Maybe.”

The mother: “Do men check you out?”

Christine: “Sometimes.”

The mother: “Are you ugly?”

Christine: “I don’t know.”

The mother: “Look in the mirror. You are a catch!”

It was an amazing process of the mother taking over Christine's capacities for thinking and reflecting. Christine, on her end, had surrendered and possibly invited her mother to take over. So I turned to the mother and asked her how she got into this inquiry about Christine.

She said that she gets infuriated when Christine acts like this and if it happens in front someone outside of the family like me, she feels deeply embarrassed. She also feels very guilty that maybe she might not have raised her right.

Christine's mother was actively intervening with her projected image of her daughter, an image that was introjected and identified by Christine, unlike the image that was partly rejected by Pauline. These interpersonal interactive scripts that I named as "the mother taking away Christine's thinking capacities" were a point of therapeutic entry for me. Once the defensive intervention was observed by all participants, the projector would have the opportunity to begin an exploration of the historical roots of this significant intervention.

Session

The mother, Christine, and I am present.

Christine is silent, her mother appears as if she is barely holding herself back from a verbal barrage.

> The mother: "On the weekend I was planning to plant potatoes, tomatoes, and green pepper in my vegetable garden for the summer. I was hoping that Christine would be of some help but alas, there she was, lying in her bed till late morning while I had woken up at the crack of dawn and began working like crazy. (To her daughter): Why are you so silent? Is there something that is eating you up? Give it a chance, talk for a change."
>
> Christine: "I guess . . ."
>
> The mother: "Go ahead, talk."
>
> Christine: "I find all of this confusing."

The mother: "If you don't talk, Dr. K will never understand you. All of this is for you to get better. If you went to a doctor and had asthma, wouldn't you say what was bothering you? How can Dr. K help you?"

Christine: "I am not sick."

The mother: "You are sick in the brain."

Christine: "I think I am normal at the moment."

The mother: "Do you think so? We see that you are not normal, we see symptoms."

In the countertransference field, I wondered whether I was included in the "we." I had a vague sense that an immediate husband transference was coming from the mother. I felt as if I were the father who should have been there, one who wouldn't abandon the family.

The mother: "It was a beautiful day, why didn't you come and help me?"

I realized that mother truly didn't understand why Christine did not help her; a very common conundrum in working with severe pathology as we saw in the cases of Pauline and Judy. The patient and relatives struggle with the following dilemma: on the one hand, they wonder if the patient is pervasively damaged by the illness and has no areas of agency; on the other hand, they see the patient as all-willful, a person who is scheming and manipulating all the time. So the patient becomes a hugely confusing entity that vacillates between an omnipotent, omniscient person and impotent person who has lost her mind.

I summarized my internal thoughts: "I think Christine confuses you. You don't understand whether she can't help you because of her illness or because she simply won't."

The mother: "You are a smart person. That is exactly right. After all, Christine is back in college, trying to get a master's degree in art; she has a boyfriend with whom she gets along well. She is praised by the family of the boyfriend as a 'joy to be around.' Further, she understands what the professors at school tell her and teach her, and she gets good grades. And yet at home she turns into a moron and does not participate in anything. I don't get it."

Christine in turn continued to insist that she felt confused and attacked by the way her mother talked to her and interacted with her.

The mother on her end was becoming exhausted with the amount of work she had to do alone with hired hands on their significant number of rental properties. The father—who was a very reserved person suffering from alcoholism—when he was around, was silent all the time just like Christine. The mother said that Christine had turned out to be exactly like her father.

This was a moment when I felt we could find a red thread that lead to the creation of a projected image of Christine.

I: "How so?"

The mother then recounted the touching account of how as a native African she was seen as an "other" in this exclusively white, small town. She had to endure racial slurs, denigration, and workplace harassment as she tried to earn a living for the family, feeling all alone. The father was dealing with a patch of arable land that didn't bring any money to the family but allowed him to isolate himself and drink in a barn throughout the day, in essence hiding from his family and friends. The mother said that she was terribly pained by all of this. She had raised a family all by herself and felt very proud of her accomplishments. However now, her beloved daughter, whom she had hoped would become a successful professional, was doing some useless graduate studies and dating the son of a family that was frowned upon in the town. And she started crying. In between her uncontrollable sobbing, she expressed that she was truly exhausted.

I noticed that Christine was getting teary-eyed so asked her what was evoked in her.

Christine said she was very surprised and sad to hear her mother expressing her exhaustion. "I always saw my mother as a very strong woman, so this is quite strange for me," she said.

The mother talked about the importance of "pride" for her. In Africa, where she and her husband had met, her family belonged to a historically powerful tribe that owned large pieces of land. They would put a lot of emphasis on their heritage, the animistic religious rituals, and their slowly disappearing African dialect. The sense of belonging to that tribe was the central pride, well beyond individual pride. The tribe would shame members who did not act in conformance with their heritage and would sometimes banish them. So, now in a small, white, American mill town, as the only black person, she made it a central aim of her life to raise a family that she would be proud of. What happened after Christine developed her psychosis had ruined this project. Even though Christine was compensating back to reasonable levels of functioning, her multiple hospitalizations had irrevocably stuck with Christine and with the image of her family. The psychosis had delineated the family further as being an "other" in this small mill town.

The therapeutic intervention on the projective/introjective cycle had worked. We were now hearing the stories that were fueling the mother's anxieties that had initiated the cycle. It was a moment of authentic contact between Christine and her mother, as the following session demonstrated.

Session

Christine's sister joined the session but was silent for most of the time.

Christine: "I don't have anything to talk about."

This repetitive pattern brought back an impression from our twice-weekly psychotherapy sessions. When I would greet Christine in my waiting area, I would see a cheerful, chatty, interactive person. As soon as she sat in the chair across me, her facial expression would change. She would appear as if she was in pain; and a deep silence would invade the room. Her eyes half-closed, she would space out and sometimes she would doze off. There were other extended stretches where she would imprison me with an intense stare. Feeling overwhelmed with her silence and staring, when I asked about any thoughts or feelings she had in her mind that we could hear together, she would reply that she had nothing in her mind and would prefer that I talk to her. The observation in the family session was very important for our individual clinical work; Christine had probably developed a powerful transference/countertransference plate in the individual therapy sessions right from the start. It was difficult to talk with her; she would evoke the other to talk to or at her.

The mother: "Maybe she could talk about yesterday."

Christine: "Specifically about what?"

The mother then had an extensive, articulate, detailed narrative about what they did together, in contrast to her usual projective barrages that just focused on Christine. She told us that things were better between her and Christine the previous day. They were like good friends, talking with one another. They had wonderful conversations as they took a long walk.

And Christine appeared eager to help her mother. There was a sense of bonding.

I: "Christine, did you sense the change?"

Christine: "I have no idea."

The mother: "You were almost normal for a few days."

Christine: "Well, I felt like you were sick, so I tried to help. It was very sad for me to see you crying."

I: "You recognized the vulnerabilities of your mother."

Christine: "Yeah, it made me think . . ." When she paused her mother jumped in after a few seconds and started asking questions; "What did you think about? Trees? Your boyfriend? School? Your future?" It was quite a long list of choices she was offering to her daughter.

By now, I was aware of the pattern of the mother's effusive barrage and Christine's pervasive silence invading all of the space and had recognized that they were very similar in their aggressive aspects. The mother was actively invading the space through her ruminative verbosity and Christine through her perseverating silence. With this formulation in mind, I interrupted the mother's barrage and said it appeared to me as if she were thinking on behalf of Christine and not allowing some space for her to develop her own ideas. I added that it was a tiring effort on her part and a thwarting one on Christine's mind.

The mother found this idea of "thinking on behalf of Christine" quite interesting and said that she could see my point. But she was very worried that her brilliant daughter, this star of a person all through college, may have now lost her skills. So she might actually need to relearn how to be motivated, talk properly, and behave like the old Christine she loved.

I commented on how in fact they both were unknown to each other. Christine was clamming up, and the mother was lost behind her focus on and barrage of inquiry of Christine. The sadness she managed to display, despite the fact that it felt to her like other "common women" of the town, showed her insides to Christine and me, and in turn Christine exhibited her different capabilities of herself to her mother. The mother said it had been very difficult for her to cry in front of me; she had never cried in the presence of others but had found this space quite safe to let her hair down in.

Christine, with hesitation and in fragments, continued to articulate her experience of her mother during the last session. It was one of those rare instances when she recognized that her mother was not the person she tried to portray herself to be; confident, endlessly energetic, unbeatable. When her mother was in tears, Christine was deeply saddened and felt like crying. And it was a huge relief that she found some similarity with her mother.

The mother intervened stating that she had to be strong because of what her life had dealt to her in the small mill town with a husband who was withdrawn, drunk, unavailable, and who had finally abandoned the family. She had to carry the responsibilities of her young family and had no intention of becoming like the white American women of the town—women who loved gossiping and going to hair salons—fragile and despicable people, in her mind's eye.

As we were talking, Christine's sister Sarah was rubbing her neck. The mother immediately focused on her, began an inquiry about what was wrong with her neck, then in salvoes of advice, told her how she should take good care of herself.

I made a rather long-winded interpretation on how the mother's vigilance about her daughters took the attention away from her own serious medical problems such as her diabetes and her recent transient ischemic attack. I hypothesized that she may be avoiding a deep sense of grief by focusing on her sick daughter and the ailments of the other daughter.

The mother: "What you say makes sense. But no one is helping me!"

Christine: "Mom never asks for help, but rather will order people around to do certain chores in the house or in the yard." She continued to elaborate on this interesting differential, articulately explaining how the two were entirely different stances. Christine had made a poignant interpretation; one stance left space for autonomous thinking and decision making, but the other was a robotic execution of the mother's orders. The capacity to make a decision, a centrally important aspect of the mind, was fully located in the mother. The mother said that she had never thought of it in those terms.

As the mother allowed Christine to see some other sides of her own self, Christine was becoming less muted in the relationship, and was allowing us to see how her mind was still competently processing the world that was surrounding her.

Session

As usual, Christine opened the session declaring that she had nothing to talk about.

The mother asked whether she could talk about her boyfriend. Apparently the boyfriend had called the mother and complained that Christine was planning to move to a larger city to find a job and establish a new life for herself. This was a concern for the boyfriend as well as for the mother; she was worried that Christine's lack of skills could lead to failure that could be followed by hospitalization, as had happened in the past.

Christine countered her mother's argument; she said that she had not been able to hold on to her previous jobs because her managers at the time had been hostile and had not helped her at all.

The mother: "This is an excuse. Christine always blames others for her failures."

Then Christine attacked her mother, accusing her of not trusting and of having no confidence in her. In contrast, she continued to complain, her sister had her mother's full confidence and that was what Christine also wanted.

The mother: "There is enough evidence from the past that Christine will fail again and I am tired of this pattern."

I asked the mother whether she was tired of worrying on behalf of her daughter.

The mother: "Not really, I believe that Christine has it in her but needs to bring that side of her out."

I noted again the dual image of Christine in her mother's mind, one was a sick, incapable person, and the other was someone who had it in her and wouldn't do it. I was wondering whether Christine was sensing this dichotomy and asked her about her thoughts.

Christine agreed that she needed to motivate herself. She added that everybody was different, so she shouldn't be compared to her sister. The mother then started another monologue: she loves Christine, in fact Christine was the daughter she really wanted; she was such a beautiful girl, successful all through college and then these psychotic episodes had ruined her mind and life.

Christine reiterated her dilemma: the disability payments she received did not give her a decent lifestyle so she had to try something to make a better living.

The mother thought that this idea of Christine was just grandiose and was probably related to her psychosis.

Christine said that she felt trapped, that on the one hand she wanted a better life for herself, but wasn't getting any support, and on the other hand, she felt like she was criticized by her mother for not doing anything to change her life. It was confusing for her.

REFLECTIONS ON PAULINE AND CHRISTINE

In both of these cases, I had to shift the frame and add family work to the individual psychoanalytic therapy. Recently, we have become more comfortable in utilizing a broader range of techniques (Gabbard and Westen 2003) that would ordinarily be considered as nonanalytic, or even worse, antianalytic. I am of the personal opinion that even neurotic patients may, at least in some parts of their treatment, require some parameters, as Kurt Eissler (1953) initially coined them, and may indeed require other therapeutic approaches, as the following story of Will is a testament to.

7

PSYCHOANALYSIS PROPER

We had a small family farm in Turkey where we raised cows and chickens and had plenty of fruit trees. It was a pleasant piece of land where I had many wonderful days during my early youth and learned quite a bit about Mother Nature. The farming operation would continue year round, but we would close our little shack on the farm during winters. During my occasional visits to check out the shack, I would notice some "dead" bugs around the window sills—flies, bees, and some others I couldn't name. To my amazement, when we heated the house for a weekend visit, or when spring came back, most of these desiccated bugs would start buzzing their wings and come back alive after many months! The story of Will often reminded me of those "dead" bugs.

WILL—I AM NOT DEAD

Will was working as a senior engineer in an energy company when he first came to my office. He had a chronic, agonizing inhibition in approaching women and recently began experiencing some obsessive symptoms and depression. He sought psychoanalysis to make sense of what was going on with him.

Will (his nickname in America) was the son of white-collar parents who had gone through considerable tumult in their lives. His father was from a country in Asia, and his mother was from the United Kingdom. The couple met each other when they both were students in London, fell in love, and got married. Following graduation, they settled in the father's country of origin where they became successful academics in their respective fields. They had two children, Will and a younger daughter, and had a prosperous life until a military-Islamic coup d'état turned their fortunes around. The new regime was merciless about whom they considered as infidels, and Will's parents were at the margins of that definition. They were relieved that they had not lost their freedom or lives but they lost their reputable jobs and social status. Will's father began working as a high school teacher, and his mother began translating books from English to make some money. They became resigned to the reality of settling into a middle-class lifestyle.

Beyond the impact of the military-Islamic takeover on his parents, there was a massive transition awaiting Will. As a member of the elite of the pre-Islamic regime, he had been attending a British private school. At this school, the main science curriculum was taught in English while social studies was taught in his native language; there was a heavy emphasis on English literature, and he would be writing in the Latin alphabet whether he spoke in his native language or English. The military Islamic regime closed down his Western prep school, and Will was forced to go to a public school where he had to learn how to write and read in the Arabic script. For a ten-year-old, it had been an extremely onerous task; Will remembered returning from school in tears and spending countless evenings studying to learn the new script. He would tell his parents how he missed his British school and beg that the family move back to the United Kingdom, his mother's home, just like many of his friends' families were doing at the time.

The severe impact of the revolution on their social status made Will's father and mother much more temperamental. They would get into heated arguments over minor things and would throw temper tantrums; the father would lose control and start hitting himself on the face and the mother would throw herself on the floor, wailing, and scratching her face and neck. As a successful young couple with two promising children they looked perfect from the outside, yet within the household, they both were out of control.

During Will's high school years, the couple separated many times but ended up back under the same roof, since divorce was legally and morally shunned in the country they lived in. His grandparents were around and the neighborhood was close knit, so the loss of the cohesiveness of the nuclear family for the children was compensated by the larger set of relatives and neighbors.

Will never reflected on this massive collapse of his family but went on with his life. Being a successful student, he was accepted to a prominent university in England with a full scholarship. He left in a rush, without even saying goodbye to some members of his family. The switch back to English and being away from the restrictions of an oppressive regime was a huge relief for him. He became a stellar student right away, but within the liberal relations of a Western university campus, he was becoming self-conscious about how painfully shy he was in relating to women. So when he was approached by Anne, a classmate he had a crush on, Will was ecstatic.

Anne was his first love. They lived together for the next two years. Those years were a heavenly island in Will's otherwise bland life. They explored the wonders of late adolescence—in the ways they kissed and made love or talked about the injustices of the world, or in the ways they engaged the wonderful world of gossip, jealousies, rivalries amongst their peers, all going through a similar period of passage. It was a time of joy, wonder, hope, and happiness. There was a sense of infiniteness; it felt to both as if they would be in this heaven forever.

In the third year of their relationship, after a wonderful day together, Anne announced that it was over for her, and she abruptly left the apartment they had cohabitated for many months. Will was stunned. Unable to comprehend what went wrong, he was confused and deeply hurt.

For many months, he secluded himself in the apartment home that he and Anne had created together. This artsy apartment, this place of dreams, where they had together fantasized about their future as a family with a boy and a girl, turned into a space where he was now contemplating suicide. It was an unbearable time—"beyond agony," as he evocatively put it. He was enduring the grief of the shocking loss, barely managing to go to his classes, isolating himself in the evenings and during the weekends.

After a few months of isolation, when he could have benefited from hospitalization, he decided that this horrendous phase of his life should be over. With sheer willpower, he stopped thinking about what had happened and focused instead on his academic work and returned to being the stellar student he once was. He graduated from university with an impressive academic record and got an invitation from an oil company in the United States. He accepted the offer without hesitation and came to this country again somewhat secretively, without even saying goodbye to his friends in the United Kingdom, just as he had left his paternal homeland some years ago.

Now, in the United States, his country of dreams, he began working seven days a week, with only a few days of vacation a year. He was captivated by the challenges, was going to the refineries in the middle of the night, trying to understand and resolve the engineering problems of the infinitely complicated structure of the refinery and at the same time learning how to manage a considerably large staff. It was an exhausting but exhilarating job with substantial monetary benefits. After a few years, he became a star professional but still stayed clear of dating women. The hurt of Anne was still raw in him.

Around his early thirties, as he was rocketing to higher positions in his work, Will became increasingly anxious, indecisive, and less confident in his work. Besides feeling discontent with his life, he was having intrusive thoughts about homosexuality and obsessive wishes to harm his loved ones. These obsessive thoughts became more powerful and began flooding his mind to a point where he thought he was heading toward a nervous breakdown. He was capable of hiding these torturous thoughts so no one was able to see the internal agony from the outside. Then came a point when Will could not tolerate this confusion any longer and he sought psychiatric help.

Psychoanalysis

I worked with Will for four years: one year in psychoanalytic psychotherapy and three years in psychoanalysis proper.

During our first meetings, Will told me that he did not understand what was happening to him. For a long while he thought all aspects of his life was going well, and he thought he only had problems dating women. Then, out of the blue, these obsessive intrusions flooded his mind, and he was now at the edge of losing his enthusiasm in the area that was so important—his work.

When I asked about his problems with dating, in vivid detail he described what felt like an agonizing vicious cycle. When he felt attracted to a woman and felt some vibes that she was interested in him as well, he would make intricate plans about ways of approaching her. But these plans did not yield any results; most of the times Will would feel paralyzed and would not be able to bring himself to invite her on a date. When he managed to have a date, he would become anxious or lose interest in his date, and would break off, leaving the girl in bewilderment. On the problem of obsessive intrusions, he was at a total loss; they made no sense to him and he was hoping to find an answer to these problems through psychoanalysis.

As the psychoanalytic psychotherapy unfolded, in between his obsessive preoccupations with dating woman and making intricate plans for the dates, there emerged a fended-off process of mourning. With a deep sense of sadness, he started talking about his parents, uncle, grandfather, and Anne, all of whom he had left behind. As I listened to these undertones, I was intuitively developing a formulation that was different than Will's original formulation of what brought him to treatment. I hypothesized that while Will had a one-dimensional description of his "problem," what he perceived as the problem could actually be embedded in an obsessive character structure. And his recent intrusive thoughts, fantasies, and inhibitions could all be a part of a regression.

With this formulation in mind, I actively confronted and clarified some of his habitual patterns, conveying my impression that there was more than an inability to date; that the symptom he reported was in itself very important but probably was also a synoptic summary of a complicated set of conflicts. These early efforts of mine seemed reasonable to his perceptive mind, so with some sense of surprise and sadness, Will came to recognize that the problem was deeper and wider than he had thought and that he was not as "perfect" as he assumed himself to be.

This sad recognition opened the field for a deeper exploration; countering the stubborn ruminative style that kept him away from the emergence of affect and of thoughts that were connected to affect in the pursuit of understanding his relations to other, I repeatedly invited him to take a look at his obsessively defended, "affect-less" presentation, suggesting that he was trying to stay in a cocoon, maybe for good reasons.

In time, through my persevering attempts of resistance analysis, some poignant memories about his parents emerged. Even before the family crumbled with the impact of the military-Islamic regime, his parents had a dichotomous presentation. On the one hand were the images of successful academicians, but on the other hand, there was the somewhat hidden image of people with some serious fragilities. The father suffered from alcoholism and was prone to being absent through regular blackouts. The mother was depressed to a point where she would collapse and spend weeks at a time housebound, unable to accomplish anything. And then they would occasionally lose their control in their ever-increasing arguments. Most often though, they would appear to others, including to Will, as if they were functioning superbly in multiple aspects of their lives: as a loving couple, as wonderful parents, and as successful professionals.

As I got to hear this history from Will, I was refining my formulation. On the surface it looked as if the main culprits were his father's alcoholism and his mother's depression, but I thought these were too generic and simplistic. I commented on the conspicuous lack of a reflective space for thoughts and emotions for Will as he was going through his teens: "It appears as if there was no room for you as a young kid who needed to be listened to about what had happened to you during your day. You had so many observations, questions, thoughts, and feelings that you needed someone to think through together with you, and help you, to understand the world around you."

Will agreed. He said that he was used to logical thinking but was uncomfortable with feelings. Then he made an interesting comment: "'Feelings' is such a commonplace parlance—one that implies that if one were to talk about feelings everything would be fine." So he hated the idea for its absurd simplicity. I thought he was right. I had similar thoughts about the popularized idea of feelings and in so many words, I tried to convey to Will that I thought the concept of "feelings" was a euphemism, and the concept was not just about feelings per se. That feelings made us think about our lives, ourselves, and others and if harnessed properly, they were great guides for our minds. But if they were let loose like his father and mother were prone to do with theirs, or anaesthetized as he was trying to accomplish, we lost an important fuel and a sense of direction in life. He silently listened to my speech, and so did I, as it spontaneously came out of my mouth.

First Year of Analysis

In the cases of Al, Barbara, Judy, and Henry, we talked about how the body was a proto-language. In my therapeutic relation with Will, his idiosyncratic bodily language appeared rather early. Will had been reluctant to lie on the couch for about a year, during which we conducted face-to-face therapy. Later on, I was surprised to hear that he had actually created an unusual psychoanalytic position from day one. I had noticed that at some points in our psychoanalytic psychotherapy sessions, with him sitting across me, he would take his glasses off. This seemingly insignificant action was in fact significant, as his severe myopia would turn me into a blur, with no details of my face discernible to him.

This recognition evoked a series of theoretical notes in me: psychoanalysis, after all, is a distortion of ordinary human conversation. First, we ask the patient to free associate, and we reciprocate with our evenly hovering attention. And second, we ask the patient to lie on the couch. Will was reminding me that a well-known but infrequently discussed aspect of the psychoanalytic relationship is the loss of the faces of both the analyst and analysand to one another. Supposedly stemming from Freud's intolerance of being gazed at, the couch distorts the ordinary human communication immensely. A centrally important medium of human conversation, the human face, the grand evocateur and communicator, is lost to both.

When Will finally managed to lie on the couch, he positioned himself in a strange fashion; he would put all of the pillows available in my office under his head and shoulders so that he would almost be in a sitting position with his back turned to me.

When I introduced the rule of free association, he began talking about the endless details of his workday, making his narrative sound like an obsessive report—repetitive, boring, without specific persons, dry and lifeless.

He reported a deep sense of shame and fear over telling me everything that came to his mind, stating that he was afraid that I might lose my respect for him. Exposing some other sides of himself would make him vulnerable and weak whereas he needed to come across as an intelligent and calm person. Just as he was unwilling to lie flat on the couch, he was also reluctant to delve into some sides of himself because he did not yet fully trust me. I later learned that he only dropped this obsessive reporting when he was with his gay uncle who had immigrated to Australia to escape the severe persecution of gays under the Islamic regime.

If he abandons his obsessive ruminations and tries to be in the moment, then many memories and reflections surge as if coming from the depths of his self; so he has no choice but to try to push away these contents of his mind in order to avoid this overwhelming tsunami. Conversely, if he opens up the old memories, then he feels like his gay uncle—weird and childish. He has a deep sense of sadness and embarrassment over these thoughts. Then Will told me that he was also afraid that I may kick him out if I notice these sides of him.

When I point to the absence of particular persons in his narrative, he tells me that mentioning specific names makes him feel guilty, since it sounds like gossip and feels a bit too personal. That is an intimidating idea, one that he again connects to his gay uncle. He is afraid of his thoughts that remind him that he has some similarities to his uncle even in the way he talks or handles himself, in the way he dances with girls at parties.

Occasionally surfacing in his narrative were his mother, father, and aging grandfather. Each time they appeared with some sense of sadness and then quickly disappeared. I recognized the instantaneous defensive repression of his sadness; it was like a flicker that is put out, as soon as it appears, by a counter idea. In his mind, these experiences were universal, so there was no need to delve into them. When I interfered with his narrative and pointed out his sadness, he would break into tears but would quickly compose himself. I tacitly would note the sudden retrieval, but decided not point to it out again to him, thinking that I might in the process make him more self-conscious and enhance his defense.

Will Is Married!

When in between the lines of his dry, repetitive, boring narrative that was punctuated with some patches of connectedness, Will told me that he had recently gotten married, I was absolutely stunned. Then I saw the slim silver ring on his wedding finger that had skipped my attention; as he lay on the couch, he had managed to keep it out of my sight.

Will recounted the story: his long-time, long-distance girlfriend who was sick and tired of Will's obsessive indecision had finally shown up at his doorstep with her belongings, leaving him no option but to let her in! Will had not previously reported this to me. Now, after several months of living together, Will had agreed to get married, and they had done so with a few friends witnessing their ceremony.

Will's "secret" wife, Ginger, was a professional cellist, a member of an orchestra and a chamber group. She was deeply invested in her work and would spend many hours every day of the week practicing or playing.

She was attracted to Will because they were similar—young professionals who had outstanding accomplishments in their respective fields, and used to working extensive hours.

Defenses Challenged

Will was talking about how his analysis was like his marriage. He felt as if he "has to do it." On a different level, Will was now feeling anxious over losing the sight of my face and my body. He would lay on the couch in front of me, with minimum access to the sight of my shoes as I rested them on the ottoman next to the couch. He would try to decipher my bodily cues that were now barely audible, barely visible: a sigh here and there, the shuffling of my legs, or a series of vocalizations that we spontaneously use in ordinary human discourse. But my face, the grand container and communicator, was gone for him. My physical presence used to give him many cues, now he didn't know what we should talk about. He thought that losing me in the field of his sight, reminded him of losing his parents when he left the paternal home country. And he was also reminded of the exciting, scary, and deeply sad times when he was sent from his elite private school to the public school, where he felt all alone in a deeply religious culture with a different alphabet.

He remembered the gay uncle. He loved talking with him, but his mom and dad were vehemently opposed to it. His parents had told him that he was a bad influence on Will's mind and was interfering with his studies. He continued to associate as to whether his thoughts are weird or not, arousing strong temptations in me to respond to his queries, to tell him his thoughts were ordinary and normal.

Then an interesting shift occurred in the sessions as his obsessive style of living and thinking was challenged by analysis and by his increasingly intimate relationship with his wife. Some prolonged pauses and drowsiness emerged. In the midst of a stream of associations he would pause, space out, and gave me the sense that he was dissociating in front of me on the couch.

The Second Year of Analysis

Will reflected on the agonizing time of transition to a new alphabet. Through the end of his middle school years, he had read and written everything in Latin script. Whereas in the post-Islamic period, his new alphabet was Arabic, and he had extreme difficulties adapting to this colossal shift. In my mind, I associated to his moving from the playful narrative of his youth to his usual obsessive narrative. And now he was resisting my invitation for a more spontaneous narrative as if he feared the transition, and I wondered about the parallels.

As he continued complaining about the absence of joy in his life and about feeling "dried out," I noticed the parallels to our own dry work together. I provided a synoptic summary of his narrative to him intermittently, to make sure that I had understood him and also to make him aware that I was listening to his story. I tried to empathize with the subject of these repetitive complaints, observations, and themes. Yet all the while I felt as if I were left out. I was not sure if he was listening to me.

Slowly Will managed to stay with the experience of sadness as it appeared in flickers in the session. However, after a few minutes of staying with the affect, he would start beating on himself, complaining that he was inefficient, obsessive, and not living up to expectations. Using my Grayian lenses of close process monitoring, I pointed to the switch from sadness to ruminations and self-criticism (Gray 1990, 1994; Busch 1999). Will recognized the switches and said he felt as if we were talking to one another. He found my observation very helpful, and then he fell back asleep.

Then drawing from another revered teacher, Anton Kris, ideas about severe self-criticism (Kris 1990), I pointed to his endless complaints about himself, and told him that he sounded like he kept an eye on himself all the time and he probably didn't like himself. Will agreed with me, laughed, and expanded on my observation—at least nowadays he wasn't cursing himself all the time as he had in the past. Then, as he slipped into the dissociated/sleep state, left alone with my thoughts, I realized that I was calling great teachers of mine for their help—a sign that I was lost.

The Narcissist

On many occasions, Will had told me that he was a narcissist. When we explored what he meant by that, an aspect of him came out that made me quite irritated; he said that would never prepare his meals, he would just tell his wife that he wanted a breakfast and even at this age she would prepare it and inform Will when the breakfast was ready. When I asked him what would happen if she did not do that, Will said he would simply avoid the meal and make his wife feel terribly guilty. He would never help with any chores in the house and would even ask for a cup of water sometimes, all of which drove his wife insane.

I offered the interpretation that he was a slave to his mind as if he were just that, a mind. That is why he treated ordinary activities like preparing a breakfast, shopping, helping with the dishes, and so on with contempt. In order to interfere with the bipersonal defense, I encouraged him to start doing some house chores. This interpretation and recommendation surprised him. In the next session he told me his wife had laughed her head off when she was told of my comment. I thought about how he had been using her as a chauffeur and recently out of exhaustion she had protested, and Will had begun using his bicycle to come to his sessions. Then came the memories of his grandfather who, unlike his parents, was a person who would acknowledge and praise Will for whatever he did, never scolding him on any wrongdoings.

These rare moments of contact were followed with sleepiness on both sides—he spaced out, and I felt sleepy. Then, some other material came out in patches; his mother was not communicating with him anymore, Will did not call her much either since he was busy. In a disjointed way, he then recalled his previous therapy in London. He was worried about "losing it." When I inquired about what he meant by "losing it," his dad's emotional outbursts came to his mind: he was trying to learn how to drive as an adolescent, having his father as his teacher. Whenever Will made a minor mistake, his father would start crying, yelling, and hitting his own face with his fists, causing his face to swell. That was how Will had lost interest in driving.

I observed his reluctance to expand his thoughts beyond his usual complaints about his work, life, and self. When some other themes appeared in flickers, he quickly snuffed the fire out. Will agreed that he too noticed that about himself and continued with the ruminative narrative.

Then a sexually tinged memory surfaced. When he was twelve, he had been attracted to a young maid who lived with them. One time, as they were playing like any two teenagers, chasing one another, he had crashed through a glass panel, injuring his right wrist. He showed the deep scar on his arm to me. His parents had fired the maid and shamed him, and locked him in the cellar for a day after the surgery.

In my excited mind, I noted the multiple meanings of that memory: if you follow your desire, you get castrated and punished, and your object of desire disappears. As I invited him to follow this evocative memory with the hope of reaching potentially rich associations as mine, to my great disappointment he became drowsy. He told me that he needed to keep his mind busy with work. As we go through these oft-repeated cycles of sleeping/spacing out/dissociating, I was noticing an increase in his capacities for self-observation.

Reveries

In the sessions, as he absented himself, I was increasingly drawn to my reveries: I feel as if I am invited to see glimpses of his life and then I am excluded. It feels like a tease. Then I am reminded of my ancestors, the Ottomans, besieging cities. Am I besieging him to extract information about his life? Am I sadistically attacking, attempting to penetrate his mind? Is there a budding sadistic homosexual countertransference?

He opens the doors and then closes them. He lets me in, or comes out, then kicks me out and goes back into his mind. He tells me that after talking to me he sees things in a different perspective and that feels good. But it also makes him vulnerable. Then he wonders whether he is trying to impress me by showing me that he is making progress. I recognize the irresistible sleepiness in me. As he disappears in the session, in my mind I move from the benign, understanding symbol of doors to an angrier one; I feel like an empty cartridge, I have the images of my warrior ancestors besieging cities and conquering them. There is no way in.

The sense of helplessness, powerlessness that had emerged early on in the treatment continues to plague me and I recognize that a major cause of my fatigue is the barrenness of his narrative, the absence of specific persons with their names, colors, the gossip like structure of ordinary analytic narrative. My mind goes to sophisticated cultures of reverence of the Middle East or Far East, where people may also display severe forms of aggression, like hara-kiri, kamikaze, and the self-beatings of some religions around religious events. Is he attacking me or himself?

Ancient Hysteria Revisited

Then I go back to my younger years. During my psychiatry training in the mostly rural, isolated, developing Turkey of the 1970s, I had treated classical hysterical pathology. I had seen many patients who had hysterical paralyses, aphonia, trances, fugues, arc de cercle, and other exotic presentations. As Turkey became more integrated with the world and started emerging as an increasingly urban society, the nature of psychopathology shifted considerably and hysteria had become extremely rare. After I moved to the United States in the 1980s, I saw only one case of hysteria, and that was in the medical wards of a general hospital. So in time, I developed an impression that for some obscure reasons, classical hysteria had disappeared (Laplanche 1974; Öztürk 2002).

Now I was surprised to face this fugue-like phenomenon on my couch, in a big American town, at the edge of the twenty-first century. I speculated that Will, coming from an Asian country, was not too different from the patients that Freud (1893/1940) had seen Charcot treat and himself treated in the late nineteenth century. Nor was he very different than the ones that I had treated in the Turkey of the 1970s. As I was drawn into struggling with these fascinating historical correlations in my mind, I slowly became aware of my internal vacillations between thinking about Will as a case of generic psychopathology on the one hand, and my capacity to hearing his unique personal narrative on the other.

Once I managed to pull myself out of the attempt to "categorize" him, shifting my theoretical lens, I mulled over the absence of specific persons in his narrative in my mind: Will told me that he was afraid that if he mentions specific names, I may think that he is not a nice person, that he will be gossiping about someone else, which is not cool. If I, as his analyst, recognize that he can hurt someone's image by talking about him, he will lose the self-image that he is trying to keep alive all the time—a kind, nice person who does not think evil about others and a person whom others like and love.

I told Will that he was constantly working on narrowing his presentation to a simplified image with me. He agreed with my interpretation: that he was disemboweling his narrative.

He always played with his "thoughts," he didn't think about "people." Quite often he was mad at his wife and his colleagues, but he was not talking about them in person because there was nothing he could do about it. And he became very self-conscious while talking with someone in a position of authority. He had mixed feelings about scholars, and he presumed that I was one, as a respected professor. He thought he would be on dangerous ground here if he lets himself loose—then he may get out of control and become like his dad or mom. He preferred to keep his composure and provide a detailed, meticulous narrative to me.

In his mind's eye, Will always tried to think like a "Lord," making reference to royalties of his maternal culture or an "Aga" in his paternal culture—both titles of reverence. That revelation surprised me. Aga was the same term in my culture, and I associated to my father who was jokingly called an "Aga," in Turkish of course, due to his strong opinions and influence on the extended family.

Parallel to my sporadic inclusion into his internal world, his parents surface and recede in his narrative. He is trying to forget them. It is intolerably painful for him to think about his paternal home, to hear songs from his country of origin, or to watch their national team in the international soccer tournament. He blocks them out, sleeps, or maybe dissociates. He is reluctant to come to sessions. He feels very dependent on these sessions, although he feels better, lighter after revealing certain things. But he is also worried that I could see him as defective. He is worried about crying, looking vulnerable. He is afraid that his weakness will make him easy prey. When I point to his choice of word, he realizes that "prey" is a strong word, but remembers that he felt like prey when his mother and father would attack him if he showed any weakness.

In time, he recognizes a potential connection between being busy and sadness. He wasn't this busy in London or in his beloved paternal country. He recognizes sides of himself that are like his dad. He sulks, pouts, and feels he is close to fits of rage just like his dad. As soon as he recognizes these deep, old identifications and acknowledges missing his parents and his free-spirited times, he gets embarrassed. It feels like time stopped when he came to this country. His wife, he notices, has different relationships with her parents. She is more warm and cuddly. He envies that, but it is scary to him. I point to his deep, complicated mourning of his loved ones in different continents.

Gradually Will became aware of his ego-syntonic "niceness." He reported a core fantasy: "If I act like a good and helpless child, others will help me when I need them." He studied people and tried to behave in a way that won't be upsetting to them. It was constant, hard work for him.

He told me that he was hiding his sadness, missed the times he saw me face-to-face. Now he didn't know how to read me. He always felt alone. He was ambivalent about psychoanalysis as he continued to sleep in our sessions and then cursed at himself for doing so.

Somewhat bored, frustrated, and angry, I became more active and mentioned some themes over the course of several sessions; that he was focused on his self, that he never forgot about himself, that he was always in his own mind. I also said that it was as if he was trying to evoke a response from me and say "Will, you have to study or stop beating yourself." I made a note of what was absent from his associations; fantasies, dreams, playfulness. I told him that it was as if he is taking his thoughts extremely seriously, to the detriment of some other aspects of his mind.

Will agreed. He told me that he was scared in the United States. He felt comfortable in his country of origin and later on in the United Kingdom. Now it was all shattered.

He admitted that he missed me during absences. But he immediately added that he did not want to get to a level of attachment to me as he had with Anne. He recalled how he and Anne had lived together for some years, and she had abruptly left him. Will had felt that Anne was the love of his life, and her abrupt departure led this man of a few words to write a one-hundred-page passionate love letter in his mother tongue. He was surprised to recognize, as he was reflecting on his past, even when he wrote to his parents, he had not been able to express his love for them.

I hypothesized that he was possibly defending against a deep attachment to me, the multiple motives of which were not yet explored. It could have meant that I might leave him, or it might have meant that he may have to leave other old loves behind. I wondered whether I should use some of these internal notes interpretatively but intuitively shied away from doing so and simultaneously, I had the troubling thought that I might be reverting to my own usual, habitual cocoon.

Marriage and Analysis as Parallel Challenges

In parallel with his analysis, Will's marriage continued to challenge his character style. Will complained that his wife was interfering with his daily routine. He thought that maybe they should have a schedule, plan their day in such a way that Will would know when they would eat, sleep, or have sex. And his wife now wanted to open a joint account, but Will didn't want to do that, and after a few such interesting associations he drifted again into sleep. When he awakened, he stated that he felt selfish for seeing me so often, four times a week, unlike the earlier part of therapy when we met twice a week.

Despite my continuing hesitation, with the support from peer supervision, I persevered in my work with the "absences." When I again remarked on his excluding me from the details of his daily life, Will told me that he didn't want to bore me, nor did he want to feel like he was betraying others. A lively narrative unfolded; in an unusually forthcoming manner, Will associated to his first adolescent love, to playing soccer, to memories from his first work in London as a young engineer, to his love for his wife, to his feminine sides like his uncle's, to a colleague trying to seduce him, and to his resistance to being seduced.

I was left with a sense of pleasant surprise, wonder, and curiosity. Maybe he was interpreting my listening, silent stance as absence, I thought.

Then followed the deepening mourning of Anne. Thinking about their time together, to my surprise, Will cried. Following this period of open mourning, he reverted back to his cocoon, ruminating and reporting on his day in phrases so familiar that by now I could recite those sentences for him. I nevertheless managed to notice that he was not putting so many pillows behind him and was getting closer to lying on the natural contour of my couch.

When I pointed to the shift from mourning to the ruminations, he disappeared again. When he came back, I pointed out to him the sequence of my intervention and his falling asleep, and asked for his thoughts. Will said he didn't have any. Having used all of the technical tools at my disposal, from Kohutian (Kohut and Wolf 1978) empathic immersion to Grayian (Gray 1994; Busch 1999) close process monitoring, I realized that I was becoming bored in the sessions and had called again on the ideas of some master clinicians for help.

As I repeatedly pointed to absence of fantasies and dreams in his narrative, he told me that he thought they were a waste of time. With the ongoing consultative help of my peers, I recognized his "trench-war"-like stance, his opposition, and his dismissiveness more clearly. When I offered these as interpretations, he retorted that he didn't feel that way.

Sporadically, a subtle shift in his narrative emerged. Will began giving some hints of his enviable sides. It was slowly becoming clear to me that this young man who portrayed himself as desperate, dependent, and a failure on many grounds was also a man with impressive professional accomplishments. He was probably as intelligent as I am, if not more so in certain ways. He was ten years younger than me when he arrived in this country, was already making much more money than I ever would, and had a great adventure ahead of him. I felt warmly happy for this young patient of mine, and as I heard more of his story, I noticed I was quite envious.

My invitations to "play" with his associations were initially accepted by Will with some joy but his thoughts soon ended up retracting to his obsessive/schizoid cocoon. He repeated that he was scared most of the time, he was also afraid of making mistakes: "If I make a mistake then it is irreparable," he said. Then he recalled being locked in a cellar at the age of four by his grandfather, after biting his mother's leg. We both recognized that he had internalized his parents. He was thinking and talking about himself in the way that they would think about him. It was painful for him to engage in fantasy talks with his parents but it kept him in good company; there was no one else around to guide him, or to criticize him.

Connecting the theme of loneliness with the recurrent countertransference wishes to give advice, I was now much clearer about this particular transference-countertransference script. As an opening to an interpretation from countertransference, I asked him what he thought about my not giving him advice.

Will: "I truly would love to hear some advice from you. I would argue with my dad but trust his advice one hundred percent. He turned out to be right about many things. I miss him. He is moving farther away . . ." Then, as he recognized that he was becoming more emotional, he dozed off. And with a sense of accomplishment, I realized that in a slow but steady fashion, he was catching his dissociative defense earlier.

In the following sessions, we uncovered some regressed aspects of his complicated relationship with his parents. His mother and father had given Will the impression that if they didn't guide him, he would create an irremediable disaster and embarrass the family in the eyes of their neighbors. He would disagree with this infantilizing assumption and get into heated arguments with his parents. And now, in a fascinating way, he was operating with the same assumption that he would create a catastrophe. With a deep sense of mistrust of his mind, he felt crippled and paralyzed in his capacity to make decisions. He felt as if he had lost his anchorage. He realized that if his beloved mom and dad were not around then he did the only thing he could: behave like them. Will was recognizing that he missed those fights that he had hated while he was still living with his parents. He was close to tears and trying to stay awake.

I pointed to his dilemma: he fought with his parents but found them very helpful in his decisions. If he gave in to his desires and the parents didn't guide then he would fail. "It sounds like you brought mom and dad with you," I observed. He agreed. He complained that his wife also shied away from giving advice: she acted like an entourage, leaving him alone to make decisions.

Reveries

The scenes and the soundtrack of our conversations were playing back in my mind, as Will was abandoning me and coming back in the sessions' hours, as he was mightily struggling with his dissociative defense.

Will feels that the time in these sessions belongs to him, but at the same time he is conflicted about our conversations and feels guilty. He feels relieved on the one hand and embarrassed on the other. Also he is anxious—afraid that he may sound stupid. In his usual style, in between the lines, Will tells me that he is getting very tired of his perennial indecision. Observing that he sounds tortured, I invite him for exploration, but he dozes off, yet again.

I feel lost. When he awakens he tells me that he can't trust people. He has been taking care of things on his own for so many years. He has protected himself from depending on others. He recognizes that I may die, and he will, one day. We are both getting old, and death is becoming a palpable reality for him.

These revelations evoke a pang of fear in me. I wonder whether I had missed a regressive pocket in my understanding of Will and ask him to tell more about his painful thoughts around death and abandonment. Will tells me that he sometimes feels there is no reason to be alive. He doesn't have the motivation to change and all our efforts are futile. He just can't get off this torturous road. He feels as if someone always puts him back to where he started. He is trying to be a good, polite, and obedient boy so that maybe people might like him and help him. Then he ponders: what if Dr. K says these thoughts are rubbish and irrelevant, and gives a warning that he is getting tired of the whole process? I think to myself, he is not totally off in his guess about what I feel inside of me.

As Will is talking about his fears of forgetting his family, an interesting fantasy emerges: he is afraid that if he changes, his loved ones may die. He continues: "It may sound odd but it is very real and deep for me." He catches himself as he is about to doze off. He tells me that he does not really fall sleep. He just drifts off, maybe because he doesn't want to discuss certain things with me.

Asia

Will is on the eve of a month-long business trip to Asia and anticipates our separation. His drifting off into a daze becomes more frequent. I point to the possibility that he may be defending against the loss of me during the break. He agrees. Just before the Asia trip, an unusual thought emerges in his mind: maybe he is not that incompetent of a man he portrays himself to be, maybe he is denying that he is actually quite a successful man, a person not so much in need of his parents, of Dr. K, or of others. I empathically support the thought with "hum, uhm." And the thought makes him shudder.

When Will returns from his successful visit to Asia, he acknowledges me as a person for the first time: "I am glad to see you." As he experiences the separations and their impact on him, the names of people slowly appear in his narrative; the names of his parents, friends, relatives. It is apparent that he is letting go of his parents as he mentions them by their names. He recognizes that he has the fantasy or fear that if he mentions them by their names then he has to acknowledge that they are getting old. And he realizes that he is changing. He dozes off as he names people. Then he expresses his embarrassment over sleeping.

Absence of Play

I comment on his attempts to be in full control of his self and his mind, and that he is not allowing any space to be playful or spontaneous. Will in turn tells me that after he came to this country those sides of him died. He decided to be in full control, and strived to become a serious person and a superb professional. Then he reminisces about how he had felt like he was a real person during his years with Anne. After Anne, he thinks he behaves like the characters in movies; the tough cowboys, cut-throat competitive businessman, and it is all an act. I can feel his narrative in my body; it is alive and evocative. It is in stark contrast to his usually dry obsessive style, and Will is still struggling to stay awake. And when I point to the presleep pause, he recognizes that he always wants to say something worthwhile at those moments before he drifts off; as if he wants to bury some aspects of his mind very, very fast.

As Will is developmentally progressing through our work, his wife is still deeply engaged in her partially defensive, hypomanic investment in music. Breaking the unconscious agreements of projective-introjective aspects of their relationship through his therapeutic transference involvement with me as his analyst, the couple's relationship sours. His wife becomes impatient and chronically angry with Will.

The marriage is under considerable strain. In the sessions, I note and interpret this dyadic strain with increasing regularity and recommend that we initiate couples work with a colleague of mine. As they begin regular couples work, the regressive pull softens, and we have more space to focus on the transference in the here and now of the psychoanalytic space. Yet Will's wife is still deeply reluctant to get into a personal psychoanalysis.

Some prominent companies are after Will and make him attractive offers for senior positions in Europe. He becomes indecisive again and procrastinates in his response to these offers. He wishes that someone, maybe Dr. K, would show him the way to go. I remind him that his father had played that role for him and he expects the same role from me. He agrees with my interpretation and tells me that he misses his dad terribly. He is worried that he might make a mistake and choose the wrong company. Despite the termination regression, I have an internal sense that he is becoming more attentive, interactive, and authentic.

We both recognize the "lack of anger" despite his continuing, ordinary frustrations in his marriage and in his work life. Will tells me that he is trying to be fair to everyone. If he disagrees with someone, he tries to see their side too, unlike his dad and grandpa who would flare up even over minor disagreements. He is aware of getting angry inside but mostly keeps the anger in, and he doesn't express it to me. I ask whether that is because he wants to come across like an honorable, somewhat aloof, contained, royalty, like a prototypical "Lord." He agrees then adds that another worry: if he gets angry he is afraid he may just lose it. He recalls the incident in fourth grade when he slapped a kid several times when he mocked Will over his accent. He sure does have fantasies of beating and yelling; he just doesn't articulate those to me.

He catches some glimpses of his style of connecting with people around him: either he gets attached head over heels like he did with Anne, or he is cold and aloof. He has a lot of anxiety about his styles of attachment so he is afraid of getting involved. If he gets involved, what happens next? Thoughts of abandonment, and to my surprised ears, death resurface in his associations.

I underline a significant shift in him: "You are beginning to notice that you like people and get attached."

Although Will now utters names more comfortably, he remains embarrassed to talk about women. In parallel to his increased ability to give names to persons in his life, he starts showing more interest in me; my office, my books and whether I read them all. He comments on our separations over the weekends and treats me as an "other." With reversions back to his ruminative style, he asserts that he tries to give me a responsibility when ruminates. He wishes that I would join and interrupt his ruminations, as his parents would. As I stay away from these strong pulls to enactment, he recognizes the nature of his "loneliness." To avoid the intense pain it might evoke, he doesn't call any relatives, some of whom are influential people in the United States. If he calls them, then he would be reminded of his country, his parents, and other people and things he had left behind.

As he is becoming affectively alive, demonstrating increased self-analytic capacity and seeing me as an "other," Will creates an evocative metaphor. He likens this state to thawing. As if he had been frozen for many years and the recent warming up was causing considerable pain in his hands and feet.

With a warm sense of fulfillment over what we have accomplished together and a sense of sadness that we are approaching the end of our relationship, I think to myself: what he thinks of thawing is in essence allowing another person to become a part of his story, a part of a new set of object relationships; settling deep jealousies in his mind; creating the potential of gaining a new set of representations as we call it in our rather dry theoretical language. These will be further sources of transferences and resistances and inquiries of new objects throughout the rest of his still very young life. As I awaken from these theoretical ponderings, I notice I am thinking about his life in a very similar way that I think of my sons'.

It was into his third year of psychoanalysis as he was approaching the end of his work at his company that pervasive themes of termination began to emerge in Will's mind. He recalled the many painful transitions earlier in his life. He remembered the time he had to shift from Latin to Arabic alphabet at the age of ten. He recalled having to switch from his beloved mother tongue to English when he got a scholarship from a prominent university in England. Then he recalled his remarkably secretive departure from the United Kingdom to the United States. As he was departing he was full of excitement, joy, and sadness, but he was unable to share either his joy or his sadness with any loved one. He felt he was leaving a country where he felt good about himself; as a perfect student, athlete, and a man. I note to myself that as he was reflecting on these painful separations, he manages to stay awake.

The Drawer

As the termination drew closer, Will's increased awareness of his proclivity to ruminations and indecision brought out another poignant memory: in his teens, he had a drawer where he would stuff his chocolates, chewing gums, candies, and his little toys. In time, some of the items would become stale but he wouldn't throw them away, thinking that he may use them sometime in the future. So this drawer would eventually overflow with stuff.

He drew a parallel between throwing his thoughts into the drawer. He had not used many of his own thoughts and impressions about the world to guide him; it felt like he was depositing them in the drawer and to his mind's eye, the process of thinking would mean throwing some things out of his drawer. Will was now contemplating some further self-analytic interpretations in my presence; his mother and father had done the same thing; they had dismissed Will's quite impressive mind, stating: "You will have your opinions when you grow up, so keep them to yourself." Thus he had difficulties in learning what things to put things into his drawer and what to throw out. He was instead mightily trying to keep everything in the drawer of his mind without differentiating between what was useful and what was not.

I was encouraged with Will's increased capacity for self-observation. The way he played with the "drawer" was a good metaphor for his character style so I was feeling more comfortable with the idea of leaving him and letting him grow, and with the idea of me maybe throwing some out of my own drawer. Then there appeared a worrisome increase in his obsessionality to the point where he started displaying some overt compulsive symptomatology—washing his hands more often, worrying about whether he had locked the door as he left the house and driving back to check, and wondering whether we had accomplished much during our years of work. However, these periods were followed by sessions where I felt he was alive and we were connected. Will was clearly going through a termination regression.

Will had been offered a senior position in Europe, and by coincidence at around the same time I had received an invitation to join a prominent therapeutic hospital. He recognized that I was slowly packing my office and commented on it. Then came moments when he isolated himself into his ruminative cocoon but then recognized it and self-interpreted with a giggle; "I am keeping you out again." I felt hopeful that our work had an impact of increasing his capacity for self-observation and a germinating sense of self-deprecatory humor. And for the first time, he developed revenge fantasies toward Anne. He wanted her to know that he can live a decent life without her. He had found her on Facebook and thought he should maybe contact her and tell her he was doing well.

Will also became more comfortable with taking pride in his accomplishments: he stated that maybe he was quite successful because he was getting invitations from many top companies in the country. He was not too worried about my envy of him. Now he was concerned that I may in certain ways be better than him as he witnessed my advancement in my own field. I was reflecting on envy of a senior versus envy of and competition with a peer and recognized that these two were different from each other. In the case of a developmental senior, one has a chance of "beating" them in time or not, whereas in relation to a peer it becomes a different issue—you had to do it now.

I: "At the beginning of our work, it felt easier for you to beat on yourself in front of others whereas you secretly despised them. And after so many years of work, instead of despising yourself publicly and admiring yourself secretly, you are learning how to be content with who you are, without making it an issue of deadly shame or pride. You are becoming aware of different sides of yourself—excited, bored, embarrassed, proud, vengeful, forgiving, playful, and serious."

Will: "Yes. I didn't even celebrate my birthdays. For many years enjoyment was banned in my thoughts and in my mind. Just like my parents did in the past, I was shunning it myself."

Now we were conversing; he was hearing me, and I was also hearing him. I realized that I was more active, making what felt like long-winded genetic/dynamic interpretations that connected his past to his current transferential relation with me. I contemplated that maybe I was clearing out of my hopelessness in regard to our work. I commented on how he was more capable of throwing away some stuff from the drawer as he left behind his relationship with Anne, his loved ones, and me.

Will acknowledged that it was terribly sad, and somewhat relieving that he would be leaving me. As he was moving to Europe and I to another town, it was unclear in my mind who was leaving whom behind. Would he have stayed around if I were to stay around? Had he announced his departure first or had I? It was all a blur. I was feeling guilty about abandoning him to his new life in Europe and at the same time had a pang of jealousy over whom he might work with as his next analyst.

As we sailed through this rather unusual termination where both of us were leaving each other, as we were going through a process that was full of affect and fantasies on both sides, Will made another visit to the memories of his first love, Anne. This time around he was not spaced out and painfully sad and in tears, he was able to talk about her.

REFLECTIONS ON WILL

Hypomanic-Obsessive Character Organization

Will had what I would call an "obsessive-hypomanic character organization." It is a constellation that has caught the attention of some authors who propose to place it as a subtype of bipolar illness (Akiskal et al. 2000; Gartner 2005). I view this as a chronic character trait, not an episodic one as one would usually see in bipolar spectrum disorders. And I am tempted to think and talk about the defensive/adaptive elements in this "personality organization," aspects that are amenable to analytic work.

Hypomanic-obsessive character organization is a constellation that is quite common in high-achieving professionals: constriction of affect, powerful defenses against mourning, some awkwardness in the interpersonal realm, and an immense capacity for work that has important defensive aspects and on the adaptive front, brings forth significant professional achievements.

In this category of patients, in contrast to the false-self formation of Barbara, splitting and substantial externalization of the internal world is less pronounced. However, there are pockets of split, repressed representations that could be awakened in the intense transference developments of psychoanalysis and some aspects of their interpersonal life, be it in their marriages or in their relationships with some colleagues at work. This development is along the Kernbergian differential of neurotic personality organization that may regress to borderline personality organization (Kernberg and Caligor 2005).

Developmentally, these individuals don't have an overly traumatic early life like Barbara. They come from families where the triadic structure is somewhat maintained. These are the cases in which there was an internal permission from the parents to develop other attachments in the extended family or among their peers.

The importance of this character style is that the pathology can easily get lost in the contemporary cultural ethos that celebrates hard work and professional accomplishment. So these individuals, after a long stretch of a "successful" life, may end up stalling in an aspect of their life as was seen in Will. Or they may end up in a massive collapse if not intervened therapeutically and may even need hospitalization. The Professionals in Crisis Unit at the Menninger Hospital that I directed for some years had many patients who fit this profile.

In the analytic office work then, the technical task is to be aware of these pockets as they surface and push the patient from a neurotic level of functioning to a borderline configuration, just like the point when Will regressed to a level where he was bringing material on his deep sense of loneliness and hopelessness. As a rule, besides being an intrapsychic representational script, these pockets are interpersonal, a series of relationships that involves the patient and another person from his life (wife, friend, parent, mentor, or a sibling). In other words, the intrapsychic is also anchored through projective identification in a relation with another. This actual person with whom the patient has a fixated, regressed relationship is a significant source of resistance to the development of the patient in analysis as many of the cases I talked about demonstrate.

Technically, when these pockets emerge, there are different ways of approaching them. One may choose to work through them in the analysis by approaching this dyadic relationship in the office. Then the exploration and interpretation has to shift from the here and now of the transference-countertransference in the hour to a relationship outside of the office, to extra-transference work (Blum 1983). Or as Otto Kernberg (2008) points out in his work in Transference Focused Therapy, to the transferences outside of the therapeutic matrix. This may have some impact on the work on the resistance in the session.

Yet another efficient therapeutic intervention is to initiate couples work or to get the other person in the projective identificatory relation into psychoanalysis: when Will and his wife agreed to get into couples treatment, it enabled Will to continue progressing in his work with me.

The most difficult case is probably the one in which the patient is under the impression that he has already severed the ties with the central archaic object and resolved his problem. It may need prolonged efforts on the part of the therapist to confront the patient and remind him that the relationship is still alive and that it still has an impact. It is a condition that I am tempted to call a "frozen/distant regression" for the lack of a better term. It is in contrast to the proximate, enmeshed, hot regressions that we are accustomed to, as in the cases of Judy and Kate.

Al was a good example of this "frozen/distant regression" with an archaic object. He had not talked with his parents for many years, had enough money to live on, and thus had created the illusion that he had solved the problem. However, internally he was torturously involved with his parents; he would ruminate about them every day, for many hours. Thus, they were like ghosts haunting him (Loewald 1960). With Will, this was less of a problem. He was aware of the fact that he was trying to forget them; yet his parents, with whom he had minimal contact, were a presence in his mind, albeit not as painfully as in Al's mind. In other words, Will's parents occupied a space that made him feel guilty and mournful whereas Al's parents were like "introjects"; mummies or zombies that he was not reminiscing about but rather ruminating about, and they were haunting him.

Probably the most poignant example of the impossibility of this "freezing," "forgetting" solution was another patient of mine, Art.

Art was a successful surgeon, a professor in a teaching hospital, and happily married to a fellow physician. They had two sons, and Art was on the track of becoming the next CEO of his hospital. He had a tremendous capacity for work; he would do rounds at four in the morning every day of the week, driving his junior colleagues and residents to exhaustion. He had only taken a few weeks off in the last ten years and took enormous pride in his work ethic.

His father was a blue-collar worker, and his mother was a housewife who suffered from chronic schizophrenia and developed a unique relationship with her son. In Art's younger years, during her psychotic episodes when she was unable to attend to her needs, as an able teenager Art would take care of her to the point of giving her baths. He would take care of the chores of the house and was a parental figure to his younger siblings, protecting them from the wrath of their out-of-control mother. When he became a doctor, he took his mother to many doctors, but she quickly become noncompliant with their recommendations.

By his mid-thirties, unable to convince his mother to get appropriate treatment, feeling terribly guilty but helpless, Art had given up on his parents and severed his ties with them. He limited their relationship to periodic phone contact. He would regularly call them every other month and would briefly talk to his father. His mother would never talk to him. Art felt that this was evidence that his mother had fully forgotten about him. He felt somehow sad but also relieved.

When Art was briefly hospitalized after the collapse of his hypomanic defensive style, he could not call the parents at his regular time. In a surprising but telling way, his mother got into a frenzy and attempted to call Art. When she was not able to get ahold of him, she then called his wife, then his friends, and then finally the police, who ended up knocking on the door of the parents' home, asking whether everything was alright. This mother who had refused to talk to her son for so many years made over one hundred calls in a matter of twenty-four hours when her son had broken the rule of calling at regular intervals!

8

ODE TO AN ESTEEMED TEACHER

I began this book with acknowledgments of some great teachers of mine, and will end it with my farewell to one of them, the psychotherapeutic hospital. It is first and foremost a personal goodbye; a few years ago, I closed my hospitalist career in psychoanalytically informed hospitals. But sadly, this may be well beyond a personal farewell; these amazing human ecologies are in a course of attrition, and they may be extinct in the next few decades. Thus perhaps it is timely to offer some personal thoughts while the memories of my experiences in these unique human ecologies are still fresh.

This section is the story of my relationship with the psychotherapeutic hospital and how I came to understand her remarkable workings. And neither the object nor the subject is fictional.

DR. K—WHAT IS THE MYSTERY OF THE PSYCHOTHERAPEUTIC HOSPITAL?

I worked in a few psychotherapeutic hospitals for well over two decades: the main ones were Hacettepe psychiatric inpatient unit in Ankara, Turkey; the Austen Riggs Center in Stockbridge, Massachusetts; and the Menninger Clinic in Houston, Texas.

A Curious Lack of Recognition of the Hospital

While I was working in these hospitals, I also kept a busy practice in psychotherapy and psychoanalysis. An intriguing observation emerging from this dual engagement was the fact that the world of psychoanalysis proper had virtually no information about or interest in the unusual, heroic human experiment of the psychotherapeutic hospital. Similar to the disappearance of psychoanalytic group work from the world of mainstream psychoanalysis, the psychoanalytically informed hospitals had vanished from the awareness of psychoanalysis, there was no interest to learn from this unique psychoanalytic experience.

On the other hand, it seemed equally puzzling that these hospitals did not have substantive theories of their own; competent clinicians, teachers, or colleagues of mine, who were well versed in the classical psychoanalytic theory as it was taught in the psychoanalytic institutes, were at a loss when they were invited to theorize on how and why the hospital worked. Instead, they were borrowing the sophisticated, elaborate theories of psychoanalysis proper, the two-person theories of therapy, and they were interpreting their work through the lens of that dyadic space.

Dr. Martin Cooperman, an outstanding clinician, was a model for this limited dyadic approach. He had come to Riggs from Chestnut Lodge where he had worked with legendary names of the times like Frieda Fromm-Reichmann, Harry Stack Sullivan, and Otto Will. During our fascinating supervisory sessions, besides offering many wise suggestions, he would talk about a central belief of his that I felt was his doctrine about therapy in the hospital: everything, according to Martin, was in the "transference with the therapist." The patient's involvement with the rest of the complicated structure of the hospital—the nurses, the peers, the activities staff—was, in his charming World War II Navy Captain lingo, pure "hogwash."

Cooperman's was a radical statement, but it still represented a deeply ingrained theory amongst a substantial proportion of hospitalist clinicians, as the monograph of Fromm-Reichmann illustrates (Fromm-Reichmann 1960). In this classical text, the theory is developed through the lens of individual psychoanalytic psychotherapy and there is not a single reference to the "hospital" as a system. Fromm-Reichmann also wrote about the importance of the hospital, but she did not articulate the importance of the system as clearly as her sophisticated theories on individual psychotherapy (Fromm-Reichmann 1947). Other influential psychoanalysts from Chestnut Lodge similarly focused on the analytic dyad without any significant references to the hospital as a therapeutic system (Pao 1979). Will (1964), who emphasized the importance of the context that enveloped the dyad, is one of the exceptions among the prominent clinicians who have mostly ignored the importance and the workings of the larger system.

While Fromm-Reichmann remained exclusively focused on the individual work, there were some other budding trends amongst hospitalists; in striking contrast to the "dyadic" perspective of Reichmann, Will Menninger was developing a sophisticated and meticulous guide for an effective integration of therapeutic community into the patient's treatment at the Menninger hospital in Topeka (Menninger 1939/1982). And in contrast to the predominantly dyadic theories of clinicians from Lodge, over the course of decades, the staff at Menninger continued to highlight the importance of the substructures of the whole system (Kernberg 1973; Gabbard 1992). The Cassell hospital in the United Kingdom also developed a long tradition that gives equal importance to psychotherapy, nursing, and social treatment (Main 1957/1989; Griffits and Pringle 1991; Day and Pringle 2001).

The most recent effort to theorize on the psychotherapeutic hospital, which I was a part of, came out of Riggs (Plakun 2011). My main critique of this excellent group work is the lack of a cohesive theory shared by most. As I read through the chapters, I notice two main theoretical threads. The dominant one, perhaps including myself to a degree, is a common trend in the writings of individual therapists: it is a modified Coopermanian stance that takes the individual psychotherapeutic work as the central intervention. By placing individual psychoanalytic psychotherapy in the context of a holding/containing environment, this stance is a step more integrative than Cooperman's but lacks an elaborate understanding of the therapeutic functions of the containing structure. These structures are formulated as a nonspecific support system in which patients need to be "attended to" in between therapy sessions, or at the most, they are a venue for "displaced or dispersed transferences" of the therapeutic dyad (Shapiro 2011). The second, more silent theoretical thread emerges in some other chapters written mostly by staff working in the community and with families. In these chapters, the attempt to formulate the significant multiple therapeutic venues of the hospital becomes more dominant (Tillman 2011; Krikorian and Fowler 2011; Schwartz 2011; Elmendorf et al. 2011).

Multiple Therapeutic Planes, Multiple Transferences

As I approached the end of my active hospitalist career, I began to take stock of that phase of my work, and I sluggishly articulated to myself what I thought was a different and original way of thinking; a synthesis of what was somewhat dormant in the way I intuitively operated throughout many decades.

However when I decided to turn these personal reflections of mine to the project of a book, a systematic review of the literature and conversations with clinicians like Glen Gabbard made me realize that some previous clinicians had developed approaches similar to mine (Gabbard 1992, 2014; Griffits and Pringle 1991; Day and Pringle 2001). It was an ambivalent surprise; I was somewhat disappointed over the loss of the fantasy of my originality, and at the same time felt solidly supported in my thinking.

This recognition reminded me of the wise words of Merton Gill, an alumnus of my alma mater, Riggs: "The points I have made are not new. They are present in varying degrees of clarity and emphasis throughout our literature. But like so many other aspects of psychoanalytic theory and practice, they fade in and out of prominence and are rediscovered again and again, possibly occasionally with some modest conceptual advance, but often with a newness attributable only to ignorance of past contributions" (Gill 1979, 286).

At this point in my professional life, as I close the chapter of my active hospitalist career with this book, I am of the opinion that we still do not have a good theory of the workings of these unique human experiments, and there clearly is need for scholarly historical evaluation. To contribute to this historical evaluation, I will summarize my understanding of the workings of the hospital as follows:

1. I hold on to the surprisingly simple "equipotent" view that all of the available therapeutic interventions in the therapeutic hospital—individual therapy, family work, nursing, groups, milieu, and art departments—are potentially equally powerful and important.

2. These therapeutic planes have the capacity to potentiate the efficacy of the work of each other.
3. With certain patients, some venues may become centrally important.
4. With most patients, the centrality of the venues may wax and wane; the focus of the work tends to shift in the hospital as demonstrated by some treatments I have written about.

To demonstrate these assertions:

Individual psychoanalytic therapy may be the central element for a deeply schizoid woman who can barely get out of her room or is silent in the group meetings and in the community. But the same patient may find a second venue of help in the arts department through a very solid friendship with an art instructor.

Another patient wreaks havoc in the community by acting out and getting into aggressive confrontations with the staff and peers; and at that moment the core learning may be the way in which the community develops firm boundaries around the patient's aggression. The staff and peers, either individually or in meetings, confront the patient in a nonretaliatory way. And then once the patient retreats out of a deep sense of humiliation, the peers and the staff do not allow the patient to disappear by isolating himself in the room either. Thus, a perfect opportunity for containment emerges, as it is described Wilfred Bion (1962), to help the patient to tame, learn about, and talk about his aggression as it explodes and implodes. In other words, the milieu tackles the transference/countertransference scripts of the patient and offers the opportunity of the development of new ones.

Or one might have a sixty-year-old female patient who is in the hospital after an impulsive suicide attempt. The work stalls after several months of steady progress, and she starts feeling more depressed. After a thorough evaluation as a team, the therapist realizes that the husband is struggling with unresolved grief and is unconsciously projecting an aspect of this to the patient in the hospital. This projective nidus of resistance to the development of treatment is effectively brought into treatment through regular, intense couples work. Then the patient gains momentum once again.

Last but not least, there may be a person with quite severe psychosis, who is only capable of coming to his sessions but utilizes the night nurse as another important person. This relationship with the night nurse becomes as important as the therapeutic dyad.

Hence the hospital provides an enormous array of transference potentialities in the persons of staff and peers, and offers opportunities to work on group transferences.

Now, let us try to deepen our analysis a few steps further.

Who Benefits from the Psychotherapeutic Hospital?

Ernst Simmel, the founder of Schloss Tegel, the first psychoanalytic hospital, had a prescient answer to this question. He wrote about a subset of patients in psychoanalysis where the clinical problem that presented itself in the person of the patient was, in actuality, one symptom of a "collective neurosis." In contrast to the "manifest" neurosis of the patient, the people around the patient had complementary "latent" neuroses. Simmel further stated that every movement in analysis had corresponding movements in the mental lives of important others, and made another prescient formulation: "It is true that sometimes analytic treatment of the individual as an out-patient has succeeded in effecting the psychic cure of a whole circle of people. But more often in the cases which I have known I have observed a 'negative-therapeutic result' in the other people (those associated with the patient)" (Simmel 1929, 73). To avoid this negative outcome, he recommended treatment in a psychoanalytic sanatorium (Simmel 1929).

In contemporary writings of psychoanalytic hospitalists, the psychotherapeutic hospital as an alternative to some aspects of biologically driven psychiatric treatment is a notion that is well articulated. What I would like to expand on is the less studied observation that Simmel (1929) alluded to some ninety years ago, an observation that seems to have receded to the sidelines: psychotherapeutic hospitals are powerfully effective when the patient has been in long-term psychodynamic work or in psychoanalysis with competent clinicians.

In fact, in my experience, a substantial proportion of the patients come to the psychotherapeutic hospital mostly because they have stalled in outpatient long-term psychodynamic therapy or psychoanalysis; these are patients who are, for a number of reasons, in need of "multiple treater settings" (Gabbard 2014). These stalled treatments are reversed and significant intrapsychic/interpersonal development is achieved through the massive intervention of psychotherapeutic hospital (Blatt and Ford 1994).

Why and How Is the Psychotherapeutic Hospital Effective?

One interesting window into understanding the efficacy of the psychotherapeutic hospital is an observation made by a few clinicians.

In his classical essay, Tom Main (1957) observed that there was a subset of patients who would evoke intense interest and grandiose aspirations in their treaters. The patient would often be referred to them after a failed treatment effort, and the new team who took over the treatment would feel that all of the previous persons who tried to help the patient had failed to understand her. Their initial therapeutic exhilaration would be followed by a series of fascinating group dynamics that would end up with the development of an "in group" surrounding the patient with therapeutic zeal and an "out group" that would be quite hopeless about the treatment, and sometimes outright hostile to the patient. The treaters with the therapeutic zeal would eventually feel they were ineffective, and with a deep sense of resentment, defer the patient to another set of treaters. And the cycle would go on.

Gabbard expanded on this observation with the concept of the "special patient," evocatively describing the regressed relationships within the therapeutic dyads: "The referring clinician is often unduly optimistic about the prognosis of his patient, but only if the patient is treated in a highly sensitive manner. The referrer often attempts to stipulate in great detail exactly how the patient should be handled and provides dire admonitions if there is any departure from the stipulated approach. He will typically assert that the reason for previous treatment failures is because the treaters were not sensitive to the proper way to approach the patient. Frequently, the referring clinician has become overinvolved with the patient to an alarming extent" (Gabbard 1986, 339).

The phenomena that Main and Gabbard are referring to is what I call the "lowest common denominator of hospital patients": Regression to dyadic symbioses through the primitive defenses of splitting and projective identification.

If we were to agree with this hypothesis, then one way to look at a central function of the hospital is that it serves as a "third" to the regressed dyads as they evolve in transference, through "repetition compulsion," within the matrices of the hospital. But the therapeutic environment of the hospital, the "third," provides an opportunity to go beyond repeating; it is an opportunity for repetition and reparation.

In the writings of some clinicians, the "third" has a different meaning as it applies to the dyadic psychoanalytic space (Ogden 2004; Muller 2011). I am proposing to concretize and expand it further beyond a concept that is held within the minds of a twosome; the third as an actual person or group or a system, with its counterregressive capabilities that can supplement the Ogdenian "third" as a moral, ethical, clinical treatment concept held by the minds of the twosome in the dyadic therapeutic space.

Let us go back to another of Simmel's observations through the case of Al to expand on this.

The "Negative Therapeutic Reaction"

> *Porphyria's Lover*
> That moment she was mine, mine, fair,
> Perfectly pure and good: I found
> A thing to do, and all her hair
> In one long yellow string I wound
> Three times her little throat around
> And strangled her . . .
> —*Robert Browning*

It is a mystery why some of our patients, when provided the best of treatments, get worse after an initial significant positive response (Riviere 1936; Bird 1972; Cooperman 1989; Grabel 2008). At first sight, it was not clear why Al or Judy deteriorated after several years of good therapeutic work and substantial improvement, or why Henry attempted suicide after stabilization in the therapeutic farm. These were all probably cases representing the enigmatic phenomenon of the "negative therapeutic reaction."

The work in the psychotherapeutic hospital suggests a surprising paradoxical linguistic solution to this perennial dilemma; these patients probably get worse "because" they were provided the best of treatments and had an initial significant improvement.

Hypotheses on the Negative Therapeutic Reaction: The Object-Representation

It is clear to all of us analysts that in psychoanalysis, as we offer ourselves as potential new transference objects, we evoke a jealous competition with the object pole of the "self and object representational scripts." As the patient tries to accept us as a new object in the psychoanalytic matrix, the old intrapsychic/interpersonal object scripts are awakened, and the new love object settles into the internal/external life of the patient with extensive reshuffling.

In the realm of severe pathology, in contrast to the neurotic "reshuffling," there is deep, deadly jealousy over including a new love object amongst the old loves of the patient. To use a visual metaphor, the intrapsychic/interpersonal space is limited, and it is almost impossible to include a new love object into that space, unless an old object is discarded. Thus the transference invitation of the therapist evokes a deadly competition as suggested by the stories of Al, Judy, and Kate. When the analyst attempts to become another important person in the patient's life, the fantasy that "somebody has to die" emerges with force, evoking annihilation anxieties. Annihilation anxieties (Benveniste et al. 1998; Hurvich 2003) are not just intrapsychic dreads, but also literal interpersonal anxieties. And thus the "negative" therapeutic reaction. If we carry this line of thinking further, the so-called negative therapeutic reaction may in fact be a "positive" reaction because it prevents death.

Hypotheses on the Negative Therapeutic Reaction: The Self-Representation

In the area of primitive pathologies, the situation is further complicated because the "self" pole of the internal object relations gets into the mix. One of Al's roots of resistance to his attachment to me as a new object was his deep sense of jealousy over cathecting anyone but himself, or more specifically, any mind other than his. Harold Searles (1986) pointed to this phenomenon with his concept of "intrapsychic jealousy." A triadic concept, jealousy, in the world of primitive pathologies can easily become a dyadic phenomenon. Similarly envy, a dyadic concept, may regress to an intrapsychic phenomenon and become self-envy, as Al was unable to hold his mind and his body together in his mind at the same time (Maizels 1985; Kernberg 1980).

To summarize, with our invitation of becoming a new, good-enough object that will help the patient repeat and repair the self and object representational scripts, we get into an intrapsychic and interpersonal decathexis and recathexis that inevitably evokes internal and external jealousies, competitions, and resistances within the old internal scripts and actual relations of the patient. This may lead to a psychotic breakdown, an immediate negative therapeutic reaction, before the therapy starts, as the work of Daniel Schwartz demonstrates (Schwartz 1990).

How Does the Psychotherapeutic Hospital Interfere with Annihilation Anxieties?

Freud taught us about the power of transference, of bringing the history of the patient alive between the person of the analyst and the patient (Freud 1912). In the psychotherapeutic hospital, we go a step further and bring the actual actors of the transference script on the scene through family work. When these important others, who carry an aspect of the defensive constellation, are brought to treatment, the bipersonal defenses are directly confronted and analyzed. Thus we create an opportunity to tackle the severe anxieties of all relevant persons; not in the effigy of transference but in their real, actual selves. In this process, the parents' differentiation from their own parents is also facilitated as a parallel processes that goes hand in hand with the patients' differentiation from their parents.

Second, in the dyadic maternal/paternal transference with the therapist, the patient has the option of experimenting with different intrapsychic/interpersonal solutions than those he had encountered in his historical development. He is allowed and even encouraged to further expand his attachments, to explore and find new objects amongst the many available in the hospital beyond the person of the therapist. As demonstrated by the patients' histories recounted here, these new objects might be found in the person of a nurse, a friend in the milieu, a substance abuse counselor, and many others.

Third, the patients who need the intervention of the psychotherapeutic hospital have, to use it as a shorthand, "fixations" in many layers of their development. Their treatment in the hospital allows the simultaneous evocation of vertical, lateral, and group transference scripts to address these; the pre-Oedipal tasks of developing a solid dyadic relationships, and then moving to the resolution of the triadic structure of Oedipal development, sibling dynamics, and transference scripts with the other important persons in the family, then the post-Oedipal, latency, adolescent tasks of establishing relationships beyond the family, and so on. Thus many of the stages of development are addressed in parallel, unlike the sequential transference plates that develop in individual therapy

All of these make the psychotherapeutic hospital an impressive therapeutic human ecology capable of achieving what we can't in our offices.

Risks of Psychotherapeutic Hospitals—Creating Excessive Dependency

The therapeutic hospital can bring enormous benefits to the stalled/deteriorating outpatient psychotherapeutic treatments. Nevertheless, like any other powerful therapeutic intervention, psychotherapeutic hospitals have their unique risks.

The most important risk is probably the potential for the supportive aspect of the hospital to develop into an endless source of dependency for the patient (Chiesa et al. 2003). As an example, a central problem in Al's development was that a whole set of human relationships were brought to him, he had not sought them on the outside; the immigrant family and his uncle were implanted into his household. Thus the hospital, in certain ways, became a repetition of the regressed aspects of his life where the outside world was brought to him. Hence, a central task for Al became to figure out ways to get out of the house/hospital. He managed to accomplish it through his love affair and joining the band and the golf club where he became a member of some peer groups—tasks he had missed out on during his adolescence.

To address this potential problem of excessive dependency, these hospital systems have developed spaces where the therapeutic reflective activity is suspended, regression is stemmed beyond a point, and the patient's autonomy and mature interdependence is supported. At Riggs, through the activities department and the concept of "resident patient," the adaptive capabilities of the patient are nourished as a counterbalance to the therapeutic regression (Sacksteder, personal communication 2015). At Retreat, there are active Eastern-philosophy-oriented modalities that encourage spaces of nonlinear reflection (Ross, personal communication,

2015). At Menninger, patients are encouraged to be involved in rigorous physical exercise and meditation on a daily basis. And the Cassell hospital encourages patients to actively participate in the daily routines of the hospital, from cooking to cleaning (Griffits and Pringle 1991; Day and Pringle 2001). In addition, all of these systems have stepdown programs through which the patient is gradually exposed to life outside of the confines of these campuses, thus helping the patient to gradually come out of dependency on the hospital and reintegrate with the outside world.

One interesting historical experiment on how to counter the regressive pull of the hospital comes from the seemingly unrelated field of military psychiatry. During the World War I, before any psychotherapeutic hospital was around, French military doctors developed some fundamentally important insights into the problem of dealing with "shell shocked" soldiers. These military doctors noticed that the patients would exhibit enormous amounts of resistance to going back to the battlefield if they had been evacuated to a hospital that was far away from the war zone. Gaining historical support from the observations made during the 1905 Russo-Japanese war, the French doctors came up with the ingenious idea of keeping the treatment close to the war zone, naming the idea as the "principle of proximity." This central dictum of warfare psychiatric treatment proved to be an effective intervention in restoring the soldiers back to their roles. In time, through many wars in many different lands, military psychiatrists developed some other principles for dealing with psychological trauma during combat (Binneveld 1997). This fascinating work seems very familiar to the struggles of a hospitalist psychoanalyst, where we always try to find an optimum level of therapeutic regression.

Risks—Destructive Regressions of the Staff and the Milieu

The interpersonal matrix that treats all members as citizens regardless of whether they are members of the staff or patients is a double-edged sword. This type of environment can be very helpful, but it can also easily become stagnant or hostile as we know from the dynamics of group regressions, seen in the cases of Al and Henry. It is easier to think about patient regressions, but what is subtler and more destructive is the propensity for nontherapeutic regressions in staff (Kernberg 1973; Shapiro 1987).

In these systems, the personal lives of the staff are deeply affected by their work, much more so then acute inpatient units or private practitioners. This phenomenon is partly due to the staff developing strong, unique attachments and transferences to the patients with whom they work with for prolonged periods. It is also facilitated by the fact that, with the group structures of team and the therapeutic community, the staff develop intra-staff connections and dynamics. While this experience is necessary for the treatment of serious pathology, it carries the unavoidable risk of group regressions within the staff, much more frequently and intensely than other hospital or outpatient settings. This propensity for staff regression can easily turn therapeutic capabilities to mediums of attack and destruction.

Risks—Transferences to the Hospital as an Encapsulated System; Idealization/Devaluation

These unique systems that can work with patients for extended periods are rare in contemporary psychiatry, so they become magnets for idealization and devaluation. In the eyes of outsiders, the hospitals may become objects of admiration; they may be seen as "the" places for ultimate treatment, places that are unique in what they can achieve. Or they may be seen through the lens of hostile envy and contempt; as "dinosaurs," places for the "worried well." The staff may also vacillate between a sense of guilty entitlement, grandiosity, and irrelevance amongst the larger panorama of contemporary psychiatric treatment.

In parallel, in this lonely space, the lack of sister systems may push the psychotherapeutic hospital to severe intellectual and clinical isolation as a system, further fueling the dynamics mentioned above. In other words, these wonderful systems show a dangerous tendency of treating the vast majority of the general psychiatric system as an "other" and thus inviting being treated as an "other" by general psychiatry. It is important, therefore, that we all be reminded of the larger context in order to help the staff to have a realistic view of their central functions: psychotherapeutic hospitals are not institutions where the cure of the psychiatric ailment is achieved. Rather, they are places where stalled outpatient psychotherapeutic treatments are put back on track.

I will end with the wise warning of Dr. Harry Stack Sullivan. Sullivan, through his pioneering work with schizophrenic patients, reminded us that "we are much more simply human than otherwise." It is important that those of us who are working in psychotherapeutic hospitals should remember that "we are much more simply a hospital than otherwise."

9

CONVERSATIONS WITH PSYCHOTHERAPEUTIC HOSPITALISTS

As can be seen in my communication with Dr. Gabbard, I posed a series of questions to some psychoanalytic hospitalists. I asked these clinicians, who have led prominent systems, to use my questions as a loose scaffolding and talk about their experiences in, and ideas about, psychotherapeutic hospitals. In this appendix are the responses of these clinicians.

THE MENNINGER CLINIC

Glen O. Gabbard, MD

Glen O. Gabbard, MD is a clinical professor of psychiatry at Baylor College of Medicine in Houston. He is also a training and supervising analyst at the Center for Psychoanalytic Studies in Houston. From 2001 to 2011, he was Brown Foundation chair and director of the Baylor Clinic before going into private practice. From 1989 to 1994, he was director of the Menninger Hospital and vice president for Adult Services. From 1996 to 2001, he was director of the Topeka Institute for Psychoanalysis.

1) *Please provide a summary of current general parameters of your hospital; the number of beds, yearly admissions, length of stay, staffing, and basics of programming.*

I do not know the current parameters of the Menninger Hospital. I can only answer the questions based on the era in which I worked there.

When I was there, it was a 166-bed hospital with an average length of stay that started out at eleven months and fell precipitously during my five-year term. We also had to close units and lay people off because Topeka was a nonmetropolitan area. So as the length of stay fell, the occupancy fell since it was hard to get local admissions. I don't remember the details of staffing or the yearly admissions. When I started in 1989, there were four long-term units, one chemical dependency unit with shorter stays, one crisis and emergency unit with very short stays, and one intermediate unit with six- to eight-week stays and a therapeutic community that relied heavily on groups. While I was in the position, I started the PIC unit, replacing the intermediate unit, a self-mutilating unit, and a trauma unit.

2) *How would you define and differentiate your hospital in the larger scheme of therapeutic hospitals in history?*

Menninger was one of the earliest psychoanalytic hospitals and was based on the work of Simmel. It then progressed to a drive-based approach under the direction of Will Menninger. When I inherited the hospital, Kernberg had transformed it into an object relations approach, which I continued.

3) *How are you, at the moment, different from other residential settings and other psychotherapeutic hospitals?*

I don't know enough about the current situation.

4) *Why/when is there a need for hospital in the treatment of an individual? Differentiate the hospital in relation to psychiatry and psychoanalysis, psychodynamic psychotherapy.*

Psychodynamic psychotherapy does not provide an around-the-clock structure like a hospital does. Neither does outpatient psychiatry or psychoanalysis. In ego psychology terms, the structure and the relationships and activities build ego for patients who have ego deficits. There are reparative techniques that address ego weaknesses like judgment, impulse control, etc. with peer pressure brought to bear. There is also a reparenting aspect to the treatment. It goes without saying, of course, that the structure prevents (sometimes) a chronically suicidal patient from acting on the wish to die.

5) *How do you formulate the mechanisms of effectiveness of your psychotherapeutic hospital?*

When I was running the hospital, I met once a month with the psychiatrists who ran the teams, and we would make a systematic effort to apply psychoanalytic thinking to hospital treatment. Much of it was based on a combination of object relations theory and ego-building as described above. The patient comes into the hospital and unconsciously recreates his internal world in the milieu. Different internal self and object representations are projected onto others in the milieu, and then via projective identification, that which is projected comes alive in another person and can be understood and processed. Splitting is a good example of this phenomenon as described in my paper Splitting in Hospital Treatment in the 1989 *American Journal of Psychiatry* and in the 1986 *International Review of Psychoanalysis* called "The Treatment of the Special Patient in a Psychoanalytic Hospital." The milieu offers an opportunity for the patient to understand his longstanding relational patterns as they are played out with others and systematically examined.

6) *What kind of patient population is the psychotherapeutic hospital good at working with?*

When I ran the hospital, personality disorders were the group that the hospital did the best work with. I don't know about now.

7) *When is the hospital ineffective or may even be destructive?*

When the patient is psychopathic or when the patient has absolutely no motivation for treatment. Also when a patient is unreachable because of schizoid or autistic phenomena.

8) *What does the future hold for the psychotherapeutic hospital?*

I do not know, but the economics of long-term care is a huge problem.

HACETTEPE

M. Orhan Öztürk, MD, professor emeritus of psychiatry and former chairman, Department of Psychiatry, Hacettepe University School of Medicine, Ankara, Turkey

I completed my psychiatric residency at the Department of Psychiatry, University of Tennessee Medical School in 1957, and had an advanced fellowship training in psychoanalytic psychotherapy at the Austen Riggs Center (1957–1959) where I later worked as a member of staff (1970–1972).

My first experience at the Austen Riggs Center was at a time when Riggs was at the height of her fame as a psychoanalytic hospital and was an elite training and research center under the leadership of Robert P. Knight. As a brilliant clinician and tactful administrator, Knight had created a distinguished institute in the small New England town of Stockbridge and made it an attractive center for some very influential psychoanalysts of the times such as Erik H. Erikson and David Rapaport, amongst others. In the early 1970s when I came back as a member of staff, Riggs was still a highly respected training and treatment center under Otto A. Will and Erik H. Erikson.

In 1960, I became a faculty at the Department of Psychiatry in Ankara University Medical School, and in 1964, I joined Hacettepe Medical School. Hacettepe was a recently founded system, an ambitious project targeting to be the top hospital/medical school in the country and I was recruited as one of the founders of the Department of Psychiatry. General psychiatry in Turkey at the time was heavily influenced by the biological approach of French and German schools. Psychoanalysis was known in intellectual circles but was almost nonexistent as a clinical approach. Within this larger context, I felt it was an opportune time to create a new system that had a strong psychodynamic ethos and I initiated a conversation with my colleagues, some of whom were also psychoanalytically trained. The task ahead of us was an exciting and challenging one.

Turkey was a different culture, thus it was obvious to me that we had to create an amalgam that needed some modifications of the model I worked in at Riggs. This required intense and extended group thinking; we had endless discussions and debates with colleagues on how to create a psychotherapeutic structure from ground up. Interestingly, these extended to some architectural consultations on the internal physical structure of the new psychiatric unit we were developing.

We were able to bring this new project to life, at least in terms of the basic principles of psychoanalytically based dynamic psychiatry, in a few years. And at the core of our endeavor was our twenty-five-bed unit located in the Hacettepe General Hospital. It was a semiopen unit, with about an added load of twenty-five daytime patients. All patients were assigned a primary therapist and a primary nurse. We had psychologists, art instructors, and some mental health workers involved in the care. Individual dynamic therapy, cognitive behavioral therapy, groups, family work, and therapeutic community were the main psychotherapeutic structures of the unit. We were providing state-of-the art medication management and other biological services to the patients. The therapies were mainly conducted by psychiatry residents and psychology fellows while they were working under the intense supervision of faculty. The whole didactic teaching and clinical training curriculum for the medical students, clerks, interns, and residents was prepared with essentially psychodynamic orientation with special emphasis on the psychosocial developmental concepts such as the one formulated by Erikson.

We were trying to develop a new culture of a therapeutic environment, and this was initially mainly achieved through active training as well as group participation in evaluating and treating patients. We had to join the staff, residents, interns, students, nurses, activity teachers, and other personnel like secretaries and attendants in a common understanding in regard to approaching patients. Our intense initial educative efforts paid off, and in time we created traditions of a new culture that were now organically transferred from one generation to the other within the department.

One central aspect of Hacettepe philosophy was our respect for patients' autonomy and dignity as persons. Notwithstanding that they were suffering from serious conditions, we tried to convey to our younger colleagues and the patients this sense of commonality. With our residents, basic principles and subtleties of doctor–patient relationships were continuously emphasized in different venues such as team rounds, meetings, case conferences, and supervision sessions.

A brief description of the physical structure of the twenty-five-bed inpatient unit with an additional twenty to twenty-five partial patients in it may more concretely clarify the nature of the psychotherapeutic hospital in Hacettepe. As we were working on the philosophy and the therapeutic programs of the new unit, a central task was to create a unit in a general hospital where the patients would not regress to excesses of dependence like the medical surgical wards, but have their adaptive capabilities active all throughout their stay. So, we made significant physical alterations to the unit. We created large living spaces where the patients would gather with staff, have friendly conversations, and join group or therapeutic community meetings. There was also a substantial space allocated for art where the patients would get involved in various arts-and-crafts projects with the help of instructors. As we tried to keep patients from isolating, we had a similar approach to the staff. We placed the nursing station and the consulting rooms in the middle section of the unit, again to avoid staff isolation. We were striving to develop a physical structure that would enhance the sense of a small staff and patient community living together in a ward of a massive general hospital.

Our patients were initially a bit surprised with this arrangement. Having been to hospital wards where the delineation between staff and patients were dramatic, in a culture where the "doctor" is almost deified, this democratization of relations, without necessarily blurring of the roles, appeared as an interesting experiment for our patients. I would like to remind the reader that when this system was built, Turkey was still a mostly rural country, and we had many patients coming from villages and small towns.

After fifty years, I am quite fulfilled with the end results of this experiment that I led with other dedicated colleagues. The psychodynamic approach is established as a solid part of Turkish psychiatric thinking and was influential in changing the approach to hospitalist work in Turkey. When I reflect back on this half a century of work, all of these developments that I have been a part of give me a sense of integrity, as my esteemed teacher Erikson (1956) would put it.

THE AUSTEN RIGGS CENTER

James L Sacksteder, MD, former medical director/CEO, The Austen Riggs Center, Stockbridge, Massachusetts

The Center's mission is threefold.

First, it is to provide superb clinical care to patients with very serious emotional difficulties. Second and third, to engage in research and education about the issues that are raised by the patients' clinical problems.

Here are some of the defining aspects of Riggs:

Riggs is an open hospital. The patient has to decide to seek treatment here and has to decide to remain in treatment. By an open setting we mean we have no seclusions or restraints, and we do not take any patient on a commitment basis. People are free to come and go twenty-four hours a day, seven days a week. So they are actively deciding each day to stay and engage in treatment.

The other important element is our psychodynamic approach to understanding the nature of the difficulties of the patients and intervening with them. Psychodynamic approach integrates contributions coming from nursing, therapeutic community program, social work departments with their work with the families of our patients, the psychopharmacological interventions, and individual psychoanalytic therapy. Our patients are in four-times-a-week therapy, something virtually unheard of in contemporary American psychiatry.

Another part is that we offer a therapeutic community where the patient engages in a process that we call "examined living." That involves patients as active agents of change with one another as well as members of staff as agents of change. It is a centrally important venue where the behavior of patients and staff are translated into words, and the patient has a chance to understand how he is impacting others through his actions and behavior. Patients and staff give feedback in relation to how they relate to one another all the time.

We have an activities program that is located in a separate building where the patient becomes a student in relation to a teacher in painting, weaving, and woodworking, amongst many other arts-and-craft forms. It is a staff-free zone of the hospital, a space that exclusively belongs to teachers and their students.

So in our system, the person admitted to Riggs is a patient in treatment, and at the same time a citizen in the open hospital and a student in the activities program. This helps the patients maintain their highest level of functioning and counterbalances the ordinary therapeutic regressive pulls of the hospital.

Finally, our approach is not additive but integrative. The patient works with the same team throughout the entire course of her stay, from highest level of care to the point where she may be in our day program where she is virtually an outpatient with minimal ties to the hospital.

THE RETREAT AT SHEPPARD PRATT

Donald Ross, MD, former medical director

Medical degree: Michigan State University, graduated 1978
Psychiatric residency: Duke University, completed 1982; chief resident 1983
Psychoanalytic training: Washington Psychoanalytic Institute, completed 1989

Sheppard Pratt Hospital: staff psychiatrist, 1983–present
Director of education and residency training: Sheppard Pratt, 1987–2001
Medical director: The Retreat at Sheppard Pratt, 2002–2015
Clinical associate professor of psychiatry: University of Maryland SOM
Director of psychotherapy training: UMD/Sheppard Pratt Psychiatry RT Program
Supervising and training analyst: Washington Psychoanalytic Institute

Sheppard Pratt Health System is a large, multicenter, comprehensive mental health center with its main campus in Towson, Maryland, where it is anchored by a psychiatric hospital that has been in service since 1891. For many years, it was a national tertiary site for long-term treatment using a psychoanalytic framework. Harry Stack Sullivan did his pioneering work on interpersonal psychiatry in the 1920s as the head of the men's long-term unit. These patients were thought to be schizophrenics who had little chance of recovery; Sullivan saw them as "much more human than otherwise" and developed ways of engaging them in dynamic psychotherapy. There was a close relationship with Chestnut Lodge (fifty miles away in Rockville, Maryland), both competitive and cooperative. In the 1960s, Bob Gibson and Clarence Schulz came from Chestnut Lodge and assumed leadership of Sheppard, Gibson as medical director, and Schulz as director of training. Both trained at the Washington Psychoanalytic, and both were strongly influenced by Frieda Fromm-Reichmann and Otto Will.

Schulz was my mentor, along with Jane Lichtenberg and Judith Chused at the Washington Psychoanalytic Institute. I spent a number of years working on a long-term adult unit just around the time managed care came in and rearranged how inpatient psychiatry was practiced (1985–2000). We went from a 323-bed hospital (95 percent filled), dedicated to long-term dynamic work with a national patient base (and a vestigial outpatient program) to a regional-based institution with a new integrated continuum of care and specialty units (eating disorders, trauma disorders, neuropsychiatry, dual diagnosis, etc.). We had less actively filled beds (closer to two hundred) and many, many more admissions and total patients. Under the remarkable leadership of the new medical director Steven Sharfstein (1986–present), we evolved quickly and stayed relevant during this period of rapid change in American psychiatry. Long-term hospital treatment was relinquished, and alternatives using other residential and intensive outpatient options were explored and embraced. We grew as a health system even as the "hospital" part was reduced.

In 2002, the Sheppard leadership felt there was a need (and an opportunity) to revisit long-term dynamic residential care outside of the purview of third-party payment. Enough families would pay privately for the care that was missing. The Retreat was born under my leadership and involved the following principles:

1. Safe, intensive residential treatment for patients who have been unable to benefit from the new model of brief inpatient stays;
2. Intermediate stays (one to three or more months) with equal emphasis on building mastery alongside allowing necessary therapeutic regression;
3. Intensive, expert psychodynamic psychotherapy (individual, group based, and milieu based);
4. Expert biomedical assessment and state-of-the-art medical and psychopharmacological interventions;
5. Adjunctive use of "Eastern wisdom" approaches to treatment such as yoga, t'ai chi chuan, and mindfulness meditation, along with a wellness focus from the alternative medicine perspective;
6. Later, a robust CBT/DBT component was added and then expanded to complement the other three pillars of treatment philosophy; and
7. Finally, an integrative rather than competitive approach, recognizing that all therapy happens through a healing relationship. Everyone (doctors, nurses, and therapists) would embrace the values of compassion, respect, and mutuality in the treatment of patients.

We became licensed as an extended-care facility (not a hospital unit) for various reasons, including reimbursement options and the relationship to the larger Sheppard Pratt Health System. There is no seclusion room and the doors are unlocked. We have excluded patients we felt needed a more contained environment, such as acutely suicidal, actively psychotic, and organically confused patients. We have had such patients stabilize on one of the acute inpatient units at Sheppard and later transferred them to the Retreat when appropriate. We also have excluded patients we felt would not be able to work in a therapeutic milieu.

Over time, we have found we are particularly helpful to patients with complex mood disorders, complex anxiety disorders, borderline personality disorder, and patients with co-occurring psychiatric and substance abuse disorders. Many of our patients have other personality disorders complicating their initial presenting complaints, which has made it difficult to treat them under more typical outpatient conditions. We do not do as well with withdrawn covertly psychotic patients, although we have had some success here. We do poorly with "toxic" negative personality disordered patients, who have proven too powerful in "poisoning" the therapeutic milieu. (Part of this may be due to our small size.) We handle narcissistic personality disordered patients relatively well most of the time, and that could be considered a strength of the program.

One of the unique aspects of the Retreat is that all primary therapists are board certified psychiatrists trained in psychodynamic psychotherapy. We have a strong sense of team and an ethos of egalitarianism with other therapy staff and nursing staff. There is a strong effort to empower staff to use all of their innate talents and healing qualities in their work. We emphasize learning from the patients and from each other. Consequently, the team is able to absorb the tensions of long-term work with very difficult-to-treat patients and maintain a sense of compassion and positivity. We have also been able to develop some unique integrative treatments on our unit, including creative uses of DBT, art therapy, equine therapy, healing the self (combining psychoanalytic and spiritual perspectives), psychophysical balance (combining t'ai chi chuan principles and existential psychotherapy), and so on. Much of this has come about from staff feeling empowered to develop programming that connected with their interests and clinical needs.

The future is exciting and uncertain (as it always is when seen with open eyes). We recently opened Ruxton House, a group home for Retreat "graduates" who need more time to heal in a therapeutic setting, but are able to work more independently and begin to integrate into community-based life (school, work, volunteering, etc.). There is room to expand this. We have a collaborative relationship with Clearview Community in Frederick, Maryland, which is a private-pay program for patients with chronic mental illness that involves several levels of residential and outpatient care. We are building our co-occurring disorders programming, and we have a good relationship with Kolmac Clinic on our campus. There are opportunities to promote other collaborations, such as with the

Anxiety and Stress Disorders Institute and our Neuropsychiatry Program. On the other hand, the world of private-pay "premier" units is growing; they are potential competitors. We need to be more effective in differentiating ourselves from these programs and marketing our advantages to the appropriate referring therapists, families, and patients.

REFERENCES

Akhtar, S. (1987). Schizoid Personality Disorder: A Synthesis of Developmental, Dynamic, and Descriptive Features. *American Journal of Psychotherapy* 151:499–518.
———. (Ed.). (2011). *Unusual Interventions: Alterations of the Frame, Method and Relationship in Psychotherapy and Psychoanalysis*. London: Karnac.
Akiskal, H. S., Bourgeois, M. L., Angst, J., Post, R., Moller, H. J., Hirschfeld, R. M. A. (2000). Re-Evaluating the Prevalence of and Diagnostic Composition within the Broad Clinical Spectrum of Bipolar Disorders. *Journal of Affective Disorders* 59 (Supplement 1): 5s–30s.
Allen, J. G., Fonagy, P., and Bateman, A. W. (2008). Mentalizing. In *Mentalizing in Clinical Practice*, 25–71. Arlington, VA: American Psychiatric Publishing.
Arlow, J. A. (1995). Stilted Listening: Psychoanalysis as Discourse. *Psychoanal. Q.* 64:215–33.
———. (2002). Transference as Defense. *J. Amer. Psychoanal. Assn.* 50:1139–150.
Bell, D. (1997). Inpatient Psychotherapy: The Art of the Impossible. *Psychoanal. Psychother.* 11:3–18.
Benveniste, P. S., Papouchis, N., Allen, R., and Hurvich, M. (1998). Rorschach Assessment of Annihilation Anxiety and Ego Functioning. *Psychoanal. Psychol.* 15:536–66.
Binneveld, H. (1997.) The Basic Principles of Military Psychiatry. In *From Shell Shock to Combat Stress: A Comparative History of Military Psychiatry*, 137–59. Translated from Dutch by Jon O'Kane. Amsterdam: Amsterdam University Press.
Bion, W. R. (1962). *Learning from Experience*. London: Tavistock.
Bird, B. (1957). A Specific Peculiarity of Acting Out. *Journal of the Psychoanalytic Association* 5:630–47.
———. (1972). Notes on Transference: Universal Phenomenon and Hardest Part of Analysis. *Journal of the Psychoanalytic Association* 20:267–301.
Blatt, S. J., and Ford, R. Q. (1994). *Therapeutic Change: An Object Relations Perspective*. New York and London: Plenum Press.
Blos, P. (1976). The Split Parental Imago in Adolescent Social Relations—An Inquiry into Group Psychology. *Psychoanal. St. Child* 31:7–33.
Blum, H. P. (1983). The Position and Value of Extratransference Interpretation. *J. Amer. Psychoanal. Assn.* 31:587–617.
———. (1994). The Conceptual Development of Regression. *Psychoanal. St. Child* 49:60–79.
Bollas, C. (1987). *The Shadow of the Object: Psychoanalysis of the Unthought Know n*. London: Free Association Books.
Boston Change Process Study Group. (2010). Non-Interpretative Mechanisms in Psychoanalytic Therapy. In *Change in Sychotherapy: A Unifying Paradigm*, 1–29. New York and London: Norton.

Bowen, M. (1978). Toward the Differentiation of Self in One's Family of Origin. In *Family Therapy in Clinical Practice*. New York: Jason Aronson.
Boyer, L. B. (1979). Countertransference with Severely Regressed Patients. In L. Epstein and A. H. Feiner (Eds.) *Countertransference*, 347–74. New York: Jason Aronson.
———. (1986). Technical Aspects of Treating the Regressed Patient. *Contemp. Psychoanal.* 22:25–44.
Busch, F. (1999). *Rethinking Clinical Technique*. Northwale, NJ and London: Jason Aronson.
Canestri, J. (Ed.). (2006). *Psychoanalysis: From Practice to Theory*. Chichester, UK: John Wiley and Sons.
Chiesa, M., Fonagy, P., and Holmes, J. (2003). When Less Is More. *Int. J. Psycho-Anal.* 84:637–50.
Cooperman, M. (1983). Some Observations Regarding Psychoanalytic Psychotherapy in a Hospital Setting. *The Psychiatric Hospital* 14 (1): 21–28.
———. (1989). Defeating Process in Psychotherapy. In *Psychoanalysis and Psychosis*. A. L. Silver (Ed.). Madison, CT: International Universities Press.
Couch, A. S. (2002). Extra-Transference Interpretation: A Defense of Classical Technique. *Psychoanal. St. Child* 57:63–92.
Daehnert, C. (1998). The False Self as a Means of Disidentification: A Psychoanalytic Case Study. *Contemp. Psychoanal.* 34:251–71.
Day L., and Pringle, P. (Eds.). (2001). *Reflective Enquiry into Therapeutic Institutions*. The Cassell Hospital Monograph Series No. 2. London and New York: Karnac.
Devereux, G. (1953). Why Oedipus Killed Laius—A Note on the Complementary Oedipus Complex in Greek Drama. *Int. J. Psycho-Anal.* 34:132–41.
Eissler, K. R. (1953). The Effect of the Structure of the Ego on Psychoanalytic Technique. *J. Amer. Psychoanal. Assn.* 1:104–43.
Elmendorf, D., and Parish, M. (2011). A View from Riggs: Silencing the Messenger—The Social Dynamics of Treatment Resistance. In E. M. Plakun (Ed.) *Treatment Resistance and Patient Authority: The Austen Riggs Reader*, 204–23. New York: Norton.
Erikson, E. H. (1956). The Problem of Ego Identity. *J. Amer. Psychoanal. Assn.* 4:56–121.
———. (1970). Reflections on the Dissent of Contemporary Youth. *Int. J. Psycho-Anal.* 51:11–22.
Feldman, M. (1992). Splitting and Projective Identification. *New Lib. of Psycho-Anal.* 14:74–88.
Fenichel, O. (1945). Neurotic Acting Out. *Psychoanal. Rev.* 32:197–206.
———. (1997). Projective Identification: The Analyst's Involvement. *Int. J. Psycho-Anal.* 78:227–24.
Fonagy P., and Target, M. (2003). *Psychoanalytic Theories: Perspectives from Developmental Psychopathology*. New York and London: Rutledge Taylor and Francis Group.
Freud, A. (1968). Acting Out. *Int. J. Psycho-Anal.* 49:165–17.
Freud, S. (1912). The Dynamics of Transference. *The Standard Edition of the Complete Psychological Works of Sigmund Freud, vol. 12 (1911–1913): The Case of Schreber, Papers on Technique and Other Works*, 97–108. London: The Hogarth Press and the Institute of Psychoanalysis.
———. (1918 [1914]). From the History of an Infantile Neurosis. *The Standard Edition of the Complete Psychological Works of Sigmund Freud, vol. 17 (1917–1919): An Infantile Neurosis and Other Works*, 1–124. London: The Hogarth Press and the Institute of Psychoanalysis.
———. (1925). An Autobiographical Study. *The Standard Edition of the Complete Psychological Works of Sigmund Freud, vol. 20 (1925–1926): An Autobiographical Study, Inhibitions, Symptoms and Anxiety, the Question of Lay Analysis and Other Works*, 1–74. London: The Hogarth Press and the Institute of Psychoanalysis.
———. (1940). Sketches for the "Preliminary Communication" of 1893. *The Standard Edition of the Complete Psychological Works of Sigmund Freud, vol. 1 (1886–1899): Pre-Psycho-Analytic Publications and Unpublished Drafts*, 145–54. London: The Hogarth Press and the Institute of Psychoanalysis.
Fromm-Reichmann, F. (1947). Problems of Therapeutic Management in a Psychoanalytic Hospital. *Psychoanal. Q.* 16:325–56.

———. (1960). *Principles of Intensive Psychotherapy*. Chicago: University of Chicago Press.
Gabbard, G. O. (1986). The Treatment of the "Special" Patient in a Psychoanalytic Hospital. *Int. R. Psycho-Anal.* 13:333–47.
———. (1992). The Therapeutic Relationship in Psychiatric Hospital Treatment. *Bull. Menninger Clinic* 56:4–19.
———. (1994). Sexual Excitement and Countertransference Love in the Analyst. *J. Amer. Psychoanal. Assn.* 42:1083–106.
———. (2000). What Can Neuroscience Teach Us about Transference? *Canadian J. Psychoanal.* 9:1–18.
———. (2014). Treatments in Dynamic Psychiatry: Multiple Treater Settings. In *Psychodynamic Practice in Clinical Practice*, 163–84, fifth edition. Washington, DC and London: American Psychiatric Publishing, American Psychiatric Press.
Gabbard, G. O., and Westen, D. (2003). Rethinking Therapeutic Action. *Int. J. Psycho-Anal.* 84:823–41.
Gartner, J. D. (2005). *The Hypomanic Edge: The Link between (a Little) Craziness and (a Lot of) Success in America*. New York: Simon and Schuster.
Gill, M. M. (1979). The Analysis of the Transference. *J. Amer. Psychoanal. Assn.* 27S:263–88.
Gilmore, K. (2005). Play in the Psychoanalytic Setting: Ego Capacity, Ego State, and Vehicle for Intersubjective Exchange. *Psychoanal. St. Child* 60:213–38.
Grabel, S. (2008). When Analysis Makes Patients Worse: The Negative Therapeutic Reaction Revisited. *J. Amer. Psychoanal. Assn.* 56:583–94.
Graham, I. (1988). The Sibling Object and Its Transferences: Alternate Organizer of the Middle Field. *Psychoanal. Inq.* 8:88–107.
Gray, P. (1990). The Nature of Therapeutic Action in Psychoanalysis. *J. Amer. Psychoanal. Assn.* 38:1083–96.
———. (1994). *The Ego and Analysis of Defense*. Northwale, NJ and London: Jason Aronson.
Griffits P., and Pringle, P. (Eds.). (1991). *Psychosocial Practice within a Residential Setting*. The Cassell Hospital Monograph Series No. 1. London: Karnac.
Grinberg, L. (1968). On Acting Out and Its Role in the Psychoanalytic Process. *Int. J. Psycho-Anal.* 49:171–78.
Heede, T., Runge, H., Storebø, O. J., Rowley, E., and Hansen, K. G. (2009). Psychodynamic Milieu-Therapy and Changes in Personality—What Is the Connection? *J. Child Psychother.* 35:276–89.
Hurvich, M. (2003). The Place of Annihilation Anxieties in Psychoanalytic Theory. *J. Amer. Psychoanal. Assn.* 51:579–616.
Johnson, A. M., and Szurek, S. A. (1952). The Genesis of Antisocial Acting Out in Children and Adults. *Psychoanal. Q.* 21:323–43.
Jones, M. (1953). *The Therapeutic Community: A New Treatment Method in Psychiatry*. New York: Basic Books.
Kayatekin, M. S. (2008). Christian–Muslim Relations: The Axis of Balkans and the West. In S. Akhtar (Ed.) *The Crescent and the Couch: Crosscurrents between Islam and Psychoanalysis*, 199–216. Lanham, MD: Jason Aronson.
Kayatekin, M. S., and Plakun, E. M. (2011). From Acting Out to Enactment in Treatment Resistant Disorders. In E. M. Plakun (Ed.) *Treatment Resistance and Patient Authority: The Austen Riggs Reader*, 24–41. New York: Norton.
Kernberg, O. F. (1972). Early Ego Integration and Object Relations. *Ann. N. Y. Acad. Sci.* 193:233–47.
———. (1973). Psychoanalytic Object-Relations Theory, Group Processes, and Administration: Toward an Integrative Theory of Hospital Treatment. *Ann. Psychoanal.* 1:363–88.
———. (1980). *Internal World and External Reality*. New York: Jason Aronson.
———. (2001). Object Relations, Affects, and Drives: Toward a New Synthesis. *Psychoanal. Inq.* 21:604–19.
Kernberg, O. F., and Caligor, E. (2005). A Psychoanalytic Theory of Personality Disorders. In M. F. Lenzenwenger and J. F. Clarks (Eds.) *Major Theories of Personality Disorders*, 114–56. New York and London: Guilford Press.

Kernberg, O. F., Yeomans, F. E., Clarkin, J. F., and Levy, K. N. (2008). Transference Focused Psychotherapy: Overview and Update. *Int. J. Psycho-Anal.* 89:601–20.

Kohut H., and Wolf, E. S. (1978). The Disorders of the Self and Their Treatment: An Outline. *Int. J. Psycho-Anal.* 59:413–25.

Krikorian S. E., and Fowler, J. C. (2011). A Team Approach to Treatment Resistance. In E. M. Plakun (Ed.) *Treatment Resistance and Patient Authority: The Austen Riggs Reader*, 245–68. New York: Norton.

Kris, A. O. (1990). Helping Patients by Analyzing Self-Criticism. *J. Amer. Psychoanal. Assn.* 38:605–36.

LaFarge, L. (2014). Defense and Resistance. In G. O. Gabbard, B. E. Litowitz, and P. Williams (Eds.) *Textbook of Psychoanalysis*, 93–103. Washington, DC and London: American Psychiatric Publishing.

Laplanche, J. (1974). Panel on "Hysteria Today." *Int. J. Psycho-Anal.* 55:459–69.

Little, M. I. (1951). Countertransference and the Patient's Response to It. *Int. J. Psycho-Anal.* 32: 32–40.

———. (1985). Winnicott Working in Areas Where Psychotic Anxieties Predominate: A Personal Record. *Free Associations* 1D:9–42.

———. (1987). On the Value of Regression to Dependence. *Free Associations* 1:7–22.

Loewald, H. W. (1960). On the Therapeutic Action of Psycho-Analysis. *Int. J. Psycho- Anal.* 41:16–33.

Loewenstein, R. J., and Ross, D. R. (1992). Multiple Personality and Psychoanalysis: An Introduction. *Psychoanal. Inq.* 12:3–48.

Main, T. (1957/1989). The Ailment. In J. Janes and E. Rayner (Eds.) *The Ailment and Other Psychoanalytic Essays*, 12–35. London: Free Association Books.

———. (1989). *The Ailment and Other Psychoanalytic Essays*. J. Janes and E. Rayner (Eds.). London: Free Association Books.

Maizels, N. (1985). Self-Envy, the Womb and the Nature of Goodness—A Reappraisal of the Death Instinct. *Int. J. Psycho-Anal.* 66:185–92.

McLaughlin, J. T. (1991). Clinical and Theoretical Aspects of Enactment. *J. Amer. Psychoanalytic Association* 39:595–614.

McLaughlin, J. T., and Johan, M. (1992). Enactments in Psychoanalysis. *J. Amer. Psychoanal. Assn.* 40:827–41.

Menninger, W. C. (1939/1982). The Menninger Hospital's Guide to the Order Sheet. *Bulletin of the Menninger Clinic* 46:21–112.

Modell, A. H. (1976). "The Holding Environment" and the Therapeutic Action of Psychoanalysis. *J. Amer. Psychoanal. Assn.* 24:285–307.

Muller, J. P. (2011). Why the Pair Needs the Third. In E. M. Plakun (Ed.) *Treatment Resistance and Patient Authority: The Austen Riggs Reader*, 97–120. New York: Norton.

Munich, R. L., and Green P. K. (2009). Psychosocial Approaches in Inpatient Psychiatry. In F. Ovsiew and R. L. Munich (Eds.) *Principles of Inpatient Psychiatry*, 17–41. New York: Walters Kluwer/Lippincott Williams and Wilkins.

Nahum, J. P. (2008). Forms of Relational Meaning: Issues in the Relations between the Implicit and Reflective-Verbal Domains. *Psychoanal. Dial.* 18:125–48.

Ogden, T. H. (1989). *The Primitive Edge of Experience*. Northvale, NJ: Jason Aronson.

———. (1990). Instinct, Phantasy and Deep Structure in the Work of Melanie Klein. In *The Matrix of the Mind*, 9–39. Northvale, NJ: Jason Aronson.

———. (2004). The Analytic Third: Implications for Psychoanalytic Theory and Technique. *Psychoanal Q.* 73:167–95.

———. (2005). On Psychoanalytic Supervision. *Int. J. Psycho-Anal.* 86:1265–80.

Ornstein, P. H. (2008). Heinz Kohut's Self Psychology—And Ours. *Int. J. Psychoanal. Self Psychol.* 3:195–214.

Öztürk, M. O. (2002). Dissociative (Conversion) Disorders. In *Ruh sagligi ve bozukluklari* (*Mental Health and Disorders*), 389–411. Ankara, Turkey: Nobel Tip Publishing.

Paniagua, C. (2012). The Ripple Effect: Patients Influencing Others. *Psychoanalytic Quarterly* 81:849–74.

Pao, P. N. (1979). *The Schizophrenic Disorders*. Madison, CT: International Universities Press.

Plakun, E. M. (Ed.). (2011). *Treatment Resistance and Patient Authority: The Austen Riggs Reader*. New York: Norton.
Popper, K. R. (1963). *Conjectures and Refutations: The Growth of Scientific Knowledge*. New York: Harper.
Racker, H. (1968). Transference and Countertransference. *Int. Psycho-Anal. Lib.* 73:1–96. London: The Hogarth Press and the Institute of Psycho-Analysis.
Renik, O. (2001). The Patient's Experience of Therapeutic Benefit. *Psychoanal Q.* 70:231–41.
Richards, A. D. (2003). Psychoanalytic Discourse at the Turn of Our Century: A Plea for a Measure of Humility. *J. Amer. Psychoanal. Assn.* 51S:73–89.
Riviere, J. (1936). A Contribution to the Analysis of the Negative Therapeutic Reaction. *Int. J. Psycho-Anal.* 17:304–20.
Robertson, S., and Davison, S. (1997). A Survey of Groups within a Psychiatric Hospital. *Psychoanal. Psychother.* 11:119–34.
Roudinescu, E. (2002). France and Psychoanalysis. In E. Erwin (Ed.) *The Freud Encyclopedia: Theory, Therapy, Culture*, 208–12. New York and London: Routledge and Taylor and Francis.
Sandler, J. (1976). Countertransference and Role-Responsiveness. *Int. J. Psycho-Anal.* 3:43–47.
Schwartz, A. (2011). Working with Family Resistance to Treatment. In E. M. Plakun (Ed.) *Treatment Resistance and Patient Authority: The Austen Riggs Reader*, 224–44. New York: Norton.
Schwartz, D. P. (1983). The Open Hospital and the Concept of Limits. In H. Stierlin, L. C. Wynne, and M. Wirching (Eds.) *Psychosocial Intervention in Schizophrenia: An International View*, 83–92. New York: Springer-Verlag.
———. (1986). Loving Action and the Shape of the Object. In D. B. Feinsilver (Ed.) *Towards a Comprehensive Model for Schizophrenic Disorders*. Hillsdale, NJ: The Analytic Press.
———. (1990). Psychosis and Adolescence: The Relation of Intrapsychic Structure Formation and Change to Action and Task. *Psychiatric Clinics of North America* 13 (3): 401–14.
Scott, M. E. (1998). Play and Therapeutic Action: Multiple Perspectives. *Psychoanal. St. Child* 53:94–101.
Scott, W. M. (1975). Remembering Sleep and Dreams. *Int. Rev. Psycho-Anal.* 2:253–354.
Searles, H. F. (1973). Concerning Therapeutic Symbiosis. *Annu. Psychoanal.* 1:247–62.
———. (1986). Jealousy Involving an Internal Object. In *My Work with Borderline Patients*, 99–155. London: Jason Aronson.
Shapiro, E. R. (2011). A View from Riggs: Examined Living—A Psychodynamic Treatment System. In E. M. Plakun (Ed.) *Treatment Resistance and Patient Authority: The Austen Riggs Reader*, 269–84. New York: Norton.
Shapiro, E. R., and Carr, A. W. (1978). Disguised Countertransference in Institutions. *Psychiatry* 50 (1): 72–82.
———. (1991). *Lost in Familiar Places*. New Haven, CT: Yale University Press.
Shapiro, E. R., Zinner, J., Shapiro, R. L., and Berkowitz, D. A. (1975). The Influence of Family Experience on Borderline Personality Development. *Int. R. Psycho-Anal.* 2:399–411.
Shapiro, R. L. (1987). The Family in the Psychoanalysis of the Young Adult. *Psychoanal. Inq.* 7:59–75.
Simmel, E. (1929). Psycho-Analytic Treatment in a Sanatorium. *Int. J. Psycho-Anal.* 10:70–89.
Skogstad, W. (2003). Internal and External Reality in In-Patient Psychotherapy: Working with Severely Disturbed Patients at the Cassel Hospital. *Psychoanal. Psychother.* 17:97–118.
Stern, S. (2009). Session Frequency and the Definition of Psychoanalysis. *Psychoanal. Dial.* 19:639–55.
Tillman, J. G. (2011). Integrative Psychodynamic Treatment of Psychotic Disorders. In E. M. Plakun (Ed.) *Treatment Resistance and Patient Authority: The Austen Riggs Reader*, 178–203. New York: Norton.
Tindle, K. (2006). Negative Therapeutic Reaction. *Brit. J. Psychother.* 23:99–116.
Tronick, E. Z. (2003). "Of Course All Relationships Are Unique." *Psychoanal. Inq. Psa Inquiry* 23:473–91.

Tyson, R. L. (1996). The Good Boy Syndrome and Malignant Academic Failure in Early Adolescence. *Psychoanalytic Study of Child* 51:386–408.
Vivona, J. M. (2007). Sibling Differentiation, Identity Development, and the Lateral Dimension of Psychic Life. *J. Amer. Psychoanal. Assn.* 55:1191–215.
Volkan, V. D. (1984). *What Do You Get When You Cross a Dandelion with a Rose? The True Story of a Psychoanalysis*. New York: Jason Aronson.
———. (1987). "Six Steps in Treatment." In *Six Steps in the Treatment of Borderline Personality Disorder*, 85–104. London: Jason Aronson.
———. (2014). *Animal Killer: Transmission of War Trauma from One Generation to the Next*. London: Karnac.
Will, O. A., Jr. (1964). Schizophrenia and the Psychotherapeutic Field. *Contemp. Psychoanal.* 1:1–29.
Winnicott, D. W. (1947). Further Thoughts on Babies as Persons. In *Child and the Outside World*, 134–40. New York: Basic Books.
———. (1949). Hate in the Counter-Transference. *Int. J. Psycho-Anal.* 30:69–74.
———. (1953). Transitional Objects and Transitional Phenomena—A Study of the First Not-Me Possession. *Int. J. Psycho-Anal.* 34:89–97.
———. (1960). Ego Distortions in Terms of True and False Self. In *The Maturational Processes and the Facilitating Environment*, 140–52. New York: International Universities Press.
Zetzel, E. R. (1968). The So-Called Good Hysteric. *Int. J. Psycho-Anal.* 49:256–60.

INDEX

ABOUT THE AUTHOR

Dr. M. Sagman Kayatekin trained as a medical doctor and psychiatrist and has held faculty positions at prominent institutions in Turkey: the Department of Psychiatry, Hacettepe University Medical Faculty (Ankara), and Bakirkoy Hospital for Nervous and Mental Disorders (Istanbul).

Dr. Kayatekin repeated his adult psychiatric training at the Medical College of Wisconsin. He had advanced training in psychoanalytic hospital work at the Austen Riggs Center and graduated from Boston Psychoanalytic Society and Institute as an adult psychoanalyst. Dr. Kayatekin has held senior staff/faculty positions at the University of Massachusetts Medical School, the Austen Riggs Center, and the Menninger Clinic. He is associate clinical professor of psychiatry at the Menninger Department of Psychiatry and Behavioral Sciences, Baylor College of Medicine, and has a full-time private practice of psychoanalytic work (adult individuals, couples, and family).

Dr. Kayatekin has published, presented, and lectured locally, nationally, and internationally and won numerous teaching awards at the institutions he worked at in the United States.

Also contributing to this volume is **Z. Emel Kayatekin**. She is an adult psychiatrist, psychodynamic therapist, family therapist, and a staff member at the Menninger Clinic. She is associate professor of psychiatry at the Menninger Department of Psychiatry and Behavioral Sciences, Baylor College of Medicine.

M. Sagman and Z. Emel Kayatekin are associate professors of psychiatry, Turkey; and visiting professors of psychiatry at Wuhan Mental Health Center, Tongji Medical College, Peoples Republic of China.

www.ingramcontent.com/pod-product-compliance
Ingram Content Group UK Ltd.
Pitfield, Milton Keynes, MK11 3LW, UK
UKHW042059210926
475826UK00001B/8

9 781442 238343